THE AWFUL RISE OF TH

'Mr Wilson has brought a lo
to bear . . . a genuine effort
of social disease'
Times Literary Supplement

'Like everything Mr Wilson writes, it is full of ideas'
The Observer

Also by Colin Wilson in
Panther Books

The Mind Parasites
The Philosopher's Stone

Colin Wilson

Order of Assassins

The Psychology of Murder

Panther

Granada Publishing Limited
Published in 1975 by Panther Books Ltd
Frogmore, St Albans, Herts AL2 2NF

First published in Great Britain by
Rupert Hart-Davis Ltd 1972

Made and printed in Great Britain by
Cox & Wyman Ltd
London, Reading and Fakenham
Set in Intertype Pilgrim

For Andrew Crawshaw

Acknowledgements

I wish to thank Roger Staples, for sending me press cuttings of the Collins case, Steve Geller, for press reports of the Manson case and for the loan of the typescript of his book *Musical Impressions of Murder*, Henk Van Gelre for securing me details of the Hans van Zon case, Brian Marriner for practical and theoretical help on the pornography chapter, Alan Brooke for valuable help and suggestions, Dan MacDougald (of Atlanta, Georgia) for sending me material on his attitude psychotherapy (see bibliography), A. E. Van Vogt for permission to quote his unpublished essay on The Violent Male, and *The Observer* and *Sunday Times* for permission to quote material published in their respective colour supplements. My wife Joy prepared the bibliography.

C.W.

Contents

Introduction

The present book completes my 'murder trilogy' – the first two volumes of which were *An Encyclopaedia of Murder* and *A Casebook of Murder*.

The *Encyclopaedia* was intended as a basic reference book; its index classifies murderers under method, weapon and motive. The *Casebook* was a study in the social history of murder, the changes in the styles and motives of murder since the fourteenth century. This volume is concerned primarily with the psychology of murder. Or rather, of assassination, which might be defined as murder committed for its own sake.

Most murderers would prefer not to kill. If Frederick Seddon could have obtained Miss Barrow's money without killing her, he would have done so. If Brown and Kennedy could have knocked P. C. Gutteridge unconscious (at least, before he saw them) they would have left him alive. But when John Wilkes Booth entered Lincoln's box, his aim was murder. When Jack the Ripper left home with his black bag, his aim was murder. When the Manson family entered Sharon Tate's home in Benedict Canyon, their aim was murder. This places Booth, the Ripper and the Manson family in the smallest group of murderers: the category of assassins. The assassin is a man for whom murder is not only an ultimate purpose, but also a means of self-fulfilment, a creative act.

This sounds paradoxical: the notion of destructiveness as a creative act. But creation itself often has an element of destruction, a welling-up of violence. It can be seen in the paintings of Van Gogh, Soutine, Edvard Munch. A dictionary of painters remarks of Munch that he 'saw life as a constant threat, a war of the sexes, a long-drawn-out tale of sickness and death'.[1] Such a view could obviously lead to murder just as easily as to art. The odd thing is that before the mid-twentieth century, there were so few murderers who killed out of this kind of motive – disgust with life or hatred of society. Dostoevsky *wrote* about such people; he is the first writer for whom murder takes on a quality of metaphysical evil. Dostoevsky's murderers – whom I discuss in a later chapter – are true assassins: they understand the quality of their deed; they accept the knowledge of good and evil; they think as well as act. Such men did not actually exist in the 1860s; even Netchaev, the 'tiger cub' on whom Dostoevsky based Verkhovensky in *The Devils*, was little more than a confidence man. But a century after *Crime and Punishment* (1886), the creatures of Dostoevsky's imagination had become a reality. The twentieth century has seen the emergence of a new phenomenon: the high I.Q. murderer: Leopold and Loeb, Melvin Rees,[2] Klaus Gossman,[2] Ian Brady, Charles Manson, Hans van Zon, Norman Collins, Arthur Hosein. Such men are not necessarily brilliant intellectuals; nevertheless, there is a 'cerebral' element in their crimes, a tendency to argue that crime is a legitimate response to a corrupt and decadent society. It is this that distinguishes them clearly from the majority of murderers. In 1912, a writer on crime analysed sixty-two murders; he discovered that twenty were committed during quarrels, thirteen due to alcohol, nine to jealousy over women, four to disputes about money, one to race antagonism, three to negligence, two infanticides, five committed during robbery, five due to 'general causes'.[3] A similar survey, conducted today, would show an increase in sex murders and race murders, but the overall picture would remain surprisingly unchanged. Most murders are still committed during family quarrels or disputes over money; they are committed under the stress of violent emotion, not out of a generalized resentment against society. But this should not be allowed to obscure the central fact: that the 'cerebral' murder, the resentment-murder, has become the typical crime of the twentieth century. If their significance is out of all proportion to their number, this is not because their actual number is small, but because there has been a general crime increase since the second world war. In recent years, this increase has become so steep that it would be more accurate to call it an explosion. Between 1940 and 1954, crimes of violence rose by 35 per cent in America; but between 1968 and 1970, the murder rate rose from 10,000 to over 15,000 – more than 50 per cent in two years.[4] By far the most significant feature in this changing crime pattern is the increase in 'resentment crimes' by men whose intelligence is slightly above average.

In my first book I called these misfits 'Outsiders'; they are inbetweeners, too clever and dominant for the place society has to offer them, but not clever – or perhaps stable – enough to compel society to accept them on their own terms. When such men become killers, they are 'assassins' rather than ordinary murderers. They share certain characteristics of the artist; they know they are unlike other men, they experience drives and tensions that alienate them from the rest of society, they possess the courage to satisfy these drives in defiance of society. But while the artist releases his tensions in an act of imaginative creation, the Outsider-criminal releases his in an act of violence. While the artist's acts may have the effect of integrating him into society, the assassin always walks alone.

It may seem that my use of the word 'assassin' is so remote from its ordinary usage – a hired killer – that it would be better to find some other word – for example, the German 'lustmörder' (joy-murderer, or someone who kills for pleasure). But this would not meet the case either; for I am concerned with the criminal whose motive is *frustration of the will-drive.*

In fact, the sense in which the word is used in this book is not far from its original meaning. The Assassins were a Moslem religious sect; they killed as a matter of conviction, and in obedience to the orders of their leader and prophet. Their name is a corruption of *hashishin,* a user of hashish, for it was believed they killed under the influence of drugs. (The parallels with the killers of Sharon Tate and the LaBiancas need hardly be stressed.) Since this book is concerned mainly with twentieth-century murders, it may be as well to begin with the history of the original Assassins.

1. *Picture Encyclopedia of Art,* Thames and Hudson.
2. See *A Casebook of Murder,* Chapter 6.
3. Arthur Train, *Courts, Criminals and the Camorra,* Chapman and Hall, London 1912.

4. This far outstrips population increase. In America, the population rises by about three million a year. In proportion, its murders should increase by about 150 a year; the actual increase is more than seventeen times as high.

CHAPTER ONE

Creatures of Nightmare

In the year 1273, the Venetian traveller Marco Polo passed through the valley of Alamut, in Persia, and saw there the castle of the Old Man of the Mountain, the head of the Persian branch of the sect of Ismailis, or Assassins. By that time, the sect was two hundred years old, and was on the point of being destroyed by the Mongols, who had invaded the Middle East under the leadership of Genghis Khan.

According to Marco Polo, the Old Man of the Mountain, whose name was Aloadin, had created a Garden of Paradise in a green valley behind the castle, and filled it with 'pavilions and palaces the most elegant that can be imagined', fountains flowing with wine, milk and honey, beautiful *houris* who could sing and dance seductively. The purpose of this Garden was to give his followers a foretaste of Paradise, so that they might be eager to sacrifice their lives for their leader. When the Old Man wanted an enemy murdered, he would ask for volunteers. These men would be drugged and carried into the secret garden – which, under normal circumstances, was strictly forbidden to all males. They would awake to find themselves apparently in Paradise, with wine, food and damsels at their disposal. After a few days of this, they were again drugged and taken back to the Old Man's fortress. 'So when the Old Man would have any prince slain, he would say to such a youth: "Go thou and slay So and so; and when thou returnest, my angels shall bear thee to Paradise . . ."'.

There is evidence that the story may have a foundation in fact. Behind the remains of the castle, which still exists in the valley of Alamut, there is a green enclosed valley with a spring. But it is hardly large enough to have contained 'pavilions and palaces'.

The Ismailis were a breakaway sect from the orthodox Moslems; they were the Mohammedan equivalent of Protestants. After the death of the prophet Mahomet in 632, his disciple Abu Bakr was chosen to succeed him, thus becoming the first Caliph of Islam. It is a pity that Mahomet, unlike Jesus, never made clear which of his disciples – or relatives – was to be the rock upon which his church was to be built. For other Moslems felt that the Prophet's cousin Ali was a more suitable candidate: the result was a dissension that split the Moslem world for centuries. The Sunni – the orthodox Moslems – persecuted and slaughtered Ali's followers, who were known as the Shi'a. In 680, they almost succeeded in wiping out their rivals, when seventy of them – including the prophet's daughter Fatima – were surprised and massacred. But the killers overlooked a sick boy – the son of Fatima; so the rebel tradition lived on.

All this murder and suffering produced powerful religious emotions among the Shi'a. They set up their own Caliph – known as the Imam – and they looked forward to the coming of a messiah (or Mahdi) who would lead them to final victory. Strange sects proliferated, led by holy men who came out of the desert. Some believed in reincarnation, others in total moral and sexual freedom. One sect believed in murder as a religious duty, strangling their victims with cords; these may be regarded as the true predecessors of the Assassins.

The Ismailis were a breakaway sect from the original breakaway sect. When the sixth Imam died, his eldest son Ismail was passed over for some reason, and his younger brother Musa appointed. The Ismailis were Moslems who declared that Ismail was the true Imam: they were also known as Seveners, because they believed that Ismail was the seventh and last Imam. The rest of the Shi'a became known as the Twelvers, for they accepted Musa and his five successors as true Imams. (The line came to an end after the twelfth.) The Twelvers became the respectable branch of the heretics, differing from orthodox Sunni only on a few points of doctrine. It was the Ismailis who became the true opposition, creating a brilliant and powerful organization with its own philosophy, ritual and literature. They were intellectuals and mystics and fanatics. With such drive and idealism they were bound to come to power eventually.

It was some time around the middle of the eleventh century that the greatest of the Ismaili leaders was born – Hasan bin Sabbah, a man who combined the religious fervour of

Saint Augustine with the political astuteness of Lenin. He founded the Order of Assassins, and became the first Old Man of the Mountain.

By the time Hasan was born, the Ismailis had become one of the great political powers. The Sunni Caliphs were decadent: the Ismailis set up their own Caliph and their own dynasty. They called themselves the Fatimids (descendants of Fatima, the Prophet's murdered daughter). They conquered the Nile valley, then spread slowly across Egypt, Syria, North Africa, parts of Arabia, even Sicily. By the end of the tenth century, it looked as if nothing could stop them becoming rulers of all the Moslem lands. But at that point, a new force entered Middle Eastern politics – the Seljuk Turks – who swept across the Moslem world like the ancient Romans. And the Turks, as good Moslems, decided to lend their support to the Sunni Caliphs. By the time Hasan bin Sabbah was a young man, the Ismaili empire was already past its peak.

Hasan was born an orthodox Moslem – or at least, a Twelver, which was almost the same thing. His family lived in Rayy, near modern Teheran. We know little about his early life except that he became an avid student of every branch of learning. A strong religious impulse led him to look beyond the sect into which he had been born. He was impressed by the intellectual force and mystical fervour of the heretical Ismailis. It took him a long time to decide to join them – for the Ismailis were generally regarded as outcasts and cranks. A serious illness decided him; in 1072 he took the oath of allegiance to the Fatimid Caliph. Four years later he was forced to leave Rayy – no doubt for spreading Ismaili doctrines – and started to make his way towards Cairo, a new city that had been built by the Ismailis as their capital. The journey took two years. In Cairo, he impressed the Caliph, and became a supporter of his eldest son Nizar. He spent three years in the Fatimid court; then his ardent revolutionary temperament got him into trouble – history does not go into detail – and he left Egypt and became a wandering missionary for the Ismaili cause. Legend has it that he was sentenced to death, but that just before his execution, one of the strongest towers in the city collapsed suddenly; this was seen as an omen, so he was sent into exile instead. Another story tells how the ship on which he sailed ran into a violent storm; while the other passengers flung themselves on their knees and prayed, Hasan stood perfectly calm, explaining that he could not die until he had fulfilled his destiny. When the storm suddenly ceased, Hasan got the credit, and made several converts. 'Thus,' says Von Hammer (a thoroughly hostile chronicler), 'to increase his credit, did he avail himself of accidents and natural occurrences, as if he possessed the command of both.' Von Hammer seems to regard Hasan as a kind of Rasputin figure, a trickster and a fraud who used religion to gain personal power (but then, he also describes the Ismaili religion as 'mysteries of atheism and immorality').

Hasan bin Sabbah was a highly successful missionary, particularly among his own people of Daylam, a wild, independent race who loathed the Turks. The Daylamis had been among the last to be converted to Islam, and even now they tended to be rebellious and unorthodox. Hasan saw their value. Their country was an ideal stronghold. And if Nizar failed to become the next Fatimid Caliph – which seemed highly likely, in view of the intrigues at court – Hasan might well need a stronghold.

As the number of his converts increased, Hasan selected his fortress, the castle of Alamut (or Eagle's Nest), perched high on a rock in the Elburz mountains, above a cultivated valley about thirty miles long.

His method of acquiring the castle was typical of his methods. First he sent 'dais' – preachers – to the villages around the castle, and they made many converts. Then the dais got into the castle, and converted some of its garrison. The castle's owner, Alid – an orthodox Moslem – was not sure what to do about all this. He seems to have been an indecisive man. At first he professed to be converted; then, one day, he persuaded the Ismailis to leave the castle, and slammed the gates. But he allowed himself to be persuaded to let them in again. At this point, Hasan was smuggled into the castle in disguise. One morning, Alid woke up to discover that his castle was no longer his own. He was politely shown the door and (according to one chronicler) given 3,000 gold dinars in compensation.

This was in 1090. From that time on, until his death thirty-five years later, Hasan lived in his castle. He studied, wrote books, brought up a family and planned conquests. Most of his followers never saw him. The religious rule in the castle was strict; they ate sparingly, and wine was forbidden. Hasan had one of his sons executed for drinking wine. (Another was executed on suspicion – false, as it later turned out – of having planned the murder of one of the dais.)

But if the aims were religious, the method was military. The Ismailis wanted to supplant the Sunni Caliphs of Baghdad. In order to do that, they first had to drive out the Turks who supported them. The Turks were the overlords of Persia. So Hasan's task was to extend his realm, village by village and castle by castle, until he could challenge the Turks directly. Where castles declined to be converted to the Ismaili faith, they were infiltrated or stormed. In towns and villages, Ismaili converts rose up and took control. Like T. E. Lawrence – in his own battle to overthrow the Turks – Hasan's great advantage was the hatred of the conquered people for their overlords. When he had extended his control to all the area surrounding Alamut, he sent a missionary to the mountainous country called Quhistan in the south-east, where various heretical sects were oppressed by the Turks. There was a popular rising, the Turks were overthrown, and Quhistan became the second great Ismaili stronghold. Not long after, another area of mountain country in the south-west became an Ismaili stronghold when another of Hasan's followers seized two castles near Arrajan. The Turks now became aware of their danger, and decided it was time to crush the Ismailis; two great expeditions were sent out, one against Alamut, the other against Quhistan. They soon discovered how well Hasan had chosen his fortresses. Athough there were a mere seventy defenders, the castle of Alamut was impregnable to direct attack; and the surrounding villages made sure the defenders were not starved into submission by smuggling food up to them by night. A surprise attack sent the Turkish armies flying. The expedition against Quhistan fared no better.

And it was at this point, in 1092, a mere two years after moving to Alamut, that Hasan made the great decision that may well have been his crucial mistake. He recognized that open war with the Turks was out of the question; his armies were too small. But his followers were fanatics who would give their lives for their cause. Why not use them to strike down his chief enemies, one by one? In 1092, the 'assassins' claimed their first, and perhaps their most eminent victim, Nizam Al-Mulk, the Vizier of the Turkish Sultan.

Until recent years, it was accepted that Nizam Al-Mulk had been a fellow student of Hasan's. The story told by Von Hammer – who repeats it from earlier Persian chroniclers – is that Hasan. Nizam Al-Mulk and the poet Omar Kayyam were fellow students, and Hasan suggested to the other two that if any of them should achieve eminence, he should share it with the other two. They all agreed. After some years, Nizam became the Vizier of the Turkish Sultan Alp Arslan, one of the great military geniuses of the period. When Alp Arslan died (1073) and his young son, Malik Shah, came to the throne, Nizam became the most powerful man in the land. At this point, his old schoolfellows presented themselves and reminded him of their agreement. Omar, being a poet and mathematician (one of the greatest of the Middle Ages), asked only for a quiet place to study; so Nizam gave him a pension and sent him back to his home town of Naishapur. Hasan wanted power, so Nizam found him a position at court. What happened then is not quite clear, except that Nizam realized that his old schoolfellow was supplanting him in the royal favour, and took steps to bring about his downfall. Hasan left Malik's court vowing vengeance; and that, says Von Hammer, is why Nizam became the first victim of the Assassins.

By 1092, Nizam Al-Mulk was Hasan's chief enemy, the greatest single danger to the Assassins. Hasan asked for a volunteer to kill the Vizier. A man called Bu Tahir Arrani stepped forward. He disguised himself as a Sufi – a holy man – and during the feast of Ramadan, in October 1092, was allowed to approach the litter of Nizam as he was carried out of his audience tent. He drove a knife into Nizam's breast, and was himself immediately killed by Nizam's guards. When he heard that the assassination had been successful, Hasan remarked: 'The killing of this devil is the beginning of bliss.' He meant it literally; his followers accepted that to die like Bu Tahir Arrani was an immediate passport to Paradise.

It may be that this murder showed Hasan where his real power lay. He could capture a fortress by preaching, cunning and bribery. He could destroy an enemy by sending out a single assassin. It looked like the ideal formula for guerrilla warfare.

Where he made his mistake was in failing to grasp the ultimate consequences of such a method: that if his men destroyed their enemies like scorpions or cobras, they would arouse the same loathing and detestation as scorpions or cobras. And that sooner or later, the horror they inspired would cancel all their gains. It was this that eventually frustrated Hasan's plans for conquest.

But that lay far in the future. For the moment, Hasan's method was triumphantly successful. Not long after Nizam's death, the Sultan Malik also died – of a stomach complaint, apparently. One of Nizam's sons, Fakhri, was killed in Naishapur; he had been accosted by a beggar who said: 'The true Moslems are no more and there are none left to take the hand of the afflicted.' As Fakhri reached for alms, he was stabbed to the heart. Nizam's other son, Ahmed, laid siege to the castle of Alamut; the inhabitants suffered severe hardships, but again it proved impregnable. Ahmed was later stabbed by an assassin, but he recovered.

The candidates for assassination were always carefully chosen. Hasan played his game like a master chess player. The death of Malik Shah brought on a struggle for power at court; the new Sultan, Berkyaruq, had to defend his throne against his half-brothers. Hasan lent his support to Berkyaruq, and assassinated a number of Berkyaruq's enemies. Berkyaruq's officers formed an uneasy liaison with the Assassins. So when Berkyaruq finally put down the rebellion, Hasan was allowed to operate in peace for a few years. But he continued to practise the arts of infiltration and intimidation; Ismailis joined Berkyaruq's army, and made converts. When officers opposed them, they were silenced with the threat of assassination. A point came where no one in authority dared to go out without armour under his robes. Leaders of rival religious sects were murdered. One opponent was stabbed in the mosque as he knelt at prayers, even though a bodyguard was standing directly behind him. Eventually – in 1101 – Berkyaruq lost his temper and decided it was time to destroy the Ismailis. He combined with his half-brother Sanjar to attack the stronghold at Quhistan; the armies laid waste the countryside, destroying the crops, and would have captured the main stronghold (Tabas) if the Ismailis had not bribed the enemy general to go away – a typically oriental touch. Sanjar made other attempts to subjugate the Ismailis, but eventually came to tolerate them. The historian Juvanyi tells a story to explain this. Hasan managed to bribe one of Sanjar's guards to stick a dagger into the ground near his head, when Sanjar lay in a drunken sleep. Shortly thereafter, Sanjar received a message from Hasan that said: 'That dagger could just as easily have been stuck in your heart.' Sanjar saw the wisdom of tolerating the Ismailis.

Nevertheless, Hasan's dreams began to collapse within a few years of his greatest triumphs. In 1094, the Fatimid Caliph – spiritual head of the Ismailis – died in Cairo. Nizar – Hasan's patron – should have replaced him. Instead, the Vizier, Al-Afdal, put Nizar's younger brother on the throne. There was a war, and Nizar was killed. Hasan remained faithful to Nizar (in fact, his sect called themselves the Nizari); he refused to acknowledge the new Sultan. So he was now isolated from his own co-religionists. After Berkyaruq turned against him, it was all the Assassins could do to hold on to their territories. When Berkyaruq died in 1105, he was succeeded by his half-brother Muhammad Tapar, who was even more determined to destroy the power of the Ismailis. The castle at Isfahan was besieged and taken, and the Ismaili leader flayed alive. Alamut was besieged, but managed to hold out. For several years, the Sultan sent his troops to destroy all the crops in the valley; then, when the defenders of Alamut were exhausted with hardship, the siege was started again. In 1118 the castle was on the point of surrendering when the army received news of the death of the Sultan. So they went home. The Ismailis were saved again.

The Assassins had been contained in Persia. But in the early years of the new century, Hasan sent out missionaries – and killers – to Syria. In 1103, they murdered Janah Al-Daulah, the Emir of Homs, as he prayed in the mosque. In 1106, they killed Khalaf, the ruler of a citadel called Afamiya. Their method here was again typical. Six Assassins got hold of the horse, shield and armour of a Frankish knight, and presented themselves at Khalaf's headquarters; they explained that they had killed one of his enemies, and had come to enter his service. Khalaf (himself an Ismaili, but a supporter of the present Fatimid Caliph) made them welcome. The Assassins watched for their opportunity, then murdered him. Then, with the help of other Ismailis, they seized the citadel. Their triumph was short-lived. The Crusader Tancred beseiged the town and took the Assassins captive. (They were allowed to ransom themselves.) This is the first known encounter between Crusaders and Assassins. Later on, there were many more.

Back in the castle of Alamut, Hasan was getting old. He had seen his empire rise, and then crumble. For thirty years he had directed assassinations from his castle, yet nothing had changed very much. The Turks were as strong as ever; the Sunni Moslems were still in power. And, worst of all, the Ismailis of Cairo – the men who held the power – were the enemies of the Ismailis of Persia.

Hasan's chief grudge was against the Vizier Al-Afdal, the man who had plotted against Nizar and put Nizar's younger brother, Al Mustali, on the throne in 1094. Twenty-seven years later, Hasan got his revenge; three of his Assassins succeeded in murdering the Vizier. Strangely enough, the present Fatimid Caliph was delighted; he was sick of his overbearing Vizier. He ordered the new Vizier to write Hasan a letter, urging him to return to the fold. Hasan was willing enough. At eighty-seven, he was getting tired; he could not afford to defy the whole Arab world forever. But before the Caliph and the Old Man of the Mountain could make peace, the new Vizier discovered a plot by the Assassins to murder the Caliph. In all probability, there was never such a plot. Nizar and his children were dead; Hasan had no motive for wanting to kill the man who was now offering him peace and co-operation. But the Vizier was a Twelver (not an Ismaili); he had good reason for wanting to prevent the reconciliation. And Hasan's reputation was such that any mud would stick. The Caliph took the 'plot' so seriously that he ordered that all the citizens of Cairo should be registered, and that all strangers should be carefully watched. Many 'agents of Hasan' were arrested and executed, including the tutor of the Caliph's children.

And so the last hope vanished. And in May 1194, Hasan bin Sabbah, one of the most remarkable religious leaders of all time, died in his castle of Alamut, at the age of ninety. He appointed one of his generals to succeed him, demonstrating thereby that he had learned from Mahomet's chief mistake.

This was by no means the end of the Assassins. After initial difficulties, the Syrian branch took root, and it was the stories of the Syrian mission, carried back to Europe by Crusaders, that introduced the word 'assassin' into the European languages. The event that caused this notoriety was the murder of the Christian knight Conrad of Montferrat in 1192; Conrad was stabbed by two Assassins – agents of the Syrian Old Man of the Mountain, Sinan – who were disguised as monks. (King Richard the Lion Heart of England is supposed to have been behind the murder; one of his protégés quickly married the widow, and became 'King of Jerusalem' in his place.) After this, Assassins began to figure in every chronicle of the Third Crusade, and the legend captured the imagination of Europe. They were masters of disguise, adepts in treachery and murder. Their Old Man was a magician who surveyed the world from his castle like some evil spider, watching for victims. They were without religion and without morality (one early chronicler says they ate pork – against the Moslem law – and practised incest with their mothers and sisters). They were so fanatically devoted to their master that he often demonstrated their obedience to visitors by making them leap out of high windows. Their arts of persuasion were so subtle that no ruler could be sure of the loyalty of his own servants ... A typical story illustrates this. Saladin – the Sultan of Egypt and the great enemy of the Crusaders – sent a threatening message to Sinan, the Syrian Old Man. The Assassin chief sent back a messenger, whose mission was to deliver a message in private. Aware of the danger, Saladin had him thoroughly searched, then dismissed the assembly, all except for two guards. The messenger turned to the guards and asked: 'If I were to order you, in the name of my Master, to kill the Sultan, would you do it?' They nodded and drew their swords. Whereupon the messenger, having made his point, bowed and took his leave – taking the two guards with him. Saladin decided to establish friendly relations with the Assassins ...

But by the time Marco Polo saw the castle of Alamut in 1273, the power of the Assassins was at an end. In Persia they had been slaughtered by the Mongols; in Syria, ruthlessly suppressed by Baybars, Sultan of Egypt. Some of the survivors remained in the area of Alamut – where they may be found to this day. Others scattered to distant countries, including India – the significance of which will appear in a moment.

What was it about the Assassins that made them the focus of so many legends? Something about them appealed to the mediaeval mind as Dracula or Jack the Ripper appealed to the late Victorians. In order to find an historical parallel, we have to turn to the semi-mythical figure of Rasputin, the 'holy devil' who was assassinated in 1916. The truth about Rasputin, like the truth about Hasan bin Sabbah, was interesting but unspectacular. He was deeply religious; he had a 'charisma' that attracted converts; he liked power, and was not free of human weaknesses. In short, he was 90 per cent ordinary, 10 per cent extraordinary. The legendary Rasputin is 100 per cent monster. Like the minotaur, he is a mythical archetype; he exists because people want him to exist. He has hypnotic powers and immense physical strength (in fact, Rasputin was not particularly strong); his 'holiness' is a mask that hides cruelty and power mania; he is sexually insatiable and capable of drinking vodka by the quart; he manipulates politicians and princes as if they were puppets ...

Why should people want to believe in such a legend? Because it symbolizes and objectifies a secret fear in which there is also an element of fascination; this resembles the ambiguous emotion aroused by the idea of a rapist in a sex-starved virgin. This is also true of the Assassins. 'And in the night of Friday, 23rd May, he hastened off to the fire of God and his Hell,' says Juvayni, describing Hasan's death. Murder was a sin that involved eternal damnation – and the Middle Ages took this very seriously indeed; yet the Assassins committed this sin for purely political ends. This is why the Christian chroniclers preferred to gloss over the religious motivation, and to emphasize the trickery and chicanery and fanaticism; it made the damnation so much more certain, so much more frightening.

But this is not the whole explanation. We are dealing here with deep-seated social instincts. The Old Man of the Mountain never ordered any deed of cruelty. If he had sent his soldiers to besiege a town and massacre the inhabitants, he would have aroused respect rather than horror. But he was doing something altogether more alarming. He was refusing to play the game according to the rules. The whole purpose of the social structure was to protect the citizens against evildoers. In *A Casebook of Murder* I quoted H. G. Wells: 'The early civilizations were not slowly evolved and adapted *communities*. They were essentially jostling *crowds* in which quite unprecedented reactions were possible.' Men came together into cities for protection; not from wild animals – for that purpose villages were as good as cities – but from their fellow human beings, the dispossessed who found it easier to rob and rape than to work. When the marauders were caught they were treated with unprecedented ferocity (after all, it is not so long ago that the bodies of highwaymen were allowed to rot on gibbets in England). A ruler might be cruel and arbitrary; but he was also the law-giver and protector, the foundation stone of social stability. By sending out his fanatics to murder viziers and princes, Hasan was touching a nerve of deep insecurity. It was as if – for example – some modern terrorist organization held society up to ransom by threatening to bomb school nurseries. The Assassins produced a feeling of outrage by doing something that simply 'wasn't done'. It is difficult for us, in our relatively stable and law-abiding society, to understand the feeling aroused by the Assassins in a society where stability was newly acquired. They seemed to threaten a return to chaos and violence. They were creatures of nightmare.

By A.D. 1300, the Assassins had ceased to exist in the Middle East, at least as a political force. In 1825, the English traveller J. B. Fraser remarked that although the Ismailis no longer committed murder, they were still fanatically devoted to their chief. Fraser also commented that there were Ismailis in India too. This raises a fascinating question: whether the Assassins of the Middle East formed a liaison with their Indian counterparts, the Thugs, When William Sleeman was investigating the Thugs in the nineteenth century, he was puzzled why, although they were Moslems, they worshipped the Hindu goddess Kali. One captured Thug explained that Kali was identical with Fatima, the murdered daughter of the prophet . . .

The Thugs (pronounced 'tug') came to the attention of Europe after the British annexation of India in the late eighteenth century. At first, the conquerors noted simply that the roads of India seemed to be infested with bands of robbers who strangled their victims. In 1816, a doctor named Robert Sherwood, stationed in Madras, induced some of these robbers to talk to him about their religion. His article 'On the Murderers Called Phansigars' appeared in *Asiatic Researches* in 1820, and caused some excitement. Sherwood alleged that the phansigars or Thugs (phansi means a noose; thug means cheat) committed murders as a religious duty, and that their aim was the actual killing, rather than the robbery that accompanied it.

The bizarre story caught the imagination of the English, and the word 'thug' soon passed into the language. The Thugs, according to Sherwood, lived quietly in their native villages for most of the year, fulfilling their duties as citizens and fathers in a manner that aroused no suspicion. But in the month of pilgrimage (usually November-December) they took to the roads and slaughtered travellers – always taking care to be at least a hundred miles from home.

The method was always the same. The advance guard would locate a band of travellers, then one of two of the Thugs would approach the group and ask if they might travel with it – for protection. A few days later, a few more Thugs would make the same request. This would continue until there were more Thugs than travellers. The killing usually took place in the evening, when the travellers were seated around the fire. At a given signal, three Thugs would take their place behind each victim. One of them would pass the strangling cloth (or *ruhmal*) around the victim's neck; another would grab his legs and lift them clear of the ground; the third would seize his hands or kneel on his back. Usually, it was all over within seconds. The bodies of the victims were then hacked and mutilated to prevent recognition, and to make them decompose more quickly. The legs were cut off; if there was time, the whole body might be dismembered. Then it was buried. It was now time for the most important part of the ritual – the ceremony known as *Tuponee*. A tent was usually erected – to shield the Thugs from the sight of travellers. The *kussee*, the consecrated pick-axe (their equivalent of the Christian cross), was placed near the grave: the Thugs sat around in a group. The leader prayed to Kali for wealth and success. A symbolic strangling was enacted, and then all who had taken an active part in the murder ate the 'communion sugar' (*goor*), while the chief poured consecrated water on the grave. One of the captured Thugs told Sleeman: 'Let any man once taste of that *goor* and he will be a Thug, though he know all the trades and have all the wealth of the world.'

William Sleeman was a captain in the British army; born in St. Tudy, Cornwall, he had served in India since 1809. He was fascinated by Sherwood's paper, and in the early 1820s, he began to study the Thugs in the Nerbudda Valley. The revelations he made in 1829 caused a sensation throughout India. Sleeman revealed that Thuggee was not a local religious sect, but a nationwide phenomenon that claimed the lives of thousands of travellers every year. Sleeman became the acknowledged authority on the subject, and in 1830, Lord William Bentinck appointed him to suppress the Thugs.

Fortunately for Sleeman, the organization had already become corrupt and degenerate. In its earlier days, the members of the sect had been strict in their observance of the rules. It was forbidden to kill women, because Kali was a woman; it was also forbidden to kill religious mendicants, carpenters, metal workers, blind men, pariahs, lepers, mutilated men, and men driving a goat or cow. Greed had caused a gradual relaxation of the rules (it must have been infuriating to let a rich caravan escape because it contained a carpenter or blind man); and it was to this disobedience that the Thugs attributed their decline in fortunes. In a sense, this was true. Haste and greed meant that bodies were sometimes left unburied, so a search could be instituted more quickly. And in some cases, lack of preparation meant that the killing was bungled – Sleeman mentions a case in which the Thugs were pursued back to their own village, and saved from arrest only by the intervention of the villagers (who had been well bribed). When Sleeman's researches were published, travellers became suspicious of 'holy men' or poor Moslems who asked for protection. Better roads (built by the British) meant that Thugs could be pursued more easily. Many of them became informers (or 'approvers') to save their own lives. Within a few years, thousands of Thugs had been arrested and brought to trial.

Sleeman was the first to understand the fundamentally religious nature of Thuggee: that the murders were sacrifices offered to the dark mother, Kali (also known as Durgha and

Bhowani). Because he was deeply religious, the Thug was usually scrupulous, honest, kindly and trustworthy; Sleeman's assistant described one Thug chief as 'the best man I have ever known'. Many Thugs were rich men who held responsible positions; part of their spoils went to local Rajahs or officials, who had no objection to Thugs provided they committed their murders elsewhere. Colonel James Sleeman, grandson of Sir William, described Feringheea as 'the Beau Nash of Thuggee'.[1] Like the Assassins, most convicted Thugs met their deaths with remarkable bravery, which impressed their British executioners. It is this Jekyll and Hyde character that makes the Thugs so baffling. One old Thug was the nurse of a family of British children, and obviously regarded his charges with great tenderness; for precisely one month of every year he obtained leave to visit his 'sick mother'; the family found it unbelievable when he was arrested as a Thug. For the Thugs were capable of murdering children as casually as adults. A Thug leader described how his gang decoyed a group of twenty-seven – including five women and two children – away from a larger group of travellers (arguing that they could travel more cheaply). At midnight they stopped to rest in a grove – already chosen in advance as the murder place. There the Thugs strangled the adults; the children – two three-year-old boys – were given to two Thugs; but one of them kept crying for his mother, whom he had just seen murdered. The Thug picked him up by his feet and dashed out his brains against a rock. This was one of the few occasions when retribution followed. The adults were buried, but the Thugs overlooked the boy's body. It was discovered the next morning by the local landowner, who set out to hunt the Thugs with armed men. After a chase, the Thugs were located; when the armed men opened fire, they scattered, leaving behind much of their booty. Four thugs were arrested, and kept in captivity for a few years. (Sleeman points out that the landowner's motive was not a sense of justice, but to seize the spoils.) The other boy was brought up as a Thug.

The male children of Thugs were automatically initiated into the sect. They were first placed in the care of a Thug tutor, who insisted upon absolute obedience, and acted as their religious instructor. (It must be emphasized that the killing was only a part of the ritual of the Thugs, as

Communion is of Christians.) At the age of nine or ten, the boys were allowed to act as scouts, and later to watch the killing. At eighteen they were alowed to take part in the killing and eat the *goor*.

By the year 1850, Thuggee had virtually ceased to exist in India. Over 4,000 Thugs had been brought to trial; some were hanged, others sentenced to transportation or life imprisonment. Sleeman came to know many of them – even to establish a kind of friendship; for example, he was instrumental in getting the notorious Feringheea a pardon (in the face of some opposition, for when the Thug leader was caught, he admitted that he had just returned from an expedition in which 105 men and women had died).

The mystery of the origin of Thuggee is still unsolved. Feringheea told Sleeman that all the Thug rituals were portrayed in the eighth-century carvings in the caves of Ellora. (Ellora is a village in north-east Bombay province, and its Hindu, Buddhist and Jain temples extend for over a mile, with some of India's greatest sculptural treasures, whose dates range from the third to the thirteenth century.) If this is true, then the Thugs pre-dated the Assassins by three hundred years. In his book *The Assassins*, Bernard Lewis suggests that the Thugs may have been connected with the stranglers of Iraq – the heretical sect that sprang up after the death of the Prophet. But these stranglers flourished in the first half of the eighth century, and four more centuries were to elapse before the Moslems made deep inroads into India. (The greatest of the early Moslem invaders of India, Mahmud of Ghazni – Khayyam's 'mighty Mahmud' – confined himself to the Punjab, in north-western India: Delhi fell to Mohammed of Ghur in 1192.) So it is altogether more likely that Ismailis, fleeing from persecution after the fall of Alamut, discovered that India already possessed its own Order of Assassins, and formed an alliance with the Thugs. Other Ismailis formed their own sects in India, and continued to regard the Persian Imam as their head. In 1811, the French consul Rousseau observed that Ismailis flourished in India, and that they regarded their Imam almost as a god. In 1850, a sect of Ismailis known as the Khojas decided to settle a religious dispute by their old methods, and four dissenting brethren were assassinated in broad daylight. The four killers were hanged. The quarrel centred around the question of whether the

Khojas of Bombay province still owed allegiance to the Persian Imam. This Imam was known as the Aga Khan; and a few years later, he was forced to flee to India – after an unsuccessful attempt to overthrow the Shah of Persia – and became the spiritual head of the Ismailis – not only in India, but also in Persia, Syria and central Asia. And so the homeland of the Thugs became eventually the homeland of the descendants of the Assassins.

All the chroniclers of the Thugs have talked about the 'mystery' of their psychology. And what exactly is this mystery? Not that criminals may appear to be law-abiding citizens; this is a commonplace of criminal investigation; Deacon Brodie and Charlie Peace are the rule, not the exception. But the Thugs were not criminals in the ordinary sense. What emerges on every page of Sleeman's book is that they were driven by a *compulsion* to kill. This exciting game – of stalking and strangling human beings – became a drug, an addiction. This is what troubled the British investigators, who were ordinary soldiers and civil servants – men of the Dr. Watson type. They sensed that the Thug murders were an inverted creative act, which brought its own peculiar, deep satisfaction, and the thought made them shudder.

The Thugs, on the other hand, took the obsessional nature of their vocation for granted. It was the result of entering the service of the dark goddess, and eating her *goor*. Feringheea told Sleeman: 'My mother's family were opulent, her relations high in office. I have been high in office myself, and become so great a favourite . . . that I was sure of promotion; yet I was always miserable when absent from the gang, and obliged to return to Thuggee. My father made me taste of that fatal *goor* when I was a mere boy, and if I were to live to a thousand years, I should never be able to follow any other trade.' They were the chosen of Kali; the first Thugs had been created by Kali to help her destroy a horde of demons. (These had to be strangled, for their blood, once shed, turned into more demons.) No Thug entertained the slightest doubt that the goddess accompanied them on their expeditions. She made the sacred pickaxe fly out of the well – where it was sometimes thrown overnight – into the hand of its carrier. (Many Thugs assured Sleeman that they had seen this happen.) And if they buried the pickaxe, she turned it in the night, so it pointed in the direction where the richest booty lay. Since she was a goddess of destruction, it was natural enough that her slaves should be possessed by the urge to destroy . . .

A modern psychologist would probably explain this obsession in terms of sex; for a man with a compulsion to kill is in the grip of sadism: and sadism is surely sexual in origin? This is an assumption that will be questioned in the next chapter; for the moment, it is enough to note that a Thug would have rejected this view with indignation. They were puritanical about sex, because their goddess was a woman. Sleeman says: 'No Thug was ever known to offer insult, either in speech or act, to a woman they were about to murder.'[1] A Thug theologian – if such a thing existed – would have explained the 'mystery' of Thug psychology in terms of the nature of Kali herself. She is the goddess of Time and Saviour of the Universe. (Her husband, Shiva, upon whom she stands, is the god of Space.) She represents the ultimate reconciliation of opposites: terror and motherly tenderness, death and creation. The ancient Greeks might have regarded her as an incarnation of Dionysus, the god of wine, who also induces divine frenzy in his worshippers. The Hindu saint Ramakrishna saw in her the ultimate vital force of creation, with all its contradictions, an infinite power that transcends merely human notions of good and evil.

The western mind finds this difficult to grasp, for Christianity has no counterpart of Kali. It is like asserting that God and the Devil are halves of the same godhead, both equally powerful, equally necessary to the scheme of things. The Church persecuted the heresy known as Dualism, which asserted something very similar. In *A Glastonbury Romance*, the novelist John Cowper Powys explained sadism as a consequence of this fundamental split in the godhead: 'Its primordial goodness warring forever against its primordial evil holds life up only by vast excess of energy and oceans of lavish waste. Even though the cry of a particular creature may reach the First Cause, there is always a danger of its being intercepted by the evil will of this vast Janus-faced Force . . .'[2] Powys's sadist, an antiquary named Evans, is obsessed by a certain passage in a book describing a killing blow with an iron bar. 'The nature of his temptation was such that it had nothing to redeem it. Such abominable wickedness came straight out of the evil in the heart of the First

Cause, travelled through the Interlunar spaces, and entered the particular nerve in the erotic organism of Mr. Evans which was predestined to respond to it.'[3] Mr. Evans is tortured by his obsession with killing. 'He saw his soul in the form of an unspeakable worm, writhing in pursuit of new, and ever new mental victims, drinking new and innocent blood.' The Thugs accepted their own murderous obsession, because killing was ordained by their goddess.

Whether we can accept Powys's form of Dualism as literally true is beside the point. What is important is that we recognize the *autonomous* nature of this urge to destroy, which seems to be as basic as the sexual or territorial drive. For whatever reason, man *is* capable of experiencing a morbid involvement in the act of destruction, as if some deep erotic nerve had been touched by a craving for violence. And, like the sexual impulse, this destructive impulse has the power to blind him to everything but its own satisfaction. The future becomes unimportant or non-existent; all that counts is fulfilment of the need for violence.

And it is the presence of this impulse, this 'worm of destruction', that distinguishes 'assassination' from the ordinary murder case. It can always be sensed underneath the apparent motive for the killing, whether it is sexual, or political, or simply a general resentment against society. The obvious motive is only the excuse that allows the 'erotic nerve' to be touched by the energy of destruction. In some cases, the two are so intermingled that they can hardly be separated. In Peter Kürten, the Düsseldorf sadist, the sexual impulse and the urge to violence had become interdependent: violence provoked a sexual orgasm; sexual excitement released a desire for violence. When Kürten returned to Düsseldorf – after a long prison sentence – there was a red sunset, and he saw it as an auspicious sign for the reign of terror he was about to inaugurate.[4] When he walked around the streets of Düsseldorf, he had dreams of blowing up the city with dynamite. A Thug would have recognized in him a fellow devotee of Kali.

Again, in the case of the unknown sadist known as Jack the Ripper, one recognizes again the autonomous nature of the destructive impulse. Indeed, it is difficult to form any kind of mental picture of the Ripper without assuming that he was in the power of Mr. Evans's 'worm'. The 'mystery' one senses in this case is the mystery Sleeman sensed about the Thugs. The incredible violence of the murders – the disembowelling of the victims, the hacking of the features, the removal of vital organs – all indicate a man giving expression to an urge that has become a torment. When he woke up the next morning, he probably found it unbelievable that it had actually happened, that it was not a nightmare.

The New Orleans Axeman murders, which took place in 1918 and 1919, provide an interesting parallel with the Ripper case. Jack the Ripper, writing to a member of the Whitechapel Vigilance Committee (and enclosing part of the kidney of his latest victim), begins his letter: 'From Hell. Mr. Lusk, sir, I send you half the kidney I took from one woman ...' The Axeman[5] wrote a letter to the editor of the *Times Picayune* in which he declared: 'I am not a human being, but a spirit and fell demon from the hottest hell.' It would seem that both murderers felt themselves to be demonic emissaries, agents of a dark force, sent to scourge mankind ... The parallel with the Thugs needs no underlining.

The 'demonic' element is again clearly displayed in the Ratcliffe Highway murders of 1811 – described in the appendix to De Quincey's essay on 'Murder Considered as One of the Fine Arts'. Towards midnight on 7th December, Timothy Marr, who kept a hosier's shop in the East End of London, sent out the servant girl to buy oysters; when she returned, it was to find everyone in the house dead: Timothy Marr, his wife Celia, their baby, and the apprentice boy, James Gowen. It looked as if a giant with a sledge hammer had been at work. The force of the blows had been so great that the apprentice's brains were spattered over the ceiling. The hood of the baby's cradle had been smashed, as if in a frenzy of violence; the child's head was battered, and its throat cut. The murder weapon was found in the bedroom: a type of sledge-hammer called a 'pen-maul' – which, in a poster about the murders, can be seen to bear a striking resemblance to the sacred pickaxe of the Thugs.

There was still no clue to the killer's identity – or motive – when, two weeks later, a second family was slaughtered in the same area. A publican named Williamson, his wife and their maidservant, were slaughtered with an iron bar, and their throats cut. A lodger named John Turner came downstairs while the murders were taking place, and saw a man bending over Mrs. Williamson's body, he tiptoed back upstairs, made a rope of his bedsheets, and escaped from the bedroom window. A crowd, attracted by his yells, broke into the house but the killer escaped through a rear window. (He seems to have been on the point of killing a fourteen-year-old girl in her bed when the noise disturbed him.) A certain amount of money had been taken.

The pen-maul was traced to a sailor's lodging house, and a young Irishman named John Williams arrested. He had access to the tool chest that contained the maul. On the morning of the murder, he had returned to a room he shared with other lodgers, and shouted at someone to put out a candle that was burning. The next morning, it was noticed that his shoes were muddy (the murderer had escaped by scrambling up a muddy bank); so were his socks, which he thereupon washed. A shirt was found to be bloodstained. Later on, bloodstained trousers were found in the bottom of the privy in the house. A coat belonging to Williams had heavy bloodstains in the pocket, as if it had held a knife; the bloodstained knife was later found in a mousehole. (De Quincey states, mistakenly, that it was found in the pocket.) Williams hanged himself before he could be brought to trial; his body was buried at the crossroads near the scene of the murders, with a stake driven through the heart.

In *The Maul and the Pear Tree* (1971), T. A. Critchley and P. D. James argue that Williams was probably 'framed'. The actual killer, they suggest, was a man named Ablass, a shipmate of Williams with a history of violence. The motive was robbery, and Ablass was probably aided by a man named Hart. The authors even suggest that Williams was actually murdered in jail, with the connivance of the jailer. The theory is well-argued, but the basic objections remain. If the motive was burglary, why kill the baby? If two men were concerned, why did the lodger, Turner, see only one? But the basic objection is that the murders were committed with the ferocity of a maniac; talk about 'motive' is irrelevant. It is true that Williams had no history of violence, but on examination, it turns out that Ablass's 'violence' amounted to fomenting a mutiny on board ship. Ablass had reason to dislike Williams, who had escaped punishment after the mutiny; but again, what has this to do with the violence of the murders? The Ratcliffe Highway murders fascinated De

Quincey's generation for the same reason that the Ripper murders fascinated the late Victorians: because of their 'demonic' quality, because the killer was a man obsessed by violence for it own sake.

In reading accounts of assassinations, one is struck by the assassin's indifference to his own death. In the 'golden age' of political assassination – towards the end of the last century – assassins often went to the scaffold or guillotine crying '*Vive l'anarchie!*' We have already noted the indifference to death shown by the Assassins of Persia and the Thugs of India. In some cases, this was due to genuine idealism. Kaliayev, who blew up the Grand Duke Sergius in 1904, declined an offer by the widow to plead for his life, saying that his death would do more for the cause of revolution in Russia. Sometimes, it was bravado, as when the train robber and murderer Charrier told the jury: 'I am a desperate enemy of society, and my hatred will only finish with my life. I defy you, gentlemen of the jury, to take my head.' (They obliged.) But the indifference is so general that it is tempting to conclude that the assassin hopes to destroy himself as well as his victim. It is almost as though 'Mr Evans's worm', like the monkey in Le Fanu's *Green Tea*, were a demon tempting man to self-destruction. This, again, may serve as a criterion to distinguish 'assassination' from murder.

Two examples will serve to illustrate my point. On 8th February, 1872, Lord Mayo, the Viceroy of India, spent the day inspecting the prison settlements on the four Andaman Islands in the Bay of Bengal. Towards dusk, as he was about to leave the fourth of them, Hopetown, he suddenly decided to climb a hill called Mount Harriet. As his party moved towards the summit, they were shadowed by a man carrying a long knife. The killer's opportunity came as Lord Mayo walked along the jetty, on his way to the boat; he leapt on his back, crooked an arm round his neck, and stabbed him twice in the shoulder blades. Lord Mayo died shortly afterwards. The killer, an Indian named Shere Ali, was captured, and violently beaten by the soldiers.

Five years before, Shere Ali had been sentenced to death by the British authorities for killing a relative in a blood feud; the sentence was later commuted to life imprisonment. It was his feeling that the British had no right to interfere in a hereditary feud, so although he was a model prisoner, he kept the carving knife hidden in his cell, and prayed for the day when he might murder some distinguished European. After the assassination of Lord Mayo, Shere Ali was asked why he had done it. 'By the order of God.' During the month when he awaited hanging, he remained defiant and boastful; he seemed to regard his own death as a good exchange for the murder of a British Lord. On one occasion, he succeeded in overpowering a guard and stabbing him twice with his own bayonet: on another, he showed a British officer a sharp stone which he had levered out of the floor; he said it was a good thing the officer had been civil, because he had intended to kill him.

In the early hours of 20th July, 1948, a car pulled up in front of the house of the Superintendent of the Ohio State Reformatory Farm. Two ex-convicts, Robert Daniels and John West, burst into the house, where John Niebel, his wife and twenty-year-old daughter had been sleeping. While John West pistol-whipped Niebel and his wife, Daniels beat the girl in another room, then raped her. Then all three were made to strip, and marched into a nearby field. They were made to kneel, and then shot. Mrs. Niebel was shot in the stomach, and allowed to writhe on the ground for a while before she was dispatched with a bullet in the head.

The killers were at large for another twenty-four hours, but escape was impossible. As soon as the bodies were found – early next morning – road blocks were thrown up around the whole county. During their flight, Daniels and West committed two more murders: one of them a car driver, one of them a truck driver asleep in his cab. Stopped by the police at a road block, West tried to shoot his way out and was killed; Daniels was arrested and later executed.

At first sight, there seems an abyss of difference between this case and Shere Ali's. West and Daniels hoped to escape, and nearly succeeded. But on closer scrutiny, it becomes more problematic. West was a near-moron; but Daniels was described by the prison psychiatrist as 'brainy'. Yet a few hours before the murder of the Niebels, they committed two tavern robberies in Columbus, Ohio, in the second of which they murdered the owner. Daniels was driving his own car, and its make and number were noted by customers as the bandits fled. Knowing there was a state alert out for them, they drove to the Niebels', and parked the car in front of the house, where it was observed by a neighbour. If Daniels had really been determined to escape, he would have taken elementary precautions – such as wearing a mask in the two hold-ups, using a stolen car instead of one registered in his own name, and parking some distance away from the Niebels' house. Every stage of the operation was conducted in a manner that made their capture inevitable, and the two extra murders in the course of flight – both completely gratuitous – strengthen this view. Like Shere Ali, Daniels and West thought only of the supreme satisfaction of revenge; they took no interest in what lay beyond it, because their planning of the operation made it certain that only death lay beyond it. In the sense already defined, Daniels and West were assassins rather than murderers.

This book is concerned with the psychology of 'demonic' violence, recognizing that it is the central, symbolic problem of our century: the peculiar form assumed by romanticism in an age of defeat.

1. *Thug, or A Million Murders*, Sampson Low, London, 1933.
2. 1933 edition, p. 61.
3. *Ibid.* pp. 254–5.
3. Kürten committed eight murders and many serious attacks between February and November, 1929. See *An Encyclopaedia of Murder.*
5. Like the Ripper, the Axeman seemed to select his victims at random, chiselling his way into their homes through the back door. Six of them died; others were seriously injured. He was never caught. See *An Encyclopaedia of Murder.*

CHAPTER TWO

The Philosophy of the Will

On 10th July, 1958, two Mexican children were standing on the sidewalk in the town of Cuba, New Mexico; the mother of one of them was talking to a neighbour a few yards away. A jeep drove along the almost empty street, and stopped opposite the group: the bearded man at the wheel raised a rifle, fired two shots, and then drove away, leaving one child dead, the other dying. Someone noted the number of the jeep, and later the same day, a posse surrounded its owner, an American prospector named Norman Foose, at his camp on a mountain. Foose surrendered after he had been shot in the foot. He made no attempt to deny that it was he who had shot the children; his reason, he explained, was a desire to do something about the population explosion. 'If the population increases at its present rate, there won't be enough food for everyone, and we'll all be living on a few square feet of land.' The policeman asked him if he knew that the mother of the murdered girl had eleven children. 'No, but when I saw the kids, it occurred to me that there were far too many of them in the world. I decided to make a start getting rid of them . . .'

There is something about this story that epitomizes the crime of violence in the late twentieth century. There is the dream-like appearance of logic, and then – absurdity. The motive seems elusive or insufficient, as if some vital piece of evidence is being withheld. The same was true of the Negro riots in America in the late sixties, and the I.R.A. violence in Northern Ireland, which still continues as I write this: the feeling that the violence goes deeper than its obvious motivation – as if the social discontent had produced a volcanic eruption, which then goes on to trigger an earthquake.

The Moors murder trial and the Manson case had this same elusive quality. In the classic murder case of the nineteenth century, the murderer tries to build up ambiguities, suggests doubts or extenuating circumstances. But the facts undo him; in spite of his evasions, the motive stands out like the Eiffel Tower; he is in the position of a liar who has been thoroughly found out. But even after Brady and Manson had been sentenced, there was a feeling that nothing that had been said explained what had actually been done. There were strange justifications, arguments about the sick society derived from Sade or Marcuse; but nothing that could be identified as a sufficient motive. It would have created a feeling of psychological relief if a prosecution psychiatrist had been able to show that Ian Brady had always been a sadistic pederast, or that Manson's delusions of grandeur were due to venereal disease. But it was precisely this kind of certainty that never emerged. The American public found the Manson case particularly frustrating because he seemed to be arguing according to some non-linear logic. He was innocent; not because he had nothing to do with the murders, but because society was guilty. And the underground press of California seemed to find this plea understandable and fair, even though no one actually alleged that it was society that murdered Sharon Tate and the LaBiancas.

One thing is clear: if we accept the distinction between assassins and murderers, then Foose, Manson and Brady belong with the assassins. The ordinary murderer commits his crime *looking over his shoulder*. He hopes not to be caught; if he is caught he will hang his head, and acknowledge his sense of guilt by saying, 'It's a fair cop.' The assassin peers down his rifle with the sense of justification felt by a headmaster as he canes an insolent pupil or a hangman as he releases the trap. He is punishing society. He feels he is *in the right*.

Nietzsche understood the psychology of the assassin. In a letter to Strindberg (7th December, 1888) he wrote: '. . . the history of criminal families .. always leads one back to *an individual too strong for his particular social environment*. The later major criminal case in Paris, Prado's, is a classic example. Prado was more than a match for his judges, even his lawyers, in self-control, wit and bravado. This in spite of the fact that the pressure of the trial had already affected him so much physically that several witnesses recognized him only from old portraits.' [My italics]

Prado was executed in December 1888 for the murder of a prostitute named Marie Agaetan. In 1887, Prado had been arrested as he fled from the scene of a robbery; he attempted to shoot the police who pursued him. A short time later, his two mistresses were also arrested, charged with being concerned in another robbery. Confined in the same cell, the rivals became bitter about the man who was responsible for their plight, and one of them told the other that Prado was the murderer of Marie Agaetan. After this, she decided to tell it to an examining magistrate. Jewellers were located who recognized Prado as the man who had sold them jewellery belonging to Marie Agaetan. At this trial it was revealed that besides his two mistresses (one of whom gave birth to his child in prison) he also had a wife in Spain. The public flocked to the spectacle of a Don Juan confronted by the women he had betrayed. H. B. Irving, writing of Prado in *Studies of French Criminals*, says: 'Whatever the mystery attaching to [Prado's] previous career, it had been a desperate and adventurous one. He had fought, and fought with courage and resolution, in Cuba and in Carlist wars in Spain. M. Goron, in his Memoirs, is inclined to accept . . . Prado as the son of the President of the Peruvian Republic . . . Prado . . . has something of the soldier about him; his crimes are more reckless and daring; he knows no tears . . . and brought to bay, he shows himself well-read, prodigal of words, and inexhaustible in protestations, overwhelming his judges with his torrents of argument and denunciation . . .' When sentenced to death, Prado wrote a letter to President Carnot of France, begging to be executed as soon as possible. Carnot (who was himself assassinated five years later) complied with the request; Prado met his death fearlessly. In a letter written to a friend shortly before his execution, he quoted Diderot: 'For the wise man there are no such things as laws. Since all laws are subject to error or exceptions, it is for the wise man to judge for himself whether he shall obey them or break them.' It could be regarded as the Assassin's credo.

About a decade later, the sociologist Vilfredo Pareto produced a concept that would have delighted Nietzsche – and Prado. All individuals may be rated on a scale from excellent to very bad. A man who has never committed a crime would rate zero on the criminal scale, while Jack the Ripper would come close to the top. Henry Ford would rate high on the business scale; Gandhi would rate high on the sanctity scale. All the high-raters in a society form its *élite*. And there is a governing élite, and a non-governing élite. It follows that the criminal, like the artist and the philosopher, belongs to the non-governing élite . . .

Nowadays we would refer to Pareto's 'élite' as a dominant minority. The researches of Tinbergen, Lorenz and others have made us aware of the vital role played by dominance in zoology: that the social order of most birds and animals is based upon dominance. Oddly enough, it seems that the dominant minority is precisely five per cent of the total population. This applies to human beings as well as to animals and birds. When Shaw asked the explorer Stanley how many of his men could lead the expedition if he himself fell ill, Stanley replied: 'One in twenty.' Shaw asked if this was approximate or exact. 'Exact,' said Stanley. The Chinese made use of this knowledge during the Korean war, preventing the escape of prisoners by keeping the 'dominant five per cent' in a separate compound under heavy guard; the remainder could then be left with almost no guard.

Nietzsche recognized Prado as a member of the 'dominant minority', although he knew nothing of zoology. His own philosophy recognized the will to power as the fundamental drive of all living creatures. And Nietzsche, in turn, had derived this vision of the will from Schopenhauer, whose *World as Will and Illusion* appeared in 1819. Schopenhauer had seen the will as a tremendous, blind, groping force, like some strange octopus. It drives all life, but it *has no purpose* except to endlessly renew itself. So living things are driven by endless desire, and life is pain, except when desire exhausts itself, and it becomes weariness. The will drives us on by creating illusions – religion, love, fame, knowledge, which give us a false impression of meaning and purpose . . .

As a young man, self-divided and frequently exhausted, Nietzsche accepted all this without reservation, but later, a healthy instinct turned him to evolutionism, and he saw the will to power as an expression of man's striving to become a god. It is this will to evolve that drives the élite like a thorn in the side. In healthy, evolving societies, there is always a place for the adventurer – the man with bold conceptions and the courage to realize them. In a decadent, frivolous society, such a man has no outlet, and the thorn may drive him to destroy other people, or to destroy himself. He feels no compunction in committing acts of violence, because he feels only contempt for society and its values. (Nietzsche's favourite novelist was Dostoevsky; he recognized in Raskolnikov a perfect example of his will to power.) By the time of Nietzsche's death (1900) these views had found widespread acceptance among European intellectuals.

Freud changed all that. He accepted Schopenhauer's unconscious will, and he identified it as the libido, the sexual drive. This view was so startling – after the polite repressions of the nineteenth century – and aroused so much bitter controversy, that Nietzsche and Schopenhauer were completely eclipsed – or at best, regarded as interesting forerunners of Freud. Freud identified Dostoevsky's problem as an Oedipus complex. According to the sexual theory, male violence is a form of substitute rape (although later, sensing the inadequacy of this explanation, he also introduced 'the death urge').

Freud's ex-disciple Adler suggested an alternative theory in which the will to power played a central role; but compared to Nietzsche or Schopenhauer, Adler's will to power is an apologetic shadow, an attempt to compensate for feelings of inferiority. And compared to Freud's sex drive, it certainly lacked dramatic appeal.

It is only in the second half of the twentieth century that the Freudian theory had gradually lost influence. This has been due to discoveries in zoology rather than psychology. In 1932, Solly Zuckerman published his researches into the social life of monkeys in the London Zoo – *The Social Life of Monkeys and Apes* – and his findings appeared to support Freud; monkeys seemed to think of little besides sex, and their social hierarchy was determined by it. But four years later, a young American psychologist, Abraham Maslow, studied the monkeys in the Bronx Zoo, and recognized that all the non-stop sexual activity was a way of asserting *dominance*; the dominant monkeys mounted the less dominant ones, and it made no difference whether it was a male or female on top. Robert Ardrey's *African Genesis* (1961) popularized a discovery that had been made more than half a century earlier, by the South African naturalist Eugene Marais: that among animals in their natural habitat, sex is less important than dominance and the 'territorial instinct'. Ardrey's writing produced an upsurge of popular interest in the field of animal behaviour and dominance. Konrad

Lorenz's *On Aggression* – which, a decade earlier, would have appealed mainly to fellow zoologists – became a best-seller. There were a few direct challenges to Freud; but in the face of the biological evidence, the grip of the sexual theory began to loosen.

I am here suggesting that, purely on grounds of common sense, the Freudian libido is less satisfying as an explanation of 'dominance' than the Nietzschean evolutionary drive. An Eastern despot may enjoy the exercise of power, but he keeps his sexual urge for the harem; and his sexual appetite seems to be an expression of his will to power, not vice versa. The Freudian theory looked so plausible because civilized man *is* obsessed by sex – like the monkeys in captivity. But it is more logical to suppose that sexual dominance is a part of a will to power than to regard all human dominance as an expression of sexual frustration. Men obsessed by political dominance – like Hitler and Stalin – are seldom deeply interested in sex; men obsessed by sexual conquest – like Casanova and Frank Harris – are seldom outstanding in other fields of dominant activity. *Sexual dominance is a fairly unimportant sub-department of the will to power.*

This raises again the question already discussed in connection with the Thugs: of the nature of sadism. Ever since the open discussion of sexual abnormality became permissible, towards the end of the nineteenth century, it has been taken for granted that sadism is sexual in origin. Krafft-Ebing defines it as 'the combination of lust and cruelty', Havelock Ellis as 'sexual pleasures in hurting', Ivan Boch as 'the lustful joy experienced by perverts at the sight of pain . . .' As used in everyday language, it has become a synonym for cruelty, so that anyone from a German concentration camp guard to a boy who ties tin cans to a cat's tail is described as being a sadist. Freudian psychology has conditioned us to accepting all cruelty as sexual in origin. The notion has become so much part of our thinking that most of us are not even aware of it – we simply use the terms 'cruelty' and 'sadism' as interchangeable.

But if modern violence is to be understood, it is necessary to return to pre-Freudian modes of thought – in fact, to the Will to Power of Schopenhauer and Nietzsche. Consider the following anecdote, from Ronald Pearsall's study in Victorian sexuality, *The Worm in the Bud*:

Jane Shore, aged thirty-five, lived in Shoreditch, and was the wife of an engineer in China. On her way to see a friend she visited the Lord Napier public house in Clapton, and rapidly downed a succession of ale, beer and gin. Five men volunteered to see her to her friend's home. On the way, a foreman of an oil works intercepted the party. 'What are you going to do with that woman?' he asked. 'Oh, she likes it,' one of the men replied. They threw Mrs. Shore down a twenty-five-foot hollow, and watched by a considerable crowd, the five men raped her and beat her, without anyone interfering, until she was nearly dead. The prosecution criticized the onlookers for not interfering, but the bewigged and supercilious lawyers did not live in the jungle ...

Clearly, this is sadism – as Mr. Pearsall comments – there seems no more to be said. But a Victorian, who had never read his Krafft-Ebing, might well have wondered why five ordinary workmen – presumably not 'perverts' – should have wanted to *beat* Jane Shore. The rape of a drunken woman may be understandable; but not the ill-treatment. Until we try to imagine the scene. In broad daylight, a naked woman lies on the grass, her torn clothes around her; two men hold her legs apart, while another kneels between them. At the top of the hollow stands a crowd of men and women – perhaps a few children – watching silently. Even in a 'jungle' this kind of conduct is rather shameful. So they beat her as a kind of assertion of their *right* to her; it is an assertion of their lack of guilt, an act of defiance, like a gorilla beating its chest ...

That is to say, the beating is not a *part* of the sexual intercourse; it is a kind of red-herring, designed to make the rape look like a punishment. And it would not serve its purpose unless everyone in that crowd recognized instinctively that rape is an expression of the will to power, not vice versa. If it had all taken place in the dark, without onlookers, the probability is that she would have been raped but not beaten.

What Nietzsche derived from Schopenhauer[1] was the notion that man's most powerful appetite is not the desire for security or love or beauty, but the *will itself*, a violent, permanent hunger like an empty stomach. Nietzsche came to reject Schopenhauer's belief that the will was a completely *futile* craving, fed on illusions. He recognized that happiness is the feeling we experience when obstacles are overcome, and that man is therefore a fundamentally *purposive* creature, whose will is the instrument of his evolution towards the superman. He began to see the assertion of the will as the deepest and healthiest of human instincts; so he attacked the moralists and the aesthetes – St. Paul, George Eliot, Sainte-Beuve – and glorified the adventurer and poisoner Cesare Borgia, who murdered his sister's husband in order to make her his mistress. But whether or not we agree with Nietzsche's historical judgement that 'Europe was near to greatness when it was possible to hope that Cesare Borgia would seize the Papacy', we can see that it sprang from his belief that the will itself is the deepest and greatest of all human appetites, and, that in healthy human beings, it has to be satisfied by some form of conquest. Nietzsche would have had no doubt that Cesare Borgia's seduction of his sister was an expression of the same will-drive that made him dream of becoming master of Italy.

The twentieth century has rejected the Nietzschean 'will to power', because it seems to be a licence for ruthless opportunism; this is like rejecting Freud's sexual theory because it seems to be a licence for patricide and incest. If the Nietzschean assumption is correct – *that the will itself is the basic human appetite* – then the way in which it manifested itself, in Cesare Borgia or Hitler, is irrelevant. Nietzsche's approval of Cesare Borgia may be valid ground for criticism of Nietzsche as a human being, but this is also irrelevant – as it would have been irrelevant to Freud's sexual theory if Freud had admired Casanova.

In fact, all the major post-Freudian discoveries in psychology have vindicated Nietzsche. I have spoken of these at length elsewhere[2], but they are so central to the thesis of this book that it is necessary to offer a summary.

In his important essay 'On Vital Reserves', William James recognized that the central problem of human consciousness is its tendency to fluctuate between states of great zest and vitality, and states of dullness and boredom; the latter are the 'norm'. James recognized that the 'wide-awake' states are caused by intense effort, the feeling that there is something important and worth-while to be done. On the other hand, a person trapped in a feeling of boredom and listlessness may simply 'run down' until life seems an endless series of obstacles, and every molehill seems to be a mountain. That is to say, 'neurasthenia' is due to non-use of the will.

Abraham Maslow (1908–1970) decided that Adler's 'will to power' explained the behaviour of monkeys in the Bronx Zoo better than the Freudian sexual theory: but this did not lead him to reject Freud. Instead, he decided simply that Freud was true on a lower level than Adler, and he formulated a theory which he called 'The Hierarchy of Needs'. According to Maslow, the basic animal (or human) need is for food and security; when this is satisfied, the need for sex, for a mate, takes over; when this is satisfied, the need for self-esteem, for social acceptance, becomes important. And an intelligent human being who is satisfied on all these levels will find himself developing 'meta-needs', the need for intellectual activity, for art or philosophy, for altruism or religion. Human beings become mentally sick, says Maslow, when there is some major blockage to their evolution – on *any* level. For when this happens, the will cannot find a way forward; it becomes passive, and then the Jamesian rundown follows. The vital batteries run flat, like a car left in the garage all winter. On the other hand, when the way lies open, and a human being is possessed by a strong sense of purpose, the batteries become so highly charged that any minor satisfaction causes a spontaneous discharge, a flash of pure delight which Maslow calls 'the peak experience'. The essence of psychological health is the activity of the will.

This view was also reached – from another angle – by Viktor Frankl, a Jewish psychiatrist who spent the war in Nazi concentration camps; Frankl observed that the prisoners who had nothing to *hope for* were inclined to rundown and die, while prisoners who maintained any kind of optimistic forward-drive stayed healthy. Even before the war, Frankl had observed that people who began to worry about minor problems often developed serious blockages and tensions, and that the best way to cure them was to make them *strive* to do precisely what they were afraid of doing; (so a boy who stuttered was cured by being made to play the part of a stutterer in the school play). Frank concluded that a sense of purpose is vital to mental health; a person without purpose begins to worry about nothing, in the same way that some people begin to itch when they are lying awake in the night. As soon as they are persuaded to make a real effort the blockage disappears.

William Glasser's 'reality therapy' and Hobert Mowrer's 'responsibility therapy' depends upon this same recognition: that people without purpose become breeding grounds for every kind of psychological illness, and that the cure depends upon awakening the will to a sense of reality and responsibility.

In fact, the true foundation for all this work in psychology lies in the philosophy of Edmund Husserl (whose major work, *Ideas*, appeared in 1922). Husserl's fundamental recognition was that all our mental processes are 'intentional' – active rather than passive. I tend to assume that, when I look at something, it walks in through my eyes, and imprints itself on my brain. The truth is the exact opposite. When I see something, it is exactly as if I had reached out my hand and *picked it up*. I am so used to 'seeing things' that I no longer notice the effort involved, any more than I notice the effort when I read a newspaper. But there *is* an effort; I have to continually interpret 'reality' just as I have to interpret the black signs in a newspaper.

This has important consequences, especially for poets and mystics. If I feel generally bored and run-down, I cease to put the same subconscious effort into my 'seeing', and things actually *look* duller. When I am interested and full of purpose, I put more unconscious energy into my seeing, and things seem to glow with meaning. I see more colours, smell more odours.

But *because* I am unaware of this subconscious effort, I am puzzled why the world always seems to be changing. One day life is self-evidently marvellous, the next it has gone dull. The trouble here tends to be self-propagating; because if the world looks boring and dull, my immediate response is to become passive and yawn; so the dullness may continue for years, and I shall assume it is quite normal. And if some interest or sense of purpose causes me to make an effort, and I suddenly begin to have 'peak experiences' again, I shall almost certainly fail to see the connection between my effort and the peak experience; instead, I assume the peak experience to be merely a piece of good luck, the result of some happy chance which I do not understand.

Husserl himself did not make this particular application of

his theory to psychology; but it is implicit. And his recognition of 'the intentionality of consciousness' enables us to see the connection between the question posed by William James, and the answer suggested by Maslow and Frankl. Our vitality fluctuates so much – between mystical ecstasy and complete mental breakdown – because of our fundamental error about the nature of consciousness. We think it is automatic, like our breathing. It isn't; it depends on effort, like swimming. If we stop making effort, we sink.

I come now to my own small contribution to this field. All my own work has been centrally concerned with the problem of 'life failure' – when life turns futile and sour, and no effort seems worth making. In 1957, I developed the concept of the 'automatic pilot', or the 'robot'. A 'habit' is a kind of robot in the subconscious mind. When a baby learns to walk, it has to make a painful effort with every step; then the robot takes over and it does it automatically; this applies to all the skills we acquire throughout life: driving a car, typing, learning foreign languages. The human 'robot' is more formidably efficient than that of any animal; but his very efficiency is our downfall, for he makes us lazy and dependent. I put on a record of a favourite symphony, and wonder why the music fails to excite me; it is because I am not making enough effort; consequently, the robot is hearing the symphony, and 'I' am not. The more bored and listless I get, the more the robot takes over my functions, and the more I feel myself a passive instrument in the hands of life. It can be seen how the robot explains the problem of human passivity, and the vicious circle whereby boredom can lead to life failure and mental breakdown.

For convenience, we might think of a human being as a great bank of 'receptor cells', each one like the concave reflector of a radio telescope. In moments of great urgency or excitement, all these cells are 'switched on'; but when life is dull and repetitive, most of the cells 'switch-off'. To be accurate: no cell ever switches off *entirely* (until we die); they still record information, but they fail to pass it on to the central 'I'. The robot part of us consists of these 'passive' cells.

This leads to an interesting consequence. My sense of 'who I am' depends upon *how many cells are switched-on*. So when I am bored and listless, my notion of 'who I am' is actually much *smaller* than when I am happy and excited. This is as absurd as if my physical height varied between six feet and six inches.

It is convenient to have a name for this feeling of 'who I am', and I shall refer to it as the 'self-image'.

Now my self-image depends, to a large extent, on what is going on around me. If exciting, marvellous things are happening, then most of my 'receptor cells' will be switched-on, and my self-image will be clear and satisfying; if I am depressed, my self-image becomes blurred and fragmentary.

All this was clearly expressed in a story by the Brazilian writer Machado de Assis, *The Looking Glass.* A young man from a remote country village joins the army, and returns home in his lieutenant's uniform, where he is greatly admired. An aunt invites him to stay on her farm, where the servants are instructed to address him as 'Signor lieutenant'. His ego blossoms under all this attention. Then his aunt and her husband are called away to a sickbed; the servants take this opportunity to desert; he wakes up one morning to find himself alone.

He finds it agonizing to be deprived of his daily ration of admiration. It is a remote farm, and the loneliness makes him lose his sense of identity. There is a huge looking glass in his bedroom, and one day, as he looks into it, he thinks that his outline is becoming blurred and uncertain ... Then an idea strikes him. He takes his red lieutenant's uniform, and walks up and down in front of the mirror; and so he manages to remain sane until his aunt returns ...

This is an accurate description of the psychology of the self-image. The world around us is a mirror that reflects us. But it is a magic mirror. Sometimes – when our vitality is high – it reflects us hard and clear; sometimes we are so blurred that we can hardly see ourselves at all.

But my *sanity* depends on the strength of my self-image. A man who is kept in a completely black and silent room for a few days gradually goes insane, because his self-image gradually dissolves. This also explains why most people need other people so much; they need the 'mirror'. But this obviously depends on the inner resources of the individual. A scientist or a philosopher, thinking out an interesting problem, has an inner-mirror to maintain his sense of identity. But most people are in the position of Sartre's step-father, of whom Sartre wrote: 'On Sundays, he would withdraw into himself, find a desert, and feel lost.'

It can now be seen why I regard Nietzsche's will to power as the key to human psychology. To have a blurred self-image is synonymous with feeling weak and passive. On the other hand, as soon as we experience a sense of power and purpose, the self-image becomes clear, and life is suddenly meaningful. In *A Casebook of Murder*, I pointed out how many rape-murders are committed by vagrants and tramps. When a man is 'on the road', his sense of identity becomes blurry. In this situation, his need for *purposive action* becomes acute, for it will make his image reappear in the mirror. Instinctively, he looks around for something that will galvanize him into purposeful action. The sexual instinct is the strongest of our instinctive forces; so he is more likely to commit rape than any other crime.

This leads to the formulation of another basic law of psychology: that our energies *actively seek* ways in which they can be discharged. Our receptor cells are also like radar-transmitters; they continually scan the world for satisfactory ways in which they can release their tension. This is the most fundamental part of the mechanism of evolution. It is for example, what distinguishes man from the most complex electronic brains. The electronic brain responds to stimuli; man *looks for* stimuli to which he can respond.

The self-image theory explains why so many criminals belong to one or the other of two extremes: inadequate personalities, and highly dominant personalities. The inadequate personality is only aware of the passive misery of a blurred self-image. Because he is deficient in energy and foresight, his crime is likely to be a form of short-cut to what he wants: he may snatch a handbag, smash a shop window, rape a child. But the essence of the crime is what he gains from it. The highly dominant personality commits a crime *because of the sense of purpose conferred by the act itself*. He is aware of the misery of a partial self-image. Like all human beings, he is inclined to blame this on other people. So the criminal act not only has the effect of strengthening his self-image; it also gives him a pleasant feeling of behaving logically, of inflicting punishment on a society that deserves it. Melvin Rees, the Virginia sex murderer,[3] is a clear example of this type of criminal.

According to this view of human motivation, when the self-image becomes blurred, man loses his control over his own life; he feels 'mediocre, accidental, mortal'. But since man is an evolutionary animal, whose happiness is connected with a sense of forward movement, he experiences an urgent necessity to regain a sense of control at all costs. Any action that will restore his sense of control seems, for the moment, justifiable. The hungry will, like an empty stomach, craves fulfilment.

When this is understood, it can also be seen that male sexual fulfilment is a matter of the will rather than the 'libido'. This has been caught with remarkable power in an insufficiently-known masterpiece, *A Voyage to Arcturus* by David Lindsay. In this fantasy – or allegory – set on a strange planet, Lindsay dramatizes his insights into the will to power. One scene catches the essence of male sexuality with peculiar directness. Maskull, the hero, had developed the power to suck the life out of people, 'absorbing' them by a kind of psychic vampirism. The first time he does this:

'... a feeling of wild, sweet delight immediately passed through him. Then for the first time he comprehended the triumphant joys of "absorbing". It satisfied the hunger of the will exactly as food satisfies the hunger of the body ...'

This is what the male feels as he enters a strange woman: the experience is *food for the will.*

Maslow called his theory 'third force psychology'. Frankl called his 'logotherapy'. For the sake of distinguishing my psychology of the self-image from the various other forms of 'existential psychology', I shall refer to it as control psychology.

Again, it is necessary to emphasize that cruelty and violence may have no obvious connection with sex, or even with pleasure. The James Bond novels are full of sex and full of sadistic violence, but the two are seldom connected. Fleming liked to begin a Bond novel with a shock effect. An old couple are sitting peacefully on their verandah at sundown when a bunch of sinister Chinese Negroes appear, and their leader demands that they sell the property forthwith; when they refuse, they are cut down with machine-guns. The sheer brutality leaves the reader gasping. But we have only to compare the scene with some similar catastrophe from

Sade's *Justine* or *Juliette* to see that Fleming's attitude to the violence is detached and non-sexual.

In 1971, an English newspaper published the confessions of Carlos Evertsz, a political assassin, which made it clear that such violence is not confined to the fantasy of writers of spy fiction. Evertsz, born in 1942 in the Dominican Republic, West Indies, describes how he became the friend of the youngest son of Rafael Trujillo Molina, the dictator of the Republic. At the age of fifteen, he was asked to spy on fellow students and report on those with communist leanings; as a result, two vanished, and two were released only after torture. Evertsz got to know Trujillo's uncle, a rich farmer who wanted the land of peasants adjoining his farm. 'He called two of his peons, and we got the man and buried him up to his neck. Ureña [the uncle] said, "You shoot him now." I shot him. I felt shocked – completely sick.' This attitude did not last. When Cuba invaded in 1959, Evertsz was part of the combat force that repelled them. 'We took the prisoners to the San Isidro air base . . . Some of them we chained together and threw gasoline over them and lit them up. Then we put out the flames immediately. And then we'd do it again – two or three times. Some guys died right away from the shock, others didn't.' There are times when it sounds like Rome under Nero. The colonel ordered Evertsz to execute an officer who had slept with his wife; before the man was shot, his penis was amputated; the colonel later handed it to his wife. 'His wife said nothing. She was a bloody bitch. She used to lay soldiers and have them killed afterwards so they couldn't talk.' In 1960, one of Trujillo's indiscretions brought upon his head the wrath of the C.I.A. – formerly his supporters – and he was assassinated. 'After the assassination Trujillo's wife wanted to kill the whole population. She ordered poison to be put in the water supply of the city . . .' Fortunately, she was dissuaded.

Evertsz was told that a sixteen-year-old girl had been the mistress of one of Trujillo's assassins. 'I wasn't quite sure. As a result of it, we got the girl and we killed her.' He describes how they were trained to strangle men – using political prisoners for purposes of experiment – and to torture them by peeling the skin off their chests in strips with a razor blade. He tells of the murder of an engineering student, suspected of being a communist. He kidnapped the student and chloroformed him, then killed him by pushing a four-inch needle into the brain from under his ear, the body was then dumped in a park to be found by the police; an autopsy would show death to be due to cerebral haemorrhage. Evertsz – who moved to London and became a bouncer in a West End club – estimated that he had killed between thirty and forty people.

Here, again, there is no sadism in Krafft-Ebing's sense of the word. All the atrocities described by Evertsz seem to have been committed with a certain indifference, as if it were sheep who were being butchered. Dictators who run a régime of this type are not motivated by sadism; but they *are* motivated by a fierce will to power. Such pleasure as is involved – for example, in burning Cuban prisoners – seems to spring out of the satisfaction of anger rather than some 'erotic nerve'. And it could probably be argued that the rage was due to the invasion of territory . . .

Even the works of de Sade – surprisingly enough – reinforce this conclusion that sadism is not basically sexual. At least, if sadism means a kind of neurotic pleasure in inflicting pain – usually associated with masochism and self-loathing – then it is singularly absent from his books. De Sade's sadists are aristocratic gentlemen who feel that killing or inflicting pain are a *droit de seigneur* – which sounds much like the attitude of Trujillo. Their cruelty springs from a distorted mystical idea that they are gods – ought to be. Sade's anti-heroes claim to be atheists; but in fact, they *dislike* God, because they feel a kind of jealousy. Most readers skip the part of his work that he himself considered most important: the long discourses on man's total freedom. He saw himself as a Byronic figure, shaking his fist at the sky. 'No voice save that of the passions can conduct you to happiness' he asserts in the preface of *Philosophy in the Bedroom*. His ideal is a kind of dionysiac drunkenness of delight. 'Let yourself go, Eugénie,' says Dolmancé, to the inexperienced girl who is about to be initiated into the pleasures of sex; 'Abandon all your senses to pleasure, let it be the one object, the one god of your existence; it is to this god that a girl ought to sacrifice everything, and in her eyes, nothing should be as holy as pleasure.' It seems strange that Sade – who does not lack intelligence – should be unable to see the logical objection to his philosophy: that the keenest pleasures are involved with a high degree of self-discipline, and that therefore his libertines are subject to the law of diminishing returns. Sade treats sex as if it were some forbidden nectar or ambrosia, a food of the gods that men ought to be allowed to share. If gin had been forbidden by religion, one feels that he would have written of it in the same ecstatic manner. But sex, like gin, depends on the frame of mind of the imbiber; it can be a dionysiac potion or a nasty-tasting medicine, depending upon whether you are feeling happy or depressed. Sade seems unaware of the *relative* element in sex. He would have hated Dylan Thomas's lines:

> At last the soul from its foul mousehole
> Slunk pouting out when the limp time came.

Because he was, at bottom, an idealist who felt that the female vagina is a temple of delight, a forbidden glade. He is not a sensualist in the usual sense, nor a pornographer, but a Miltonic rebel for whom 'forbidden pleasures' are a symbol of freedom. He wrote to his wife: 'This manner of thinking you find fault with is my one consolation in life; it alleviates all my sufferings in prison; it composes all my pleasures in the world outside, it is dearer to me than life itself.' Humiliated and treated as a madman, he maintained a degree of self-esteem by indulging in daydreams in which he was a kind of satanic Robin Hood. It is significant that two of his greatest admirers in the Victorian era were Swinburne and Sir Richard Burton – both men who felt violent impatience with the tame, unimaginative society of England.

I am not arguing that there was *no* sexual sadism in de Sade; after all, he was first arrested for the flagellation of prostitutes. But the fantasies of the novels reveal that he was less interested in pleasure than power.

Consider the quotation from the letter to his wife: 'This manner of thinking you find fault with is my one consolation . . . it is dearer to me than life itself.' It would be appropriate to a man who had been imprisoned for his religion. And in a sense, de Sade had. He was a sexual mystic. Saint John of the Cross says that when a man has tasted the sweetness of God, all other pleasures lose their interest for him. In some moment of sexual intensity, Sade had also glimpsed a reality that made everything else seem unreal, the vision that made Nietzsche write: 'Pure Will, without the troubles and perplexities of intellect – how happy, how free!'[3] D. H. Lawrence also describes this intensity, particularly in the later novels. To Sade, it was self-evident that the sexual orgasm is the nearest man approaches to feeling like a god. And every pretty girl who passed in the street had the capacity to awaken the sleeping god – not only in the loins, but in the heart and the brain. It was impossible to doubt that a truly happy life would be one devoted to the endless pursuit of sex, in all its varieties. The society in which he lived, although tolerant towards libertinage, regarded it as a sign of moral degeneracy. To Sade, this seemed to be a complete *inversion* of the truth; so he found himself in the same position as Nietzsche, raging against a 'mediocracy' whose values struck him as basically false. His own troubles with the law and with militant virtue (in the person of his mother-in-law) turned this dislike into a neurotic, obsessive hatred. The most interesting thing about de Sade's novels is that they are not pornography – which is written to make money – but tracts and sermons. They are written in a tone of passionate, indignant conviction.

Sade shared Nietzsche's moral vision, but he lacked his intellectual qualifications. Implicit in the long diatribes against morality there are criticisms of Descartes, Bossuet, Montesquieu, Pascal; conversely, he might have drawn support from Montaigne, Voltaire and Rousseau. Such arguments would have made him more convincing, and caused posterity to recognize in him the precursor of Nietzsche. But Sade is not particularly literate, so the sermons have a sort of Non-conformist naivety:

> In whatever circumstances, a woman, my dear, whether unwedded, wife or widow, must never have for objective, occupation or desire anything save to have herself fucked from morning till night; 'tis for this unique end Nature created her . . .

There is a tone of serious-minded, rather ponderous conviction:

> Therefore in secrecy let us compensate ourselves for all the restraint imposed by such absurd unions, and let us be

certain indeed that this species of disorders, to whatever extreme we carry them, far from outraging Nature, is but a sincere homage to render her; it is to obey her laws to cede to the desires she alone has placed in us; it is only resisting we affront her.

To begin with, one suspects that the argument is deliberately cynical. Surely no one could so fail to understand that beauty is in the eye of the beholder – and sexual desire too? It must all be part of the game – to increase his feeling of wickedness by playing the devil's advocate? But you only have to read a dozen pages of de Sade to see this is not so. No moralist was ever more sincere. In his upside-down way, he is a romantic idealist. There is even his own equivalent of lyricism:

> I've got this little virgin cunt all to myself, delicious. Oh, I'm a guilty one, a villain, indeed I know it: such charms were not made for my eyes: but the desire to provide the child with a firm grounding in voluptuousness overshadows every other consideration. I want to make her fuck to flow, it 'tis possible I want to exhaust her, drink her dry ...

If you ignore for a moment the explicit physical details, this is not really so far from the idealist feeling about the beloved in Keats and Shelley; the girl is certainly not being taken for granted. De Sade's men are, in fact, driven by a feverish romanticism about women. The gardener Augustin, called in to complete Eugénie's defloration, exclaims with his own form of gallantry: 'If it meant screwing this bonny girl, by God, I'd come all the way from Rome on foot.' Mellors could say no less about Constance Chatterley.

Once this is understood, it becomes clear that the sexual aberration to which de Sade has given his name has no real connection with the 'divine Marquis'. He was a worshipper who was as dedicated to his deity as the Thugs were to Bhavati. The underlying drive is power. Sade would have agreed with every word in the following paragraph from Nietzsche's *Antichrist:*

'What is good? Everything that heightens the feeling of power in man, the will to power, power itself.

What is bad? Everything that is born of weakness.

What is happiness? The feeling that power is *growing*, that resistance is overcome.

Not contentedness, but more power: not peace, but war; not virtue, but fitness (Renaissance virtue, *virtù*, virtue that is moraline-free[4].)

The weak and the failures shall perish; first principle of *our* love of man. And they shall even be given every possible assistance.

What is more harmful than any vice? Active pity for all the failures and all the weak: Christianity.’

If this were placed in the mouth of one of de Sade's antiheroes, nobody would notice the difference. Combine this morality of power with de Sade's sexual mysticism, and his inverted romantic idealism, and one can see how he became sadistic. The only thing that remains unexplained is the repetitive boredom of Sade's novels, the endless flogging and sodomy and gloating about deflowered innocence.

In order to understand this, one must know something of Sade's peculiar history. Most of his adult life was spent in prison (or an asylum), and it is often assumed that this was a punishment for his sexual excesses and his obscene writing. This is not true. Only his first two short periods in jail – a few weeks each time – were the result of sexual misdemeanours. (On the second occasion, he was pardoned by the king.) In June 1772, Sade and his valet went to Marseilles, and held an orgy with three prostitutes. The girls were whipped and sodomized – in one case, while Sade himself was sodomized by his valet – and they in turn whipped Sade. Sade also gave them sweets containing Spanish Fly – an aphrodisiac – which made one of them sick. Then Sade visited another prostitute, who consumed several of his sweets (she allowed him intercourse only by the normal entry. This girl later became violently ill; poison was suspected. The other three girls also gave evidence against Sade. He was tried in his absence, and sentenced to death for poisoning – which was absurd, since the victims had recovered. Sade decided to flee to Italy, taking with him his attractive sister-in-law, Lady Anne, who had been living with her sister and brother-in-law. This earned him the undying enmity of his mother-in-law, Mme de Montreuil. The indignant lady felt that he deserved life imprisonment, and she set out to see that he got it. She was rich and influential. Her spies succeeded in discovering Sade's whereabouts – in Sardinia – and she had him arrested. He spent the next eight months in prison, then escaped. After six months travelling around Europe, he returned home to his château. The whole affair would certainly have blown over, but for the vindictiveness of his mother-in-law. For the next two years, she continued her efforts to ruin him; and when he visited Paris in 1776, she had him arrested, and confined in a particularly unpleasant dungeon at Vincennes. After a year, he succeeded in getting the case heard; the court quashed his conviction, and fined him fifty francs instead. He should have gone free; but again his mother-in-law intervened, and somehow succeeded in keeping him in prison, without trial, for another twelve years. (This was due to the infamous system of '*lettres de cachet*', through which rich private citizens could have their relatives confined.) During this time, Sade came close to insanity; he also wrote some of his most bitter and violent books.

He hated the old régime, and had every reason to long for its downfall. In 1789, the wish was fulfilled; the Bastille was stormed. Sade had been transferred to another prison a few days earlier, but he was released in the following year. He was half blind and without money; his wife refused to see him. He went to live with an actress, Madame Quesnet. Some of his plays were produced with a degree of success, and *Justine* was published. Because of his revolutionary sympathies, he was made president of a tribunal – in effect, a magistrate. But he was already disillusioned with the revolution; the mass executions sickened him. In August 1793 the opportunity he had dreamed of for thirteen years occurred; his father- and mother-in-law were accused of plotting against the revolution; their lives were in his hands. The 'monster' behaved like a saint, and declined to say the word that would have sent them to the guillotine. His leniency – in this and other cases – led to his own downfall; four months later, he was arrested on suspicion of being a royalist, and again imprisoned. The efforts of his mistress, Mme Quesnet, succeeded in getting him released ten months later.

Between 1794 and 1801, de Sade made a poor living by his pen, often on the point of starvation. The most famous 'sadistic' books appeared – *Justine, The New Justine, Juliette,*

Philosophy in the Bedroom; and also some more conventional works: *Aline and Valcour* and *The Crimes of Love.* It was not these works that led to his final arrest, but an obscene pamphlet entitled *Zoloé*, in which Napoleon and Josephine take part in a typical Sadeian orgy. France's new dictator lacked a sense of humour; Sade was arrested, and spent the remainder of his life behind bars, mostly in the asylum at Charenton. He was never tried, or given the opportunity to defend himself. He died in December 1814, aged seventy-four.

All this certainly helps to explain the violence and anti-authoritarianism of Sade's novels. He had spent twenty-eight years in jail, most of it without trial. *Philosophy in the Bedroom* is not only an anti-moral tract, but also an act of revenge. This becomes very clear in the final chapter, when Eugénie's mother arrives to drag her away. She is as haughty and arrogant as Wilde's Lady Bracknell. Then – inevitably – the indignities begin; she is undressed, sodomized, violated by her own daughter (wearing a dildo) and flogged; finally, her vagina and anus are sewn up, and she is allowed to go. There can be no doubt whom Sade had in mind when he wrote the scene; he must have had even more violent fantasies about his mother-in-law during his thirteen years in prison. (Ivan Bloch is of the opinion that Sade felt the same about his mother.) Yet when he had his opportunity to destroy her, he let it pass, and confined his vengeance to paper.

Sade was certainly less black than he was painted. But when we turn to *Juliette* and *The 120 Days of Sodom*, it is clear that, in another sense, he was far blacker than he was painted. Fantasies of rape are all very well; but the violence in these books has a familiar ring; it reminds us of Buchenwald and Auschwitz, and the trial of Irma Grese, the guard who made lampshades of human skin. Suddenly, it is difficult to understand what Sade thought he was doing. The atrocities committed by Juliette and her friends are as sickening and jarring as Carlos Evertsz's story of burning prisoners alive. The degeneracy is so complete that it would turn the stomach of the most enthusiastic connoisseur of pornography. There is the crunch of broken bone, teeth snapped off at the gum, the smell of burnt flesh, entrails torn out. The philosophy preached by Dolmancé is an attempt to convert the reader to Sade's philosophy; *Juliette* seems to be a determined attempt to make the reader reject him. It seems that, like Aleister Crowley, Sade was determined to be the wickedest man in the world. In achieving this aim, he also destroyed what he had built up in other books, the Nietzschean 'revaluation of all values'. He had built up a 50 per cent plausible philosophy in which pleasure is the only good, and religion is a confidence trick. (The reader is inclined to ask: What about music and poetry? But it would be pointless; de Sade is not even aware of their existence.) Then he shows this philosophy carried to an extreme, and the result is so revolting that it becomes impossible to take him seriously. He had demolished his own edifice more effectively than Bossuet could have done.

Why? Sade was no fool; he must have understood what he was doing. And then the answer dawns. Sade's philosophy appears contradictory only so long as you assume that he was centrally interested in *sexual pleasure*. But he wasn't; he was centrally interested in power. In his daydreams, he was an absolute sultan who could order the world to be destroyed. This was why his 'manner of thinking' was 'dearer than life itself'. His books are power-fantasies, of the same type as Walter Mitty's. This is apparent even in a relatively early work like *The 120 Days of Sodom* (written in the Bastille about 1785). There is the scene in which the Duc de Blangis decides to ejaculate over the genitals of Sophie, a fourteen-year-old girl who has been kidnapped from her mother. Sophie begs the Duc to 'have pity on her tears.'

> '"Why fuck my arse," the Duc exclaimed, fondling his heaven-threatening prick. "I'd never have believed this scene could be so voluptuous. Off with her clothes, I tell you . . ."'
>
> 'Sophie's clothes are removed without the faintest regard for her feelings, and she is placed in the posture Duclos [an old bawd] has just described; the Duc announces that he is about to discharge. But how is the thing to be done? What Duclos has just related had been performed by a man who was incapable of an erection, and he had been able to direct his flabby prick's discharge wherever he wished. Such was not the case here: the threatful head of the Duc's engine had not the least

> inclination to lower the awful stare whereby it seemed bent on cowing heaven; it appeared necessary, so to speak, to place the child on high. No one knew what to do, and the more obstacles were encountered, the more the enraged Duc fumed and blasphemed ... Desgranges finally came to the rescue ... She caught up the child and set her so skilfully on her knees that, whatever the stance the Duc might adopt, the end of his prick was sure to nudge her vagina ... the bomb finally explodes on the very hole it would like to stopper, inundating it. The Duc shrieks swears, storms ... Antinous, properly situated for this function, delicately thrusts the sperm into the vagina as it flows from the spigot, and the Duc, vanquished by the most delicious sensations, dying from joy, sees grow gradually slack between the frigger's fingers, that high-spirited, mettlesome member whose ardour had just been so powerfully communicated to the rest of his being. He flings himself back on the sofa; Duclos strides back to her throne; the child wipes herself, is consoled, and rejoins her friends; and the recital marches on, leaving the spectators convinced of a truth wherewith, I believe, they have been penetrated for a very long time: that the idea of crime is able to ignite the senses and lead us to lubricity.'

Taken simply as pornography, this passage presents a number of problems. To begin with, no real 'crime' has been committed; the girl retains her virginity and is consoled. It is a kind of symbolic rape, yet no penetration takes place. This is made even clearer by the phrase: 'the bomb finally explodes on the very hole it would like to stopper'. And if this were a truly sexual fantasy, penetration *would* occur. But it is a Walter Mitty power fantasy. Sophie excites the Duc's attention because she begins to cry, remembering her murdered mother. But it is not the crime that excites the Duc (and de Sade), but the thought of being so powerful that *he can do anything he likes*. Frederick Rolfe, a failed priest, wrote a fantasy in which he became Pope Hadrian VII; Sade wrote fantasies in which he was the most powerful man the world had ever known. *Juliette* shows a development of the power fantasy to new levels of violence. It is sickening because he *wanted* to sicken his readers; why should the most powerful man in the world be squeamish? His only problem is that many readers might dismiss him as insane; to guard against this, he makes his characters break off their scourging and flogging every page or so, in order to expound their philosophy with a clarity worthy of Descartes.

This precaution failed, and he died in a madhouse. He left instructions that he should be buried in an unmarked grave, and that oak trees should be planted on it to obliterate the site. The hospital authorities ignored this, and he was buried – with the usual Christian rites – in the cemetery at Charenton.

The foregoing analyses enable us to understand Sade more fully than was possible for his Freudian commentators. The sexual satisfaction was incidental; the true role of his fantasies of violence was to *prevent the disintegration of his self-image.*

This is the vital key to the psychology of 'assassins'.

1. And probably from Edouard Von Hartmann, whose *Philosophy of the Unconscious* appeared in 1869, three years before Nietzsche's first book. Hartmann's psychology is also based on the idea of a great unconscious will-drive which underlies the desires and ideals of the conscious mind.
2. *New Pathways in Psychology: Maslow and the Post-Freudian Revolution.* London, 1972.
3. See Chapter 6, p. 118.
4. A coinage of Nietzsche's own, implying that 'moraline' is a poison and a habit-forming drug, like nicotine.

CHAPTER THREE

Pornography and the Law of Diminishing Returns

The pornography of an age reflects its fantasies and the nature of its sickness. For this reason, it is now necessary to consider some of the changes in the nature of pornography during the last century.

Ronald Pearsall's *The Worm in the Bud* and Stephen Marcus's *The Other Victorians* may be taken as representative studies of Victorian sexuality. They reveal that Victorian sexual fantasy was determined largely by a feeling of the 'forbiddenness' of sex. Because women were covered from the neck down to the toes with layers of wool and cotton fabric, the female body in itself could serve as the focus for male desire. In order to move into the realm of the forbidden, fantasy only had to envisage her removing these clothes and allowing a man to use her body. Further elaborations are hardly necessary. So *The Pearl*, the famous Victorian 'underground' magazine (1879–1880), hardly rises above the level of schoolboy dirt. There is a certain amount of 'swishing' (as was inevitable in a country that made a speciality of birching schoolboys on their naked behinds), but apart from that, the sex is remarkably straightforward, if totally unrealistic. The hero is mostly the well-to-do young man whose ambition is to possess every girl in the world. The villains – or at least, spoil-sports – are the wives and mothers-in-law who stand in his way.

> There was a young man from Ostend
> Whose wife caught him fucking her friend;
> 'It's no use my duck,
> Interrupting our fuck,
> For I'm damned if I draw till I spend.'

Its favourite convention is the notion that well-brought-up young ladies, and even pigtailed schoolgirls, are secretly lubricious and anxious for a touch of the 'sugar stick'. The Victorian misses blush and say 'Fie, for shame', but make no resistance as hands slip under their clothes. The fantasy is so straightforward as to seem almost innocent. The young man-about-town takes his pretty cousin Annie for a walk. 'How I should love to see your lovely calf at the moment, especially after the glimpses I have already had of a divine ankle.' And a few sentences later: 'Feel here the dart of love all impatient to enter the mossy grotto between your thighs.' And during the next ten minutes or so, the blushing Victorian virgin takes part in a sexual orgy that would have exhausted Frank Harris, experiencing no less than four orgasms. There is an extrovert, cheerful air about all this, so that it seems only one step away from the smutty jokes of music hall comedians, or Blackpool dirty postcards.

A similar tone prevails in *My Secret Life*, (roughly 1884–1894), the anonymous autobiography of a Victorian Casanova. 'Walter' is a hunter in the modern sex-jungle; his prey, any woman between six and sixty. His ambition is to try every sexual experience – although he admits that he was unable to develop a taste for sodomy or homosexuality. The book is written in a confidential, gloating tone, without any stylistic refinements, but it can be oddly effective. This is a description of the reactions of a country girl who has just been seduced (she is unaware that Walter is watching her):

> She sat perfectly still so long that I thought she was never going to move; then sat down on the chair and laid her head against the bed, looking down at the sovereigns at intervals: then put them down, put her hand up her petticoats carefully feeling her cunt, looking at her fingers, burst into tears, sat crying for a minute or two, then put a basin with water on the floor, and, unsteady [Walter has got her half drunk], partially upset it, but managed to wash, and got back on to the chair, leaving the basin where it was. Then she pulled up the front of her chemise and looked at it, again put her fingers to her cunt, looked at them, again began crying, and leaned her head against the bed, all in a drowsy, tipsy manner. (Vol. 1, chap. 7)

One feels that he is aware he is a coarse ruffian, and takes a kind of pleasure in the part; like de Sade, he is defying a society that disapproves of him. His freedom from literary mannerisms often lends his prose a Rabelaisian vigour: 'My prick was in such a state that it would have pierced a board ...' I threw up her petticoats ... and disclosed soiled underlinen, and stockings dirty enough to have shocked my prick if it had had eyes.' His lack of affection makes for total honesty: '... with Mary I thought of thighs, backside, cunt, and her other parts, without much liking her beyond the desire of spending in her.'

In Chapter 9 of the second volume (it runs to eleven volumes in all), he describes spending a night with a middle-aged bawd and a ten-year-old girl, and having intercourse with the girl in front of a mirror, standing up. The image catches something essential about Victorian sex: the male's complete indifference to everything but his own desires, and his need to assure himself *that it is really happening* by watching it in a mirror. He is living in a society that regards sex as one of man's lower activities, and he agrees – so much is he a child of the society. He agrees; but since he also finds it the most fascinating thing in the world, he cheerfully admits to being depraved. It is because he agrees that he needs to watch it in a mirror, and needs to ask young girls in bed to repeat obscenities: otherwise he cannot really believe that he has got the better of this frightening maiden-aunt of a society. Once again, the spirit is 'sadistic' – the expression of a will to power – but never actually cruel. He is callous, stupid and coarse-grained, but not basically a bad sort.

About two decades later, the symbolist poet Guillaume Apollinaire produced two pornographic novels* that may be considered as representative of the early twentieth century. *Memoirs of a Rakehell* is fairly certainly the earlier of the two, perhaps by as much as a decade. There is nothing in it that might not have appeared in *The Pearl* thirty years earlier. The hero is a young gentleman who describes his sexual awakening almost in the manner of *My Secret Life:* his glimpses up his sisters' clothes, early sexual explorations with one of them – of the kind that Candide carried out with Cunegonde – experiences with servant women, and finally with both sisters and an aunt. *The Debauched Hospodar,* on the other hand, is an attempt to write a Sadeian novel, but in

* Their exact date is not known, but 1910 would probably be close.

a mood of savage good humour and high spirits (which reminds us that Apollinaire invented the term 'surrealism'). The opening chapter, describing how Prince Mony Vibescu decided to leave Bucharest and go to Paris, is a masterpiece of black humour:

'One day the prince dressed himself correctly and set out for the Vice-Consulate. In the streets everybody looked at him, and the women stared and said: "What a Parisian air he has got!"'

'Indeed Prince Vibescu was walking as a native of Bucharest might suppose the Parisians to walk, that is to say, with little hurried steps, and waggling his behind. Isn't it charming! When a man walks like that in Bucharest, not a single woman, be she the wife of the Prime Minister, can resist him.

'When he arrived at the front door of the Vice-Consulate, Mony pissed lengthily against the front door and then he rang the bell . . .'

The following scene, in which he attempts (unsuccessfully) to separate two Lesbians, and ends by being sodomized under the threat of a revolver, maintains this quality of literary parody. As the book continues, the humour remains grotesque; a prostitute, forced to commit an act of fellatio on a burglar, bites off the end of his member in her excitement; a woman accidentally strangles her maidservant with her thighs when the maid is engaged in cunnilingus. But Apollinaire has set himself an impossible task: to describe necrophilia, sadistic murder, bestiality, the violent rape of children, all in a tone of humorous parody. (If, as seems probable, he wrote it on commission, then he must have agreed to include every possible form of perversion.) The humour begins to drag; one ends by condemning Apollinaire for poor judgement in going through with anything so futile. De Sade is sickening; but there is a quality of controlled hatred and violence that makes it possible to take him seriously. Apollinaire is like the second-rate comedian who insists on continuing with a feeble joke in poor taste, although no one is laughing. In view of the quality of the rest of his work, it is difficult to understand why he went through with it. Perhaps, like Blake, he assumed that 'the true soul of sweet delight can never be defiled' – that the true poet can disinfect any obscenity by treating it with detachment. The book demonstrates that this is untrue, that no one can play with this kind of pitch without getting soiled.

What is interesting is that it once again demonstrates that sadism is not a sexual perversion, but a perversion of the will to power. *Memoirs of a Rakehell* is purely sexual, based upon the assumption that all attractive women are fair game for the healthy male, even if they happen to be his sisters or aunts. *The Debauched Hospodar* begins with the usual sexual descriptions ('The red and inflamed knob of Mony's big beet had already tasted the hot wet groove between her legs'), but after the death of the burglar from loss of blood, the killing begins. In the midst of an orgy on a train, Mony's servant disembowels an actress while he defecates on her face and Mony copulates with her. Then the Russo-Japanese war is brought in as an excuse for describing Sadeian orgies of slaughter and rape. Scene after scene ends with everyone covered with blood, shit and vomit. In the last chapter, Mony, sentenced to death, takes the maidenhead of a twelve-year-old girl as he strangles her, after which he is flogged to death by the Japanese. You are aware that something odd has happened to the book; it has got out of control. Apollinaire has decided to push sex to its limit; *but that limit is soon passed*, and the will to power takes over. He seems to be possessed by a Swiftian loathing of human beings, to be straining to achieve some ultimate catharsis through disgust and violence. And in allowing his fantasy free rein, he has contradicted the assumption with which he began: that there should be no limit to man's freedom. Suddenly, the humour has turned bitter; the life-force has become stagnant and poisonous. Completely against the intention of its author, it has turned into a moral tract on the theme that the wages of sin is death.

When *The Story of O* became a best seller in France in 1954, puzzled critics pointed out that it was a piece of old-fashioned sadism, nearly two centuries out of date. This missed the point: that Sade, like Jack the Ripper, was a unique and solitary figure in his own era, completely unrepresentative; by 1954, he represented something much closer to the 'spirit of the times' – as Olympia Press sales of his books proved. *The Story of O* is a sadistic fantasy in which the girl O (even her lack of name indicates her submissive role) is taken by her lover to a Gothic castle and made to give herself to another man ('Sir Stephen') and watch her lover possessing other women. This sentence is typical: 'That evening, for the first time in Jacqueline and Nathalie's company, in René's and Sir Stephen's, O dined naked, her chain drawn back between her legs, up between her buttocks, and wrapped around her waist . . .'

But perhaps the most typical scene in the novel does not involve O: her friend Marion tells how she was masturbating one day in the office when her boss came in; he made her remove her panties, then move to a position where he could get a better view while she continued to caress herself.

Again, there is the voyeuristic motive already noted in the case of 'Walter'. It can also be seen in *L'Image*, a kind of sequel to *L'histoire D'O.*[1] This offers a series of variations on the same theme. The male narrator becomes involved with a lesbian, Claire, and with her 'slave', a beautiful young model named Anne. Anne is chained, beaten, made to urinate in front of the narrator, and so on. In a 'dignified tea-room', she is made to stand up at the table and lean forward while Claire reached up her dress from behind and fondles her genitals:

> The waiter, a very young man, came to take our order. I was obliged to remove my hand. Claire, on the contrary, had pushed her chair back against the wall to make her position seem more natural while continuing with her scandalous pursuit. Little Anne, panic stricken, tried to straighten up. But she didn't have the courage to break away completely from her friend's attentions. So she stood there, desperately clinging to the table, staring in a daze at the dumbfounded young man.
>
> I took as long as possible giving all the details of our order. The waiter, I might add, didn't seem to hear me at all, for he couldn't take his eyes off the pretty girl with the distracted face, wide eyes, parted lips, writhing in the grip of some invisible power across from him.

Anne is ordered to become the narrator's slave too; in a typical scene, she kneels in front of him, as Claire whips her buttocks, and performs an act of fellatio, while the narrator controls her head. In the climactic scene of the novel, Anne is whipped unconscious by Claire and the narrator (who then sodomizes her). In this scene, Claire herself has begun to betray masochistic tendencies; in the final chapter, she calls on the narrator, and is ordered to undress, and then tells him she loves him as he penetrates her. It could hardly be plainer; this novel is about power, about dominance.

At the same time, it is also clear that fantasies like these are based on frustration. A man dreams of a completely feminine woman, who will totally acknowledge his masculine dominance, and regard herself as his property. If he could actually discover such a girl, he would probably never even feel the need to hurt her. Unfortunately, he is married to a woman with a mind of her own, who regards him with a touch of contempt. So in his daydreams, he whips his ideal girl, and humiliates her in public . . .

The relation between Anne and her 'masters' is the normal sexual relation seen through a magnifying glass. Emotions that should be a small integral part of the relation are blown up to ten times their proper size. This can be seen very clearly in the passage from Sade's *120 Days*, where Sophie is stripped and held with her legs open; every element in the scene is magnified. In the normal act of sex, the man and woman are in the dark, entwined together, and as the woman reaches her climax, the man may wonder whether he is possessing her or being possessed by her. The details blur. His 'worm's eye view' of the act – close-upness – has diluted its meaning. A sudden glimpse up a girl's miniskirt as she bent down in the street would produce a clearer sense of over-all meaning, the desire to remove her clothes immediately; but in bed, with a girl who is no longer a stranger, a part of him is taking her for granted. The robot has taken over. His self-image fades, because it depends upon a direct sense of meaning.

And all 'sexual perversions' are simply an attempt to restore the 'bird's eye view', the direct vision of purpose; to work up the momentum that will carry the man from the beginning of the act to the end. He may simply want the girl to wear black underwear and undress in front of him. He may (like Walter) want her to use filthy language. He may want her to dress as a schoolgirl or a nurse. Or he may want her to submit to being whipped or chained before he possesses her. All these fabricated situations are the equivalent of Machado's mirror, which suddenly restores the damaged and partial self-image. As the Duc de Blangis orders Sophie to be stripped, he is suddenly the all-powerful male in his proper role as sexual aggressor.

It is important to bear in mind that there is nothing *basically* wrong with the male–female relation portrayed in *L'Image,* no matter what women's lib may say to the contrary. It is the normal male-female relation; this is why 'to do' a girl is one of the synonyms for possessing her; the male is the doer, the girl the 'done'. A frustrated male fantasizes about sex, and because it is a fantasy, it needs to be 'stronger' than reality: the girl's submissiveness has to be exaggerated; the more fantasizing he does, the more he becomes accustomed to it, and the more certain elements have to be 'magnified'. Sexual perversions like Sade's are not a sign of man's wickedness, but of the feebleness of his imagination, his inability to maintain a clear self-image.

All this is an expression of the 'law of frustration', which says that the longer frustration continues, the higher its demands become. Under normal circumstances, sexual desires become stabilized as soon as they meet adequate satisfaction. In *The Demons,* the novelist Heimito Von Doderer describes the case of a young man who has fantasies of chaining women and beating them; his secretary strongly attracts him because she is the 'victim' type. She is intelligent enough to divine his fantasies; the result is a stable and not particularly sadistic relationship. Freud describes a case in which the husband and wife had reached an exceptionally high level of perversion before they met (they had practically every perversion in the book); it was a completely happy marriage, which ended only when the husband was arrested for the murder of a rich American woman.

The 'law of frustration' explains the increase in cases of sadistic rape, in which the woman is beaten as well as violated. Jerry Brudos, of Salem, Oregon, is an example. Brudos, a thirty-year-old photographer, admitted to killing four girls in his photographer's dark room. Photographs discovered by the police revealed that he had stripped them and suspended them from a beam by means of a rope before raping them. His marriage to a completely 'normal' girl failed to satisfy him. If he had been married to a girl with masochistic tendencies, the murders would probably never have taken place.

This same increase in violence may be noted in most modern pornography. A certain degree of sadism is accepted in our society (as the James Bond novels demonstrate); therefore pornography, if it is to achieve its effect, must increase the dose. Circulars advertising 'blue films' reveal an increasing preoccupation with rape: 'The Captive', 'Schoolgirls Raped', 'All-Action (Anal) Rape'. The description for the latter runs:

> The innocent dark-haired maid doing her house chores is no match for two strong housebreakers and despite her frantic struggles she is roughly forced on to a table and tied down. Stripped of her clothes the poor girl is forced to suck first an enormous white prick and then a massive black one. As she is sucking the black prick the big white organ is forced into her cunt. Then the black man takes his turn to get up her. Finally the girl is turned over and the white cock is stabbed into her arsehole. Stretching her arse to breaking point the colossal organ is thrust right into her. Satisfied with their rape the two men complete the degredation [*sic*] as white hot spunk is splashed over her.

This is a pornographic novel in miniature; it contains all the essentials. The sexual object must be 'innocent', her mind on other things, so there is nothing to challenge the male's role as pure sexual aggressor: then she is 'degraded'. The attitude here brings to mind Patrick Byrne, the Birmingham Y.W.C.A. murderer (who raped and decapitated a girl on Christmas Eve, 1959), who told the police that he did it 'to get my own back on [women] for causing my nervous tension through sex'. It could also be compared to extreme leftism in politics: the political revolutionary who feels that the capitalists have no right to the wealth that is needed by people like himself. The sexually frustrated male feels that all girls are holding out on him; for most of the time they are not making use of their vaginas, which the males of the world need so badly; they should be taken by force . . .

'Walter' would probably find the maidservant-rape fantasy slightly disgusting. His sexuality is so normal and unabashed that he is just as happy with a fat, middle-aged whore as with a teenage virgin. He finds all women so interesting and magical that his sense of violation is fully satisfied when he has been allowed to explore their genitals. The limit of his perverseness is to watch them pissing or hear them use filthy language (a sign of their total surrender to his male viewpoint). It is an interesting measure of the difference between England in 1870 and 1970.

Even today most pornography intended for the general market remains strictly 'sexual': that is to say, it is intended as an aid to masturbation, not to shock or disgust, as in Sade. But the Victorian convention of the orgy that everyone enjoys is giving way to something more one-sided – that is to say, Sadeian. Books in which normal sex is described explicitly can be bought on any station bookstall; so the underground market has to go one step further.

Two examples will suffice, both from America. *The Man Who Raped San Francisco* by Norman Singer (no date, no publisher) simply describes a series of rapes committed by a man whose penis is so huge that he cannot have normal intercourse with his wife. It is fairly well written, as pornography goes, and after *Candy* and *Myra Breckinridge*, it is surprising that it had to be issued by an underground publisher. Its theme is an updated version of that of *Philosophy in the Bedroom*: that in a healthy society, there would be total sexual freedom; every man and woman would be prepared to have sex at the drop of a hat. So the hero, Pete Jazziewick, is portrayed sympathetically. He never uses undue force in his rapes (the women usually faint at the sight of his member), and it is implied that he is actually doing the girls a good turn. The detective who is trying to hunt him down has a penis only three inches long – the symbolism here, society versus the 'natural man', is fairly obvious. By the end of the book, his example has caused a sexual revolution; thousands of people copulate in the Golden Gate park, and when the National Guard are called in to break it up, they drop their trousers and join in. The puritanical lady mayoress and state governor have themselves frozen in a cold storage mortuary, hoping to wake up in a more virtuous age, and Pete sails away from San Francisco like a departing saviour. The Natural Man has conquered the repressive society. One suspects that the author is a follower of Wilhelm Reich, who believed that all that is wrong with the world is sexual frustration.

The New Girl, by Alex Ayers is very nearly as sick as

Juliette. Fairly obviously inspired by *The Collector* of John Fowles, this is a story of a man who kidnaps girls and ill-treats them. The ill-treatment includes removal of their nipples (which he keeps in a box), mutilation of their sexual organs, and forcing them to have intercourse with animals. He also pulls out all their teeth to make fellatio less dangerous for him. The basic daydream is common enough – having complete control over a woman (as the popularity of *No Orchids for Miss Blandish* proved[2]). What is so startling here is the writer's 'confession' of the extent of his fantasies. This is not ordinary pornography; it is closer to material from a psychiatrist's casebook. Frustration is here so in-grown, and has reached such a degree of stagnation, that the dreamer no longer experiences any contact with other people; he is like a man who wants to urinate so badly that pain has unhinged his mind. The desire for a woman – for a pretty, healthy, well-dressed girl – has soured into total defeat. He is a hungry animal surrounded by food – all of which he is forbidden by law to touch. It would be easy to believe that the book had been written by Melvin Rees, or some other sick rape-murderer.

But the will to health has not been completely destroyed. There is a description of a blue film in which three men rape a six-year-old girl, but the narrator adds that the girl is obviously an actress. And half-way through the book, the two hyenas attack the rapist, and the girl is able to overpower him. She then sets out to get her revenge, forcing the man to become her slave. There is a certain poetic justice in it, even though this part of the book is as sick as the beginning.

The most immediately striking thing about *The New Girl* is that, like de Sade, it sets out to disgust; the author enjoys describing unpleasant smells and suppurating sores. This is a description of a kind of hell. The mind is so trapped in frustration that it is like a tiny room with no windows. None of the ordinary pleasures of life are able to register on the burnt-out senses: sunlight, nature, travel, music, food – none of these can give pleasure; the mind runs in a single groove.

What becomes most clear is the disparity between the desire and its object. A girl is only a girl; anatomically she is like all other girls, and in most ways, like all other human beings. Her sexual possibilities are limited. There is something almost comically absurd about this kind of daydream – like a man setting out for a hundred-mile walk in his own backyard. Apollinaire's books are short because it is impossible to be very inventive about sex, which is basically an extremely straightforward activity, as simple as picking apples off a tree. The best erotic writing is not about the sexual act itself, but about the way in which it is led up to. Stendhal's *Rouge et le Noir* uses the basic techniques of pornography – a man's decision to seduce a woman, the planning, the scheming, the final seduction ... But it is not pornography *because it is not based upon the supposition that sex is the only interesting thing in the world.*

This leads to my central point about pornography – that it is based on a kind of *logical error*. It makes the assumption that sex is a thing-in-itself, which can be enjoyed in isolation, like eating a peach. The man sees a pretty girl; he gets her on to a bed, pentrates her ... and one more peach is gone; he throws away the stone. But sex is not like food; to begin with, a human being can go without it indefinitely without any particular harm. A woman is more conscious of the fallacy than a man, because although she may enjoy sex, she is aware that it is more than the penetration of a penis. Her enjoyment of sex is bound up with the personality of the man, and also – less immediately – with thoughts of a home and children. These are an *integral part* of her sexual response, not accidental additives. Human beings possess many levels of value-response, of potential fulfilment; they want a home and security and love and respect and a wide range of interesting experience. The most attractive sexual object, for both man and woman, is the person who seems to *symbolize* the maximum number of these values. A man who daydreams of making love to Marilyn Monroe is not simply concerned with securing an orgasm; his choice of her symbolizes what he would like to *be*: the success, glamour, fulfilment, total masculinity.

Even the appreciation of food demands the right state of mind. If your thoughts are elsewhere as you eat a good meal, you don't enjoy it. But at least, it will fill your stomach. Sex is entirely 'mental'. If your thoughts were totally elsewhere, you couldn't go through with sexual intercourse. It would make no difference that there was a naked girl in bed with you; for all practical purposes, she wouldn't be there. And if your thoughts are half on something else, t[illegible] half there, and the sex will only be half s[illegible] depends upon training the mind to completely [illegible] object; it demands imagination and discipline. O[illegible] soon palls. Casanova and Frank Harris and 'Walte[illegible] their lives chasing a will o' the wisp, because they m[illegible] same mistake as the writers of pornography: that se[illegible] is a thing-in-itself which merely depends upon having a naked female body in your bed. Roués who discovered this to be untrue tend to become pessimists, to feel that sex is based on illusion. Pornographers who pursue their theory of sexual freedom to its limits find the book turning sour on them; the life seeps out of it. On the other hand, a Casanova who had sufficient intelligence and imagination would eventually give up seduction and take to more interesting pursuits.

Pornography is mainly of interest from the 'structuralist'[2] point of view; that is, it reveals the ritual patterns that underlie sexual behaviour. Sex *is* inherently ritualistic, a symbolic act whose meanings extend beyond itself. The sexual dramas described by Sade bear the same relation to sex that morality plays bear to religion: the drama is intended to re-create the emotion by serving as a *reminder*. The purpose is to out-manoeuvre the robot and restore 'freshness' to the experience. The ritualistic nature of the situation can be seen in *L'Image*, where Anne, the 'slave', clearly enjoys the game as much as her 'masters', although she protests and begs for mercy; they are like Greek actors wearing masks.

1. *The Story of O* by Pauline Réage had an introduction by Jean Paulhan, the literary critic. *L'Image* by Jean de Berg was introduced by Pauline Réage. It is generally assumed that both books were written by Paulhan.
2. See Chapter 8.

CHAPTER FOUR

'Magical' Thinking

The change in the style of pornography, from the bottom-smacking of the Victorians to the sick violence of the 1970s, parallels the change in the type of crime, from Madeleine Smith* to Charles Manson. Jazziewick, 'the man who raped San Francisco', feels that his rapes are a protest against the social order, and a blow for freedom. The Manson family felt the same about their murders. The analysis of the ritualistic and symbolic nature of sex enables us to understand the mirror-like ambiguities of the Manson trial. The 'family' were making the same kind of logical error as the writers of pornography: mistaking a symbolic act for a concrete reality. It could be likened to throwing a stone at a mirage, which hits whoever happens to be standing where the mirage appears to be.

It is important that this should be clearly understood, for it provides the key to all crimes of violence in the twentieth century. Madeleine Smith knew exactly what she wanted to do. Her lover was an obstacle; she removed him. Her motive was also clear: she wanted a more rewarding and interesting life than her lover could offer her. She got precisely that. After her acquittal, she moved to London, joined literary and artistic circles in Soho, became a William Morris socialist, married twice, and died at the age of ninety-two. From her

* Acquitted in 1857 of the murder of her lover (by poison). The twenty-one-year-old daughter of a prosperous Glasgow architect, she fell in love with a clerk, Emile L'Angelier, and became his mistress. When her father arranged a match with a wealthy merchant, Madeleine wrote to L'Angelier, breaking off with him. In his violent misery, he threatened to reveal the affair to her father. Whereupon she resumed her secret meetings with him. It was after one of these meetings that he died, after drinking a cup of cocoa given to him by Madeleine. A large quantity of arsenic was found in his stomach. The jury decided charitably that he may have committed suicide, and a verdict of 'Not Proven' was brought in.

point of view, her murder was justifiable by results. But what exactly did the Manson family *want* when they slaughtered Sharon Tate and her friends? They already had their bohemian freedom. Logical thinking would have shown that the crime could not achieve its result (the reform of a corrupt society); but they were not thinking logically, but emotionally, or rather, 'magically' – hoping that their act would achieve a result in the face of natural laws.

Jean-Paul Sartre was one of the first to grasp the central importance of this type of 'magical' thinking – mirage-logic: and at this point, an outline of his theory is necessary. Sartre carried his theory to a pessimistic extreme that destroyed its value as an instrument of psychological analysis, but it is unnecessary to follow him to these conclusions.

In one of his earliest – and shortest – books, *A Sketch of a Theory of the Emotions* (1939), Sartre makes the suggestion that all emotion should be regarded as wishful-thinking, or 'magic'. Emotion, says Sartre, is essentially a *substitute* for action.[1] If you can do something, you go ahead and do it, and feel no emotion. It is only when we are frustrated that we feel emotion – a blockage of the energy that should go into action. The fox cannot reach the grapes, so he says 'They are sour', and experiences rage and rejection of the grapes. This is a way of discharging the energy, and preventing it from damaging him. Sometimes this emotion may lead to totally unsuitable action. A girl confronting a rapist experiences fear – the frustration of her desire to escape – and she may faint. In a sense, the fainting accomplishes her object; she 'gets rid' of the rapist; she certainly becomes unconscious of the rape. In this case, she is like an ostrich that buries its head in the sand; the 'action' she takes against the rapist is completely illogical.

This analysis is certainly accurate as far as negative emotion is concerned. Sartre tries to take it further, to cover positive emotion, happiness, etc. He sees this as a form of auto-suggestion or self-hypnosis. A man setting out for a drive on a sunny morning allows the sunlight to soothe him into a positive state, and he deliberately turns his mind towards pleasant things; he induces an 'all's right with the world' feeling, although if he is honest, he knows that millions of people are starving and children are being ill-treated . . . An adoring mother prefers to ignore the evidence that her child is selfish, spoilt and vicious in order to be able to indulge her mother love. And so on. Seen in this way, it is easy to believe that most positive emotion involves a kind of self-deception, like Nelson clapping his telescope to his blind eye. The fallacy here is the assumption that positive emotion ought to take the whole world into account. A scientist who has just made a great discovery feels a valid sensation of delight. If it is a discovery that can save lives, it would be absurd to tell him that he is deceiving himself, because it still cannot solve *all* the world's problems.

In fact, positive emotion is the delight that accompanies any step forward, any evolutionary advance. But since Sartre does not recognize evolution, he cannot be expected to see this.

Even his theory of negative emotion must be qualified. Emotion is *not* a substitute for action; many actions – in fact, most – are *accompanied* by emotion. This contradicts the basic assertion. Moreover, the fox does not *necessarily* experience rage about the grapes; he may draw a deep breath and decide to try another approach; or he may remind himself that last time he had grapes they gave him diarrhoea. This would not be 'sour grapes', for it would be true. The real 'moral' of the theory of the emotions is that negative emotions are controllable; Sartre ignores this because he wishes to use emotions to illustrate his pessimistic view of the human condition. So most of the Sartre theory must be rejected as an exaggeration. But what remains valid is the recognition that human beings may *choose* to indulge in the negative emotions and negative actions as an alternative to self-discipline. In that case, the fallacy is the same as in the case of pornography – Whitehead's 'fallacy of misplaced concreteness'. Robert Daniels and John West, the killers of the Niebels, provide an example. I have already pointed out the basic absurdity of the murder; they behaved as if their *aim* were to be caught and executed. In fact, their real aim was to discharge a violent negative emotion that had only arisen because of their inadequacy and lack of self-discipline. It was the raw assertion of the will to power, without thought of the consequences. In practice, 'magical' response to a situation means a violent and unsubtle response to a subtle problem – like a watchmaker losing his temper with a watch he is supposed to repair, and hitting it with a hammer.

It now becomes possible to see why sex crime and 'motiveless murder' are, psychologically speaking, so closely linked. Both involve the 'magical' approach to a problem. And the root cause of the increase in these types of crime is the increasing complexity of industrial civilization. Men of strong will and low intelligence prefer to smash the watch with a hammer.

In a way, it is surprising that it has taken so long for this problem to arise. The 'dark satanic mills' started their work of depersonalization in the second half of the eighteenth century; one might have expected a trend towards motiveless murder in the nineteenth century. The answer is that the psychopathic personality needs *leisure* to evolve. The Edinburgh of Duke and Hare – the body snatchers who were tried in 1828 – was as filthy and overcrowded as the Whitechapel of Jack the Ripper; but Burke and Hare murdered with the thoroughly practical aim of selling the bodies. Almost without exception, the famous murderers of the mid-nineteenth century belong, like Madeleine Smith, to the middle classes, and the motives were always straightforward: money, jealousy, fear of public scandal.

There is one noted sexual criminal who should be mentioned in passing; not a murderer, but a necrophiliac. Sergeant Bertrand, who was in the French army, was by no means a withdrawn or shy personality; on the contrary, he was an efficient N.C.O., well liked by his men, and something of a Don Juan with the country girls. His arrest in 1849 came as a shock to his army comrades, for it was alleged – and proved at his trial – that for the past two years he had been in the habit of entering cemeteries at night and seeking out the newly-buried bodies of young girls. These corpses – usually buried without coffins – excited him more than living mistresses. Of the corpse of a sixteen-year-old girl he says: 'I did everything to her that a passionate lover does to a mistress,' and adds, 'All my enjoyment with living women is as nothing compared to it.' On the first occasion when he saw an unburied corpse in a grave he was so overcome with frenzy that he leapt into the grave and proceeded to beat it with a spade. Later, he returned, dug it up, and committed acts of necrophily. The compulsion was so powerful that he once swam an icy stream in winter to get into a graveyard. He usually ended by disembowelling the corpse.

It is not surprising to learn that Bertrand's comrades found this unbelievable. Bertrand was not a brutal or violent man; he made an impression of decency and efficiency. His social personality allowed him no way to express the violent sexual feelings that lay underneath. In courting a girl, he had to play the part of a lover; in possessing a corpse, he could ignore his personality – and hers – and concentrate on the release of pure desire. The more complex personal relation with a living girl did not allow the same release; Bertrand's necrophily is a perfect example of 'magical behaviour' – a violent and unsubtle solution to a subtle problem.

The observation that the psychopathic personality needs leisure to evolve is an argument in favour of regarding Jack the Ripper as a member of the privileged classes rather than a butcher or barber (both of which have been suggested) or even a doctor. It is certainly the strongest argument in favour of Thomas Stowell's otherwise shaky theory that Jack the Ripper was the Duke of Clarence, grandson of Queen Victoria.[2] And it applies with even more force to the other chief suspect, John Montague Druitt, who became a barrister in 1885 (at the age of twenty-seven), and then sat in his office for three years, waiting for clients who never came. Druitt certainly had the leisure to brood. All that seems fairly certain is that the Ripper, whoever he was, committed suicide after the murder of Mary Kelly, a twenty-four-year-old prostitute, whose body was so elaborately mutilated that it must have taken several hours. It is as if the Ripper's career as a murderer parallels that of Sade as a pornographer: the increasing violence that fails to achieve its purpose because the purpose is the satisfaction of an immense, savage *will to power*. He is in the possession of 'Mr. Evans's Worm' – a desire for some ultimate, total *sexual* satisfaction, which he attempts to satisfy through the illogical method of destructive violence. And this kind of violence, wreaked upon the body of a half-drunken prostitute, becomes a mockery of its own aim; he ought to be destroying cities, ordering mass executions like Ivan the Terrible, raping the wives and daughters of boyars he has just seen impaled . . . The violence is 'magic'; it has no relation to reality. And each murder leaves him more deeply aware of his own absurdity, like King Canute commanding the waves.

This pattern can be discerned in most of the major sex crimes of the twentieth century. A shy or nervous man, subject to fits of depression, broods on sex until he is obsessed by thoughts of rape. The murders follow – each one succeeded by a still deeper fit of depression. Eventually, he engineers his own arrest, or commits suicide. All such cases have a strong element of illogicality, so that the normal, balanced person is inclined to fall back on the explanation of madness. But it is not madness; only 'magic', the confusion of a man who throws a stone at a mirage.

I have discussed the case of John Reginald Halliday Christie elsewhere[8], but it is worth a further consideration as a textbook case of 'magical' behaviour. Christie committed eight murders between 1940 and 1953, and was hanged in July 1953. He differed in only one respect from other 'shy killers': there was an authoritarian character structure. As a special reserve constable at the beginning of the war, he became notorious for his officiousness; he enjoyed reporting people for minor blackout offences. The first four victims were killed between 1940 and 1950, always when his wife was away on visits to relatives in Sheffield. In 1952, he murdered his wife, and buried her under the floorboards. Three more sex crimes followed in quick succession in the following months. The method was to persuade the woman to inhale gas, on the pretext of curing asthma or catarrh with Friar's Balsam, then to rape her while unconscious. The murder – by strangulation – was apparently an afterthought, to protect himself.

The interesting feature of the case is his moral collapse. The first two victims were carefully buried in the tiny back garden, and no suspicion fell on Christie. The third victim was Mrs. Beryl Evans, a woman who lived with her husband in the flat upstairs. Christie persuaded her husband that he was a skilled abortionist. The abortion was to take place when the husband – Timothy Evans – was at work. It seems unlikely that Christie intended to kill her – his chances of getting away with it were too small. But the sight of her nakedness was too much for him; he battered her unconscious, strangled her, then raped her. He later murdered the fourteen-month-old daughter, Geraldine. When Evans came home from work, Christie seems to have succeeded in frightening him so much that he ended by confessing to the murder of his wife. (Evans's I.Q. was exceptionally low, but it is still a mystery how he came to confess to Christie's crime.) Evans was hanged in 1950. Many years later, as a result of a public inquiry, he was finally exonerated.

Beryl Evans was murdered in 1949; Mrs. Christie in December 1952. After disposing of her body, Christie seems to have lost all caution, as if determined to have any orgy before he was caught. In early January, a prostitute named Rita Nelson entered 10 Rillington Place; she was anaesthetized, strangled and raped, and her body was pushed into the corner of a deep closet in the kitchen. About ten days later, Christie strangled and raped another prostitute, Kathleen Maloney. He left the body in the chair all night and went to bed; the next morning, it was wrapped in a blanket and pushed into the closet. During the next few months, the squalid little flat was allowed to become filthy and untidy. Christie had no job, and made no attempt to get one. And in the case of his final victim, he abandoned all attempt to cover his tracks. In early March, he met a girl named Hectorina Mclennan and her lover, a lorry driver called Baker. They spent three nights at his flat, sleeping in chairs or on the floor. On the fourth day, Christie approached Hectorina Mclennan outside the labour exchange, while Baker was signing on, and asked her back to the house. She told Baker where she was going, and went back with Christie. He strangled her, raped her, and put her in the cupboard. Baker called later to ask if Christie knew where she was; Christie said he didn't, and they drank a cup of tea in the kitchen; later, Christie went out with him and helped him search for her.

A week later, he sub-let the flat to another couple, collected £7 13s. for rent in advance, and wandered off, leaving the bodies in the cupboard that was now disguised by a layer of wallpaper. The owner of the house, finding the flat sub-let, told the new tenants to leave, and looked into the cupboard. In spite of the hue and cry that followed, Christie made no attempt to escape from London, even registering at a Rowton House under his own name; he walked around, becoming increasingly dirty and unshaven, until he was recognized by a policeman on Putney Bridge. What happened to him in those last weeks of freedom? It is tempting to suppose that he ceased to be responsible for his actions. Yet he continued to plan and calculate; even when on the run, he met a pregnant girl in a café, and told her he was a medical man who could perform an operation . . .

What is clear is that, beyond a certain point, Christie found himself lost in a kind of maze. His early murders – of Ruth Fuerst and Muriel Eady – were carefully planned; the women were invited back to the house when his wife was on holiday, murdered, then buried in the back garden; no suspicion fell on Christie. In his confession, Christie described his feeling as he looked at the body of Muriel Eady, after raping and strangling her: '. . . once again I experienced that quiet, peaceful thrill. I had no regrets.' It was as deliberate as a fox stealing a chicken. The murder of Beryl Evans was less calculated; but in the aftermath, Christie showed his usual skill and calculation. At the Evans trial, he was a cool and competent witness, and a barrister wrote: 'Christie bore the stamp of respectability and truthfulness.' But the murders of 1953 were neither calculated nor competent. If Christie had buried his victims in the back garden, and continued to work at his job (with British Road Services), his chances of escaping detection would have been high. None of the three women was likely to be missed. His only problem was to prevent his wife's sister from becoming suspicious; but she lived in Sheffield, and Christie had already explained that Ethel's rheumatism was so bad that she was unable to write letters. But the time for calculation was past; Christie was on the same downhill slope as Sade, driven by an obsession that turned his life into a desert. His will to destruction was also a will to self-destruction. He was no longer in control; now the 'worm' possessed him; hence the curiously aimless, head-in-sand, magical behaviour of those last months of freedom.

The case of the Thames nude murderer – sometimes known as 'Jack the Stripper' – provides an even more striking example of the build-up of a sexual obsession into aimless destructiveness. The 'Stripper's' crimes produced one of the biggest manhunts in British criminal history, which ended – typically – with his suicide.

Between February 1964 and January 1965, the bodies of

six women – mostly prostitutes – were found in areas not far from the Thames. The first of the bodies, that of a thirty-year-old prostitute named Hanna Tailford, was found in the water near Hammersmith Bridge. She was naked except for her stockings, and her panties had been stuffed into her mouth. Her jaw was bruised, but this could have resulted from a fall. On 18th April, the naked body of Irene Lockwood, a twenty-six-year-old prostitute, was found at Duke's Meadows, near Barnes Bridge, not far from the place where Hanna Tailford had been found. She had been strangled, and, like Hanna Tailford, she had been pregnant. A fifty-four-year-old Kensington caretaker, Kenneth Archibald, confessed to her murder, and he seemed to know a great deal about the girl; but at his trial, it was established that his confession was false, and he was acquitted. There was another reason for believing in his innocence; while he was still in custody, another naked girl was found in an alleyway at Osterley Park, Brentford. This was only three weeks after the discovery of Irene Lockwood's body. The dead girl – the only one among the victims who could be described as pretty – was identified as a twenty-two-year-old prostitute and striptease artist, Helen Barthelemy. There were a number of curious features in the case. A line around her waist showed that her panties had been removed after death, and there was no evidence of normal sexual assault. But four of her front teeth were missing. Oddly enough, the teeth had not been knocked out by a blow, but deliberately forced out; a piece of one of them was found lodged in her throat. Medical investigation also revealed the presence of male sperm in her throat. Here, then, was the cause of death; she had been choked by a penis, probably in the course of performing an act of fellatio. The missing teeth suggested that the killer had repeated the assault after death. It was established that she had disappeared some days before her body was found. Where, then, had her body been kept? Flakes of paint found on her skin suggested the answer, for it was the type of paint used in spraying cars. Clearly, the body had been kept somewhere near a car spraying plant, but in some place where it was not likely to be discovered by the workers.

The 'nude murders' became a public sensation, for it now seemed likely that they were the work of one man. Enormous numbers of police were deployed in the search for the spray-shop, and in an attempt to keep a closer watch on the areas in which the three victims had been picked up – around Notting Hill and Shepherds Bush. Perhaps for this reason, the killer decided to take no risks for several months.

The body of the fourth victim – Mary Fleming, aged thirty – found on 14th July, confirmed that the same man was probably responsible for all four murders. Her false teeth were missing; there was sperm in her throat; and her skin showed traces of the same spray paint. She had vanished three days earlier.

Her body was found, in a half-crouching position, near a garage in Acton, and the van was actually seen leaving the scene of the crime. A motorist driving past Berrymede Road, a cul-de-sac, at 5.30 in the morning, had to brake violently to avoid a van that shot out in front of him. He was so angry that he contacted the police to report the incident. If he had made a note of the van number, the nude case would have been solved. A squad car that arrived a few minutes later found the body of Mary Fleming in the forecourt of a garage in the cul-de-sac.

The near-miss probably alarmed the killer, for no more murders occurred that summer. Then, on 25th November, 1964 another naked body was found under some debris in a car park at Hornton Street, Kensington. She was identified as Margaret McGowan, twenty-one, a Scot. Under the name Frances Brown, she had been called as a witness in the trial of Stephen Ward, and Ludovic Kennedy described her (in his book on the trial) as a small, bird-like woman with a pale face and fringe. Margaret McGowan had disappeared more than a month before her body was found, and there were signs of decomposition. Again, there were traces of paint, and a missing front tooth indicated that she had died in the same way as the previous two victims.

The last of the stripper's victims was a prostitute named Bridie O'Hara, twenty-eight. She was found on 16th February, 1965, in some undergrowth on the Heron Trading Estate, in Acton. She had last been seen on 11th January in the Shepherds Bush Hotel. The body was partly mummified, which indicated that it had been kept in a cool place. As usual, teeth were missing, and sperm was found in the throat. Fingermarks on the back of her neck revealed that, like the other victims, she had died in a kneeling position, bent over the killer's lap.

Detective Chief Superintendent John du Rose was recalled from his holiday to take charge of the investigation in the Shepherds Bush area. The Heron Trading Estate provided the lead they had been waiting for. Investigation of a paint spray shop revealed that this was definitely the source of the paint found on the bodies – chemical analysis proved it. The proximity of a disused warehouse solved the question of where the bodies had lain before they were dumped. The powerful spray guns caused the paint to carry, with diminishing intensity, for several hundred yards. Analysis of paint on the bodies enabled experts to establish the spot where the women must have been concealed: it was underneath a transformer in the warehouse.

Yet even with this discovery, the case was far from solved. Thousands of men worked on the Heron Trading Estate. (Oddly enough, Christie had been employed there.) Mass questioning seemed to bring the police no closer to their suspect. Du Rose decided to throw an immense twenty-mile cordon around the area, to keep a careful check on all cars passing through at night. Drivers who were observed more than once were noted; if they were seen more than twice, they were interviewed. Du Rose conducted what he called 'a war of nerves' against the killer, dropping hints in the press or on television that indicated the police were getting closer. They knew he drove a van; they knew he might have right of access to the trading estate by night. The size of the victims – who were all short women – suggested that the killer was under middle height. As the months passed, and no further murders took place, du Rose assumed that he was winning the war of nerves. The killer had ceased to operate. He checked on all the men who had been jailed since mid-February, all men with prison records who had been hospitalized, all men who had died or committed suicide. In his book *Murder Was My Business*, du Rose claims that a list of twenty suspects had been reduced to three when one of the three committed suicide. He left a note saying that he could not bear the strain any longer. The man was a security guard who drove a van, and had access to the estate. At the time when the women were murdered, his rounds included the spray shop. He worked by night, from 10 p.m. to 6 a.m. He was unmarried.

This is clearly a case of the obsessive mentality – even more so than in the case of Christie. Christie's pecularity was his inability to have intercourse with a woman who was fully conscious; the Stripper was interested only in fellatio. (This was not revealed at the time of the case, and it is only hinted at in du Rose's book.) If he was the killer of Hanna Tailford and Irene Lockwood – as seems likely – then his obsession had still not reached a climax. Presumably he had been paying prostitutes to satisfy his need. The death of Hanna Tailford could have been – as du Rose says – accidental; at the height of his sexual satisfaction, guiding her head with his hand on her neck, the other probably gripping her hair, he may have lost control, and choked her with the glans of his penis – as if an apple had been jammed in her throat, as du Rose explained in an article written after his retirement. But accident is unlikely – otherwise, why should he have stuffed her panties into her mouth, presumably to make sure she was dead? When he killed Irene Lockwood, he knew in advance what he intended to do. He picked her up on the night of 7th April. The murder almost certainly took place in the back of his van. After this he stripped her, and threw her body in the river. One writer on the case has suggested that the victims were stripped to avoid identification; but this would clearly be pointless; why should the murderer care whether the women were identified, or how soon? The stripping was a part of his sexual need, the desire to feel himself totally dominant. His fantasy involved a naked woman, and it involved treating her mouth as a vagina – hence the removal of teeth. In the later murders, the bodies were kept in the warehouse for several weeks – not because he was waiting for a favourable moment to dispose of them (after all, the longer he waited, the more chance there was that they would be discovered in the warehouse) – but in order to repeat his perverse acts. The last corpse was kept longer than any of the others, and was dumped on the Trading Estate. This may have been partly out of fear of being stopped with the corpse in his van – although the police cordon had not been formed at that time. But it is more likely the same indifference that overtook Christie; murder had become a *habit*, and destructiveness involved an element of self-destruction.

It is important to understand the general psychological

principle that is involved here. Anyone who concentrates narrowly and obsessively upon a single idea runs the risk of dehydrating his soul. Human beings have the power to relax, to fling open the senses as if they were windows and allow the breath of the outside world to blow in. That feeling of *freshness* that we get on holidays is due to the relaxation of the usual tensions; it is as if we unhitch the mind from its usual narrow purposes, and allow it to *open up*, to wander freely. It is difficult to relax so completely because we are trapped by our habits and anxieties; but when it happens, it always has the same effect: to make us realize that the world is full of *meanings* that we have been ignoring. It happens most frequently when we are healthy and optimistic, possessed by a sense of purpose.

Sex can also produce this 'awakening', this sense of opening up and perceiving meanings. When Mellors makes love to Constance Chatterley in *Lady Chatterley's Lover*, Lawrence writes about 'the peace on earth of her soft, quiescent body', and 'the moment of pure peace, the entry into the body of the woman'. Christie is obviously talking about the same thing when he speaks of 'that quiet, peaceful thrill'. This was why he killed: because the sexual act was like a glimpse of a higher level of his own possibilities.

But there is a danger in becoming obsessed by the sexual act as the 'bringer of peace'. The sexual act is basically extremely simple; if it is to be fully satisfying, it needs to be accompanied by other forms of satisfaction. For Casanova, it was only a *part* of the kind of life he wanted to lead; an extremely important part, but a part nevertheless. He also enjoyed good food, luxury, travel, adventure, intelligent conversation, the admiration of men as well as of women. De Sade, on the other hand, confined in gaols and asylums, had no chance to satisfy these aspects of his nature; sexual fantasy was the only outlet left to him. Sex became the channel for completely unsuitable forms of emotional energy. His sexual palate became jaded, and then coarsened: he was like an alcoholic, on whom a good wine would be wasted, because he needs a drink that will burn his taste buds. Such a man loses not only the capacity to enjoy the 'magical' side of sex, but the magical side of life in general. The senses close up, like windows that have become too dirty to admit the light, and too stiff to open.

This problem applies to all human beings; it is one of the most basic problems of human existence. Our highly complex lives cause us to concentrate on a narrow range of experience; our frustrations prevent relaxation, the sense of wider meanings. If I write too many pages of a book in one day, I find it difficult to relax and unwind in the evening; I remain narrow and tense. In this mood, I may gulp my dinner and get indigestion, even though I have the whole evening to eat it in. With many people, tension becomes a habit, so they end in a kind of self-created prison. This state is a 'vicious circle' in the most exact sense of the term. Too much concentration upon some immediate objective causes fatigue; the senses close, so that the 'magic' can no longer get in. Unaware of the root of the trouble, we make no effort to open the windows. Instead, we harden our attitude towards life in general, taking it for granted that it is a dreary, thankless business with only a few compensations. As we concentrate obsessively on these compensations, the windows jam more tightly than ever . . . This is the psychology of all obsessives: of misers, religious cranks, women who cannot allow a speck of dust in their homes. It is also the psychology of most criminals.

Although this hardening of the mental arteries usually occurs slowly over a lifetime, it can be accelerated by obsessive behaviour, which has a reinforcement effect on the mental pattern. Most healthy males experience strong sexual desires; but the man who deliberately makes the decision to satisfy them by raping and killing women has taken the decisive step into obsessional behaviour. When his most important memories are of murder and violation, how can he avoid being an obsessive? In effect, he is like a man suffering from such a bad head cold that he can neither see nor smell nor hear nor breathe properly.

Sexual murder is the most extreme form of Sartre's 'magical' behaviour. All magical behaviour involves self-delusion, and therefore a certain conflict with reality. But a man suffering from mild delusions of grandeur may be tolerated by his fellow men; they may even humour him, so that there is no head-on clash with reality. A sado-masochist who hires a prostitute to dress up as a nurse, then to allow him to flog her, is paying for the privilege of having a partner to share his fantasies: hence he also avoids the inevitable clash with reality. But the rapist or sex killer forces the 'partner' to collaborate, and avoids payment, so the clash with reality is only deferred. In his moment of supreme satisfaction, he is Don Juan and Casanova and Haroun Al Raschid; but ten minutes later, he is only a man on the run, who may spend the rest of his life in gaol if society catches him. The strain is not merely the problem of keeping his secret; it is the problem of living permanently on two levels, like a man trying to walk two tightropes with either foot. This also explains why such a man becomes increasingly careless, or finally commits suicide. He may also develop certain delusions, which help to reconcile him to his Jekyll and Hyde personality. (According to the psychologist Robert Eisler, this is how the belief in werewolves came about – a primitive attempt by the sex maniac to understand his own behaviour.) The Jersey rapist Edward Paisnel (arrested in 1971) believed that he was possessed by the spirit of Gilles de Rais. Paisnel was charged with fifteen offences, mainly against young children; he would break into the house, carrying the sleeping child out into the garden, and commit the sexual assault. Behind a cupboard in Paisnel's bedroom there was a secret room which contained black magic paraphernalia – masks and strange clothes, an altar, a dish containing toads. Questioned by the police about a raffia cross, Paisnel's face went red and his eyes bulged; he said: 'My Master would laugh very long and loud at this.' Paisnel had literally developed 'magical' behaviour to reconcile himself to his overpowering urges. What is equally typical is that during the eleven years of his reign of terror on Jersey, Paisnel was known as a kind-hearted man who loved children; he played Santa Claus at Christmas, and was known to dozens of children as Uncle Ted. There can be no doubt that he *was* a kind-hearted man, except when possessed by his 'daemon'.

To conclude this chapter, other parallel cases should be mentioned.

Ed Gein, a lonely little bachelor of Plainfield, Wisconsin, was primarily a necrophile who ended by killing women. A deputy sheriff, searching for his mother (who ran a store), called at the Gein farm – since Gein had been her last customer; he found his mother, headless, hanging upside down from the ceiling. Other fragments of women were found in the abominably squalid farmhouse, but these had been obtained from corpses. Gein had lived alone since the death of his highly dominant mother, who had been something of a religious maniac. In spite of his mild appearance and gentle manner, Gein's sexual urges were strong. In 1942 – fifteen years before his arrest – he had been fascinated by the bare legs of a female visitor to a neighbouring house – the woman was wearing shorts. The same night, a man broke into the house, and asked the woman's small son where she could be found: the boy thought he recognized Gein. But the intruder fled before he was seen by anyone else. Three years later, Gein's mother died. Alone in the house, he brooded on sex. One night, after seeing a newspaper report of the burial of a local woman, he went and dug up her body and reburied the empty coffin. Back at the farm, he was finally able to indulge his sexual desires to the full. 'It gave me a lot of satisfaction,' Gein remarked, recalling Christie's comment about the death of Muriel Eady. Unlike Christie, Gein *had* regrets every time he gave way to the urge to visit local graveyards. Nevertheless, he ate parts of the corpses, and made waistcoats of the skin, wearing them next to his body. The compulsion occurred about once a year, usually at the time of the full moon. (In this, he resembles Paisnel.) The two women he murdered were both elderly; presumably the murders were intended as some kind of act of revenge against his mother. Gein was sentenced to internment in a mental hospital. Like Paisnel, he was universally liked in the area, and much in demand as a baby-sitter. The incredibly dirty state of the farmhouse indicates that, like Christie, he had retreated into the world of his own nightmare.

On 9th November, 1949, the body of a woman was found in False Creek, Vancouver, British Columbia. She had been strangled and beaten before being thrown – alive – into the water; missing panties and suspender belt indicated that the motive was sexual. She was identified as Blanche Fisher, an attractive woman who looked many years younger than her actual age, forty-five. She had failed to return home from a visit to the cinema on the evening before the murder.

A month later, on 5th December, a police patrol car passed a man who wore a raincoat, but whose legs appeared to be bare above rubber boots. He was caught after a chase, and proved to be wearing only a shirt under the raincoat. He claimed that he had blacked out earlier that evening, and regained his senses to find himself walking along without trousers. Understandably, the police disbelieved him. They went back to the houseboat under Burrard Bridge that thirty-four-year-old Frederick Ducharme gave as his address. On a clothes-line they found six pairs of women's panties, and in the living quarters, Blanche Fisher's shoes and watch. Like Gein's farmhouse, the boat was chaotically untidy. Ducharme (who at first gave his name as Farnsworth) admitted to being with Blanche Fisher on the evening of the murder; he claimed she had entered his car willingly, but became hysterical when he tried to make love to her and ran away. It was clear that what actually happened was that Ducharme had forced her into his car (perhaps knocking her unconscious), then taken her on to his houseboat, where she was subjected to beating and rape, as well as being cut by a knife. She was then thrown overboard.

It was never established where the panties came from, or other women's trinkets found in the cabin, although Ducharme admitted that he had stolen some of the panties from clothes-lines. The pattern is similar to that of the Gein case: a sex-obsessed man who lives alone, and who periodically wanders the streets at night, exposing himself to women, raiding clothes-lines, perhaps committing the occasional rape. The torture indicates his desire to feel himself complete master of his victim. (And in this respect, the 'victimology' deserves comment; although pretty, Blanche Fisher was unmarried. She was a shy, quiet woman who regularly attended a Christian Science church. To fellow assistants in the store where she worked, she dropped hints of romance and future marriage; but it was later established that these were pure imagination; she had no male friends. But she was an enthusiastic cinema-goer and reader of movie fan-magazines. For a man like Ducharme, she must have seemed the ideal victim.)

One also notes Ducharme's lack of foresight or caution. If he had thrown away the shoes and watch, there would have been no case against him. And the story he invented failed to explain how, if Blanche Fisher *had* run away, he came to possess her shoes and watch. The evidence suggests that he lived in a dream world, in which sex was the only reality.

The 'moonlight murderer' of Texarcana, Texas, was never caught, and almost certainly committed suicide. Between

March and May 1946, he committed five murders, two of young couples. The motive was rape; after shooting the male escort, he raped and tortured the girl. This case demonstrates the typical pattern of mounting violence. A young couple who were attacked on 20th February were only knocked unconscious, after which the girl was raped. A month later, the male escort was shot, and the girl tortured and raped for two hours before she was shot. In April, another male escort was shot, and the girl tortured and raped for four hours before she was killed. In the final case, in May (again on the night of a full moon), a farmer was shot as he sat reading his newspaper in front of an open window. The killer undoubtedly intended to assault his wife, but she ran screaming from the house. Tyre tracks outside confirmed that this murder was also the work of the 'moonlight murderer'. A few days later, a man committed suicide by leaping under a train in Texarcana. At the same time, a burning car was found in a wooded area near the scene of the earlier murders. After this, the murders ceased.

Harvey Glatman, a photographer of San Diego, California, illustrates a different aspect of this 'suicidal' tendency. Glatman, another unattractive, bespectacled little man, collected pornography and had a collection of sexy photographs. Finally, he decided to put his fantasies into effect. Three times he advertised for photographic models; on each occasion, he tied up the girl after threatening her with a revolver, took 'bondage' pictures, after which he raped the girl and killed her. The bodies were dumped outside the city, on lonely roads. A fourth girl put up more resistance; Glatman was caught before he could kill her. What is surprising is that he succeeded with three girls. Obviously, a girl who intends to answer an advertisement for modelling may well mention her destination to a room mate or friend; Glatman knew this, but he didn't care; the need for sexual satisfaction was more important than the likelihood of being caught. Such a man may be regarded as a suicide who has decided to have a good time before he goes.

In 1970, a fifty-one-year-old construction worker named Mack Edwards walked into a Los Angeles police station and admitted to a series of child murders stretching over seventeen years. He confessed to six murders – three between 1953 and 1956, and three between 1968 and 1970. His detailed knowledge of the crimes convinced police that the confessions were genuine; they also came to believe that Edwards was responsible too for a series of child murders between 1956 and 1968, bringing the total up to twenty-two. Edwards was sentenced to death, whereupon he requested to be allowed to be the next man executed in California (where there have been no executions for several years, while certain crucial appeals are heard).[4] 'My lawyer told me there are a hundred men to die in the chair. I'm asking the judge if I can have the first man's place. He's sitting up there sweating right now. I'll take his place. I'm not sweating. I'm ready for it.' He gives the impression of a man who has wakened from a kind of nightmare, whose one anxiety is to make sure it never returns.

And this enables me to state the problem of the assassin in very clear terms. Man is an evolving creature, with various *levels* of need. Physical survival is the lowest of these; once this is satisfied, he can evolve to the next level: 'territorial' security, the need for a home; beyond this, the need for sex, family, and so on through Maslow's hierarchy of values. It is also important to recognize that evolution tends to proceed in 'leaps'; I notice this if I try to master any skill, from learning a foreign language to skiing or walking on my hands: one minute I am doing it clumsily, the next minute, it has 'come to me'. The same is true of our personal evolution: we quite suddenly 'care' about something that was a matter of total indifference a few days before. A child who has always thought nothing of lying or stealing wakes up one morning to find he has outgrown them; a young man who has used his personal charm to seduce girls quite suddenly feels disgust at the dishonesty involved. Bernard Shaw was so fascinated by the abrupt nature of these overnight moral changes that he made them the subject of several of his plays.

And the basic law of moral common sense is never to do anything that will block your evolution, just as it is physical common sense not to ruin your health for the sake of some temporary pleasure. This is the real objection to crime: not a religious or moral objection, but a psychological one. For fourteen years, Mack Edwards killed children to satisfy an obsessive sexual need; one morning, he woke up and found he had outgrown it; the demon had gone. But how could he evolve into the self-esteem level – which is essentially a social level – with twenty-two dead children on his conscience? He was literally another man, passing judgement on an earlier self. His judgement was a sentence of death.

1. The Scottish novelist David Lindsay wrote in his *Philosophical Notes* (1921): 'Emotion resembles a wheel spinning free. When cogs work, action begins, emotion ceases.'
2. See Appendix, p. 225.
3. In *Origins of the Sexual Impulse* and *A Casebook of Murder*.
4. On 18 February 1972, the California Supreme Court voted to abolish the death penalty as 'unconstitutional'.

CHAPTER FIVE

The Right Man

It is now necessary to discuss in more detail the closely related questions of self-esteem and the will to power.

It is clear that what drives a killer like Shere Ali, the assassin of Lord Mayo, is a curious mixture of self-esteem and emotional self-deception (or 'magic'). This proves to apply to a surprisingly large number of political assassins (for example, Lucheni, with his 'How I'd like to kill someone – but it must be someone important so it gets into the papers'). The classic example is Charles Guiteau, the assassin of President Garfield, of whom Robert J. Donovan remarks:[1]

> Guiteau, as a young recruit unskilled in any manual craft, was given menial chores in the fields, the workshops and the kitchen [of the Oneida Community]. Under this drudgery, he took to sulking, daydreaming of future glory and tacking up on the walls of his room signs like this:
>
> CHARLES J. GUITEAU
> PREMIER OF ENGLAND
> WILL DELIVER A LECTURE IN
> ST. JAMES HALL, LONDON

It sounds like insanity; but Guiteau was not insane in the ordinary sense – only permanently tormented by a desire for 'recognition', to *be* somebody. Neither was he, in the strict sense of the word, a religious crank, although he wrote to his father: 'I claim that I am in the employ of *Jesus Christ and Co*, the very ablest and strongest firm in the universe . . .'; for Guiteau, religion was just another means of self-assertion. When religion failed to pay off, he went in for confidence swindling. After six years of this hand-to-mouth existence, he discovered the possibilities of politics as a stepping stone to eminence; he devoted a great deal of 1872 to campaigning for Horace Greeley, the Democratic candidate for the presidency. He had visions of being appointed Minister to Chile.

But Greeley was defeated, then died, and Guiteau was temporarily plunged into total depression. During Grant's two terms of office, he went back to religious oratory, billing himself as 'the Little Giant from the West', and managing to scrape a poor living by charging fifty cents for admission to his sermons on the existence of Hell. In 1880 he decided to switch back to politics, and this time to support Grant, who seemed the likely winner. Garfield was nominated as candidate instead, so Guiteau simply changed 'Grant' to 'Garfield' in the speech he had written, and hung around Republican headquarters, making a nuisance of himself and unaware that he was regarded as a joke. He had no opportunity to actually deliver his speech; but when Garfield became president, Guiteau felt nevertheless that he was due for some reward – such as a post as foreign ambassador. His first choice fell on Vienna, but he later decided that Paris would be preferable. For months he haunted the White House, becoming such a pest that the staff were finally instructed not to admit him on any account. Finally he decided that a man who could behave in this heartless way 'to the men that made him' (i.e. himself) was a danger to the American people and should be eliminated. 'Besides,' he added (in a note about his decision) 'it will create a demand for my book *The Truth.*' So he bought a revolver with borrowed money, and on 2nd July, 1881, walked up behind the President at the railway station and shot him in the back. Garfield died two months later, on 19th September. At his trial, Guiteau's defence of insanity failed – perhaps because he went to such lengths to explain that he was neither a fool nor a lunatic; it was also obvious that he was enjoying every minute of his notoriety. He was executed in June 1882.

The prosecution argued that Guiteau was completely sane in the normal sense of the term, and even the defence neurologist admitted that the chief trouble was 'the exaggerated self-feeling of the morbid egotist'. After reading a detailed account of Guiteau's life – with its endless miscalculations and humiliations – the reader comes away with the feeling that Guiteau was rebelling against fate, against life; that is to say, the murder was a 'magical' act of self-assertion; directed, like all magical acts, at the wrong person.

It should not be assumed that only males are capable of self esteem murders. In the course of revising this book, I mentioned its theme to Clive Gunnell, a reporter for Westward Television. He surprised me by saying that my theory of the self-esteem killer was confirmed by his own observation of Ruth Ellis, who was executed in 1955 for the murder of her lover, David Blakely. Clive Gunnel was the friend with whom David Blakely left the Magnolia public house in Hampstead. As they left the pub, Ruth Ellis, a pretty twenty-eight-year-old divorcée stepped forward and emptied a revolver at Blakely; Clive Gunnell was bending over him on the pavement while she continued to shoot over his shoulder.

Most writers on the case have assumed that this was a passion killing, a case of violent jealousy. Clive Gunnell denied this. Although Ruth Ellis and David Blakely had been lovers for two years, both had had other affairs; in fact, at the time of the murder, Ruth Ellis was living with one man, having an affair with another, and was married to a third. 'She just had a craving for recognition', said Clive Gunnell. 'In these days of television, she'd have probably got on to some quiz team or panel and become a public figure – which is what she really wanted. She was quite a strong personality.' In France or Italy, her shooting of David Blakely might have achieved precisely this; as a distraught and jealous woman – moreover, one who had suffered a miscarriage only a few days before the murder – she would probably have received a year in jail for second degree murder, and thereafter featured in books and articles about *crimes passionels*. The English unfortunately lack this kind of romanticism. In spite of a public outcry, she was executed.

According to Maslow, the self-esteem level of the personality lies between the sexual level and the creative or intellectual level. What this suggests is that the rapist has a low level of self-esteem, and that, conversely, a man with a high level of self-esteem (whether justified or not) is unlikely to commit rape. This seems to be borne out by police records[2]; the typical rapist is often a man of low I.Q., but he is nearly always a man of low self-esteem. Men with highly developed egos often commit crimes of violence, but rape is seldom among them.

What is also implied in the Maslow hierarchy is that men fixated at the self-esteem level should tend to show a preoccupation with the idea of intellectual or creative eminence – although they seldom show real gifts in this direction. The case of San Francisco's Zodiac killer (still uncaught at the time of writing) seems to fit this pattern. Between 20th December, 1968, and 11th October, 1969, 'Zodiac' committed five known murders, and seriously wounded two more victims. On 20th December, two teenagers – David Farraday and Bettilou Jensen – were attacked as they sat in a station wagon in a lover's lane near Vallejo, California. Both were shot dead; but the youth's wallet was untouched, and the girl had not been sexually assaulted. On 5th July, 1969, a caller with a gruff voice phoned the Vallejo police station, and said that he had just committed a double murder on the Columbia Parkway; he added that he had 'killed those kids last year'. In the car park of a golf course, not far from the spot where the other victims had been found, police discovered another couple who had been shot. Darlene Ferrin, a waitress, was dead; Michael Mageau was still alive. He was able to tell police that a man had stepped out of a parked car, fired several shots at them, then turned and walked away. A month later, three San Francisco newspapers received letters, signed with a cross superimposed on a circle (the astrological sign of the zodiac). The letters stated that the writer was the man who had shot both couples, and gave details that made it clear that he was telling the truth. Apart from the block-letter text, these letters also contained passages in cipher – a different cipher for each. A schoolteacher who cracked the code discovered that the cipher read: 'I like killing people because it is so much fun it is more fun than killing wild game in the forest because man is the most dangerous animal . . . when I die I will be reborn in Paradise and all I have killed will be my slaves . . .'

On 27th September, 1969, the same caller rang the Napa police department to report a double murder. Rushing to the scene on the shores of Lake Berryessa, police discovered a man and a woman had been stabbed. Again, the man, Brian Hartnell, was alive; the girl, Cecilia Shepherd, died soon after. Hartnell described how they had just finished a picnic when they were approached by a paunchy figure in a hood-mask; on the lower part of the hood was the sign of the zodiac, marked in white. The man asked for money, tied them both up, then stabbed them repeatedly. On the door of Hartnell's white sports car the police found a drawing of the zodiac sign, and the dates of the previous murders.

Two weeks later, on 11th October, 1969, the killer shot a taxi driver, Paul Stine, in the back of the head on the top of Nob Hill in San Francisco, then walked off, taking the driver's wallet, and a fragment torn from his shirt. The bullet was found to have come from the same gun that killed Darlene Ferrin. The next day, the San Francisco *Chronicle* received another Zodiac letter, enclosing a bloody fragment of shirt. The writer declared he was the murderer of Paul Stine; he complained of the inefficiency of the police, and went on: 'School children make nice targets. I think I shall wipe out a school bus some morning. Just shoot out the tyres, then pick off the kiddies as they come bouncing out.'

Zodiac did not carry out his threat; the murder of the taxi driver has proved to be the last to date. But on 21st October, a caller claiming to be Zodiac rang the Oakland police station, and declared that he would be willing to give himself up if he could be represented by a famous lawyer – F. Lee Bailey and Melvin Belli were his first choices. He also asked that time should be reserved for him on an early morning talk show on television. This was accordingly done. The call had come in after midnight; the show went out at 6.45 a.m. The event was announced on television; listeners were asked not to phone in with their usual questions, but to leave the line free for Zodiac. By the time the Jim Dunbar show came on, an enormous audience was watching the show. At 7.41, a call came on the line; a caller with a soft, boyish voice identified himself as Zodiac. He called back fifteen times, and talked to the lawyer Melvin Belli about his murders and the headaches he suffered from. He ended by agreeing to meet Belli in front of a store in Daly City, but failed to turn up.

Whether or not this caller (who asked to be addressed as Sam) was the genuine Zodiac, the actual killer did not disown him; two months later, he sent a Christmas greetings letter to Belli, enclosing another fragment of Stine's bloodstained shirt as identification. The letter said he needed help: 'I am afraid I will lose control and take my ninth and possibly tenth victim.' The figure alarmed the police, but a careful check of unsolved homicides failed to substantiate Zodiac's claim. In March 1971, the Los Angeles *Times* received a Zodiac letter, this time boasting of seventeen murders; but again, this claim would appear to be unfounded.

Zodiac letters have continued to be received at intervals,

some of which are regarded as genuine by handwriting experts. In some of them the writer threatens to torture future victims, and one of them contained a parody of Koko's song in *The Mikado,* describing all the people he would like to kill 'who never would be missed'.

It is possible, of course, that 'Zodiac' may be a sadist of the Kürten type, who experiences orgasm at the moment of stabbing or shooting his victims, but there is no indication of this. Kürten never used a gun; his own peculiar obsession was blood, so he preferred to stab his victims. A man who walks up to a car, empties his revolver through the window, then walks away, does not sound as if his aim is sexual enjoyment. Two youths who heard the shot that killed the taxi driver Paul Stine described how the killer emerged from the cab a moment later, reached in through the window to tear the driver's shirt, then hurried off; again, there is no indication of a sexual motive. On the other hand, the evidence *does* suggest a man who kills out of the desire for self-assertion. The killings cause shock waves throughout California; this is what he wants. He writes letters in cryptogram, and threatens that if they are not published, he will go on a murder rampage. They are published, and he has the satisfaction of knowing that thousands of people are trying to puzzle out his message; it is like being an author; in a sense, he is famous. And the taste for publicity is the most marked trait of his character, the desire to shock and to intrigue. It is tempting to assume, on the basis of the attacks on courting couples, that he enjoys killing women, and that some kind of sexual jealousy is involved; but the murder of the taxi driver fails to bear this out. This is committed for the publicity, and is followed by the threat to attack a school bus – a threat which, it seems fairly certain, he had no intention of carrying out. For a week or two, he is the most talked-about man in America. He follows this up with a television 'appearance', and has the satisfaction of knowing that the show is watched by the largest audience ever to see the same show in the Bay area. Was the caller with the boyish voice Zodiac? It seems probable. If Zodiac had changed his mind about calling the programme, and some hoaxer had taken his place, Zodiac would quickly have denounced the phoney; his highly developed sense of publicity guarantees that.

But all this exercise in anonymous publicity must have

been peculiarly frustrating. He wants to be a public figure, and in a sense he achieves this; he enters into friendly discussion with a famous lawyer on television, and later drops him a Christmas letter beginning 'Dear Melvin'. But he can advance no further into this world of celebrity – at least, not without being caught. He tries to keep the excitement alive with more letters, mentioning more murders; but as no more murders follow, the interest wanes. The logical next step would be more killings; but his ambiguous celebrity has released some of the frustration that made him into a killer. We observe again the same 'vicious circle' mechanism that we have noted in the case of sadistic pornography, and of sex crime. The killing is a response to a powerful desire whose non-satisfaction forms an evolutionary blockage. But the correct way to deal with this blockage is to find a socially acceptable way of satisfying the desire. It is true, for example, that Casanova was a sexual criminal; he admits in his memoirs that he and a crowd of friends kidnapped a girl, and all raped her. But although sexual desire dominated his life, he did not make a habit of rape; he usually found that a certain amount of effort and charm was enough to persuade a girl to give him what he wanted. A certain amount of confidence swindling was involved; he often promised marriage, with no intention of honouring his word; still, this was socially acceptable, and there was nothing to stop him from turning his attention to other fields; to cutting a figure in society, or writing philosophical essays.

For each step we take up the 'hierarchy of values' involves an *increased integration into society*. When a man thinks only of survival or security, he is thinking solely in terms of himself. When he thinks about sex, he is thinking in terms of one other person, and perhaps of a family. When the self-esteem needs become paramount, he begins to think in terms of other people and their opinion of him. And if he rises to the self-actualizing level – as a scientist or artist or philosopher – then he is thinking in terms of society, of the human race. At any level beyond the very lowest – mere survival – anti-social activity is self-defeating. *This* is the paradoxical absurdity that lies at the root of the assassin's violence.

Dr Laurence Freedman remarked of 'Zodiac': 'He kills senselessly because he is deeply frustrated. And he hates himself because he is an anonymous nonentity. When he is caught, he will turn out to be a mouse, a murderous mouse.' This may be true as far as it goes, but it overlooks one of the central points about the self-esteem killer: the 'absurd' reasoning, the 'magical' non-logic. In his letters, Zodiac attacks the police for their inefficiency, as though he is an indignant member of the public, not the man they are hunting. He implies that it takes considerable courage to kill 'that most dangerous of all animals', man, when all he has done is to shoot defenceless courting couples in their cars.

This magical non-logic is characteristic of a type that A. E. Van Vogt has called 'the violent man' or 'the right man'. Van Vogt's theory of 'the right man' is one of the most important contributions to the psychology of violence; unfortunately, it was cast in fictional form[3], and so never achieved the serious attention it deserved. A pamphlet describing the theory was printed for private circulation; the following is a summary of its contents.

In the pamphlet, 'A Report on the Violent Male', Van Vogt explains that he has been collecting stories of a certain type of violent man for more than a decade. A psychologist told him of a typical case. The man was divorced, and had set up his ex-wife in a suburban home, on condition that she did not re-marry, and should spend the rest of her life being a perfect mother to their son. The man apparently thought this was a fair arrangement.

The story of their marriage was as follows. She had been a nurse, and had had two affairs with doctors. Before marrying, she thought she ought to tell her future husband about this. He went into an insane frenzy of jealousy, and the next day, brought her a legal document in triplicate to sign. He refused to let her read it. She felt so guilty that she finally signed. Van Vogt says; 'My years of observation of other males of this type tempts me to speculate that in [the document] she agreed that she was a prostitute, and that in marrying her he was raising her from the status of a fallen woman; but she must agree that she had no rights as a wife, except what he bestowed on her.' After the marriage, the husband treated the wife as a chattel. He expected complete freedom. 'He was always driving his secretaries to and from work, and taking an unconscionable long time to do it, or visiting one or another of his women employees in their apartments. Any questioning by his wife of this activity put him into a rage that often included violence.' He roamed the country, reporting home when he felt like it. He was subject to sudden violent rages. After an evening listening to music with friends he might fly into a temper as he was preparing to leave the house for a cross-country flight, and knock his wife down. The next day he would ring up from some distant part of the country and beg forgiveness.

Van Vogt describes several other relationships with the same basic features – men who treat their wives and families in a violently despotic manner, and expect total, unquestioned obedience, becoming violent at the least sign of resistance. Such a man says Van Vogt, has an absolute obsession about being 'in the right'. He totally lacks self-criticism, and can storm and rage about some triviality with no glimmer of recognition that he is simply indulging himself and wasting everybody's time. If he has power – for example, like a Russian landowner of the last century, cited by Van Vogt – he may use it with horrifying ruthlessness, having men flogged to death for minor offences. If actually proved wrong, he is likely to evade the issue by flying into an even greater rage at some invented affront or reflection upon his dignity, his attitude being that a wife who truly respected her husband would not tell him he was wrong. If she does so, it is because she wants to insult him . . .

Van Vogt calls this man 'the right man' because of his obsessional need to be right. And he makes the interesting observation that if he is left by his wife, he goes to pieces; he may become an alcoholic, or a drifter, or even kill himself. Her submission forms the basis of his self-respect: her desertion pulls away his psychological foundations.

A point to bear in mind about the 'right man' is that he belongs to the 'dominant five per cent': but in our highly competitive world, many of these men may not possess the qualities necessary for gaining recognition from the rest of society. His immediate circle – his wife and children – has to provide the urgently needed psychological vitamin. Because they are unsatisfactory substitutes for the real thing, they also have to bear a certain amount of resentment, which may take the form of outrageous bullying. But since this bullying constitutes the last bulwark of his self-esteem, he needs the victims more than they need him. Children may leave home (in which case, they are never forgiven); but the desertion of the victim-in-chief, his wife, causes the total disintegration of his ego. Van Vogt argues that dictators – Hitler, Stalin, Mao – are often violent men. (Hitler's treatment of Geli Raubal, and his shock at her suicide, seems to confirm this: close friends thought he would kill himself; an earlier woman friend had also attempted suicide because of his unending supervision.)

Van Vogt's explanation of this attitude is that men have always dominated society, and that slightly unstable males show an exaggerated form of the normal male characteristic. He mentions that in China in 1950, the communists introduced laws designed to increase the rights of women, and that in one district alone, in 1954, 10,000 wives were murdered by their husbands for attempting to take advantage of the new law. In Italy in 1916, two women were sentenced to a year in gaol for adultery. Their defence was that their husbands were also unfaithful. The court overruled this plea on the ground that there is a legally established double standard.

I am inclined to suspect that the male attitude to women is based on something deeper than social usage, no matter how ancient. The compulsion that drives some men to rape is, oddly enough, a kind of worship of women. This probably develops in childhood – many male children think of their mother as a kind of goddess. They may be deeply shocked when they learn the facts of sex; it seems unutterably indecent that these goddesses should allow the coarse male to strip away their veils and use their bodies to satisfy his lowest appetite. A goddess ought to consort with a god. It could be argued that this sexual idealism is the result of immaturity, inexperience; but in that case, experience would be enough to dissipate it; and it doesn't. In Agnar Mykle's autobiographical novel *Lasso Round the Moon*, there is an episode that catches the essence of this male vision. He describes falling in love with a pretty girl at a party. 'He had felt as though he held an elf in his arms; the night became magical, the air was full of delicate crystal; he hardly dared touch her . . .' The next morning he overhears a conversation: '. . . two boys, who had been in the car with the girl, told how on their way home they had decided to take her to one of their homes. The girl had shown no reluctance, not to either of them. The boy's parents were away and it had taken place in the parents' room, in the double bed. She had been so hot that both the boys had to have a shower afterwards . . .' This strikes at something deeper than male possessiveness: at some vision of the eternal feminine. The same feeling emerges in Gorki's story *Twenty-Six Men and a Girl,* where the twenty-six bakers, in their damp cellar, idealize the girl Tanya – until she gives herself to a soldier, when they turn on her and call her names. Conversely, when the male finally succeeds in possessing the goddess, he may experience a sense of power, non-contingency:

What were all the world's alarms
To mighty Paris when he found
Sleep upon a golden bed
That first dawn, in Helen's arms?

If it were not for this 'magical' vision of woman, wives would have less to complain about; once the male curiosity had been satisfied, a man would lose all interest in other women. Very young men, possessed by unsatisfied desire, find it difficult to understand how a married man could commit rape or a sex crime; surely he could simply undress his wife? But this is to forget the romantic craving for the 'eternal womanly' that can turn sour and violent. The fact that these infinitely desirable creatures can offer themselves like tarts touches some nerve of morbid, masochistic pleasure which incubates jealousy and violence.

The violent man may not be particularly interested in sexual intercourse; it is the self-esteem needs that obsess him. He may care for nothing but his work. (On the other hand, there would be nothing contradictory in a violent man being obsessed by sex: by the *conquest* involved.) His violence arises from insecurity; he is like a tyrant in perpetual fear of being dethroned. His only chance of outgrowing the violence lies in success, in being accepted at his own valuation. Van Vogt summarizes: [Realize] that most right men deserve some sympathy, for they are struggling with an almost unbelievable inner horror; however, if they give in to the impulse to hit or choke, they are losing the battle and are on their way to the ultimate disaster . . .' Perhaps inner hunger or craving would be a better term than inner horror, bearing in mind that the need for self-esteem is, at its own evolutionary level, as much a hunger as the need for food.

What is being suggested here is this: A couple of centuries ago, most murders sprang out of frustration of the lowest level of the need-hierarchy: the need for food and security; the motive was economic. In an increasingly 'affluent' civilization, the next level of need has emerged: the sexual. It began to emerge about a century ago; Freud's psychology was an intuitive recognition of the emergence of this new level. The pornography boom shows it becoming accepted as a norm; so do Britain's new abortion laws, which accept that twelve-year-old girls may need advice on contraception. To be afraid of this new development is irrational. In all ages, men (and women) of talent have accepted a certain promiscuity as a norm, because it is a part of their need for self-expression. (And the greatest of them have later outgrown it.) If the whole society is slowly evolving, then a certain level of promiscuity – casualness about sex – is bound to become a norm. Sex crime is bound to increase, because there will be vast numbers of 'sexually underprivileged' males who are capable of 'stealing' their sex gratification as a burglar steals money. Logically, strictly economic crimes should decrease, while sex crimes and crimes of violence should increase. This, in fact, is what the figures show. While the number of cases of rape and violence against the person increase steeply, cases of larceny and breaking and entering show only a small increase, and occasionally even a decrease.[4]

There *should* come a time when sex crimes show a continuous tendency to decrease. In that case what kind of crime would replace them? With luck, none. The self-esteem level is a social level. It does produce crime, but this is a rarity. A man with an acute self-esteem hunger may be a boaster, a bully, an appalling husband; but his involvement with other people and his desire for their good opinion will usually prevent him from developing into a criminal.

It should now be apparent that Van Vogt's theory, if correct, may be as important to our own time as Freud's sexual theories were to the world of 1900. The violent man becomes one of the main problems of our time. The increasing number of revolution movements throughout the world, from the Tupamaros guerrillas of South America to the 'Angry Brigade' in England, is a sign of the increasing number of 'violent men' rather than of political consciousness.

Van Vogt's account of the violent man could be criticized as too restricted. The 'right man' is only a particular kind of violent man – one might call him the 'opinionated type'. The hunger for self-esteem affects different character structures in different ways. In the remainder of this chapter I will try to suggest some of these.

One of the most sensational murder trials of recent years received no publicity in the British or American press: the trial of Hans van Zon[5], the Dutch mass murderer. As in so many cases discussed in this book, the puzzling thing about the van Zon case is the motive. After his trial, his ex-headmaster remarked: 'About some boys you can, as a teacher, almost predict with certainty that they will become criminals, but I cannot say that about Hans, although I always did think that there was something mysterious about him.'

Born on 20th April, 1942, in Utrecht, Hans van Zon was something of a mother's boy – descriptions by psychiatrists of his relationship with his mother bring to mind D. H. Lawrence's self-portrait in *Sons and Lovers*. His father was a workman; the mother resented this, and dreamed of her son making a successful career. Hans was apparently a quiet and rather lethargic child, noted for his politeness to adults. He preferred to play with younger children at school. One of the psychiatrists later described him as a case of infantile autism – that is, an odd, subjective frame of mind, total lack of interest in the outside world and other people. When he left school, he went through a succession of jobs. He seemed to live in a world of fantasy – and here the literary parallel seems to be with Keith Waterhouse's *Billy Liar* who lies gratuitously, simply for the fun of it. Petty dishonesty led to his dismissal from most of these jobs.

In 1958, at the age of sixteen, van Zon went to Amsterdam, bought himself some expensive clothes, and began passing himself off as a young student. Apparently the very word 'student' had a romantic ring for him. He became a kind of con man – but without real interest in money. At one point he borrowed money from a Catholic priest, who made it a condition of the loan that he went to a Catholic institute in Doorn. He went – and ran away almost immediately.

Being a good-looking and plausible young man, he had a number of love affairs – and not always with girls. There was a distinct homosexual streak in him.

In July 1964, when he was twenty-two, he committed what was probably his first murder. Van Zon later admitted the murder, then withdrew his confession. According to the confession, he had taken out a girl named Elly Hager-Segov on the evening of 22nd July, and during the course of the evening, suddenly felt the urge to kill her. He took her home, then went off to a café, where he stayed until closing time. He then returned to Elly's lodging and told her he had missed the train. She allowed him to come in to stay the night. They made love. When he tried to make love a second time, she refused. He strangled her into unconsciousness, undressed her, then cut her throat with a bread-knife.

Later, after withdrawing his confession, he made the curious statement that he knew about the murder by a kind of second-sight, through 'visions'. This is just wild enough to be possibly true. We should bear in mind that there are two well-known Dutch clairvoyants, Peter Hurkos and Gerard Croiset, who often help the police to solve crimes, and that their method is to touch some object connected with the crime; this sometimes leads to a clear picture of the scene of the crime and of the criminal. Croiset and Hurkos both declared that one of the chief problems is that they may 'pick up' images from the minds of the police officers. Again, the English psychiatrist Arthur Guirdham has argued convincingly in a number of books that many 'mentally sick' people actually possess second sight, or other 'mediumistic' powers, and that their strange visions or dreams may be due to the operation of these powers rather than incipient psychosis. Van Zon described in detail how he had two types of vision; two dimensional and three dimensional, and claimed that his knowledge of the murdered girl's room came from such a vision. Van Zon also claimed to have been responsible for the murder of a homosexual film director called Claude Berkeley in Amsterdam in 1965, and later offered the same explanation about his knowledge of the Berkeley case.

After the death of Elly Hager-Segov, van Zon met an Italian girl named Caroline Gigli, and married her. She supported him by working as a chambermaid in hotels. In 1967, she accused her husband of planning to kill her. He was still on probation for some minor offence against morality, and the police decided to allow him to cool off in gaol for a month. After that, he returned to live with his wife.

In April 1967, van Zon murdered another girl, Coby van der Voort, thirty-seven, whom he had known for some time. They spent week-ends together periodically. On 29th April, van Zon joined her in Amsterdam; they spent a pleasant afternoon, and made love. Then he placed a pink powder on his tongue and swallowed it. When she asked him what it was, he told her it was a sexual stimulant. Naturally, she asked to try some. In fact, the powder he had taken was pink icing sugar; the powder he offered her was Soneryl, a sleeping drug. When she became dizzy, he took a lead pipe from his bag – he had made it himself from melted lead – and struck her several times on the head, killing her. He undressed her and washed the body, stabbed it several times with a bread-knife, and tried to make love to the body.

What happened next sounds like an episode from a Dickens novel. One day, when in a drunk and boastful mood, Hans van Zon described the murder of Coby van der Voort to an 'old lag' named 'Old Nol' (Oude Nol), who proceeded to blackmail him into committing more crimes. On 31st May, 1967, van Zon went to the shop of an eighty-year-old maker of fireworks, Jan Donse, known as Opa Cupido (Grandad Cupido). He seems to have taken a long time to make up his mind to go through with it, visiting the shop twice, but in the late afternoon he struck Donse with the lead pipe, and left him dead. Presumably he then robbed him.

In August, again inspired by 'Old Nol' (according to Zon and other witnesses), he murdered a forty-seven-year-old farmer, Reyer de Bruin, who lived alone in Heeswijk. Claiming to be a journalist who wanted to write about the life of a bachelor farmer, he gained de Bruin's confidence, then struck him down with the lead pipe. He also cut his throat with a bread-knife – he explained later that this was because he thought de Bruin's face changed into that of Old Nol as he lay dead.

His relationship with Old Nol seems to have been ambivalent. At the trial, the psychiatrist, Dr. Schnitzler, told the court that van Zon was fascinated by the old man, with his flamboyant manners and Dylan-Thomas-like voice. Old Nol also apparently admired Hans, or was clever enough to make him think so. He seems to have given Hans the idea of becoming a professional criminal.

It was Old Nol who suggested that van Zon kill a widow named Mrs. Woortmeyer, whom he (Old Nol) had courted. Van Zon made a mess of it – or rather (he claimed) was suddenly unable to put enough force into the blow to kill her. Pretending to be a revenue official, he got into her house and knocked her unconscious, after which he took a large sum of money from her. When she recovered consciousness she called the police. It was the end of van Zon's career of crime. He implicated Old Nol, who was sentenced to seven years. Van Zon was sentenced to 'life', a minimum of twenty years.

The most interesting thing to emerge at the trial was the curious fantasy world in which van Zon lived. He had enormous charm, and an air of being different from other men: 'he was able to get as many girlfriends as he wanted,' said a witness. He was kind and attentive to his girlfriends, and there was a touch of something Byronic, darkly tragic, in his manner. When he became interested in a girl, he began to spin elaborate fantasies: he was an orphan, and now intended to establish an import business in Iceland; he was a psychology student, an undercover detective, a C.I.A. spy hunting war criminals, a young fashion designer who would one day dominate the Parisian scene. The latter suggests the homosexual aspect of his character. Since he was fourteen he had made money by selling himself to men; but he also maintained a number of homosexual relations without expecting payment. Back in Utrecht after a short period in gaol for petty theft, he mixed with students, and could talk upon a wide range of subjects with a confidence and apparent erudition that made his claims to be a student plausible. But his understanding of the subjects was often superficial; he was interested in effect rather than in ideas.

One of the most interesting comments on him was made by a psychiatrist, Professor Kloek, who talked about van Zon's 'autism'. 'Victims of this disability are unable to see a human being *in his totality*. When he sees a baby, it is a hand or a leg he singles out. It doesn't satisfy his need to see or hear something; he wants to touch it as well. For example, when such a person is part of an audience at a piano recital, he is not satisfied to hear the music; he has a strong urge to put his hands on the piano and feel it as well. During the examinations by two psychiatrists, Hans van Zon showed an often irresistible urge to touch the clothes of the interrogators.' The same psychiatrist also mentioned that van Zon 'tried desperately to explain that he couldn't explain his feelings and share them with other people'.

All this will be of considerable importance in considering other cases besides this one. He is unable to see things *as a whole*; the world strikes him as a collection of bits and pieces. But when you respond to something – to a piece of music, or scenery – your response is a kind of electric shock that comes as you suddenly grasp its overall *meaning* – that is, grasp it as a whole. Van Zon is like a man wearing gloves, and who consequently can never really feel anything with his fingertips. And this is a description of schizophrenia – which, contrary to the usual notion, does not mean a 'split personality', but a permanent *detachment* from one's experience, as if surrounded by cotton wool. It is a lack of involvement. Van Zon's endless affairs, with men as well as women, are an attempt to remedy this. When he seduces a strange girl, he is for a moment a real *actor* in the affair, not a spectator. Emotionally, he lives in a desert; he feels that life is meaningless, and it is this that leads him to spoil chance after chance with petty crime.

But why the violence? Van Vogt's description of the 'right man' does not fit him. He is not 'opinionated' in the obsessive sense. But his psychological mainspring is the craving to be regarded with respect and admiration, and this dominates everything he does. When he reads a book on popular science, he is thinking about quoting it in a students' café. When he meets a young girl, he puts on his mysterious, Byronic air, and is not sure whether he is a secret service man or a dress designer, or some hero out of a romantic novel ... And periodically, his frustration boils over into violence. Whether the violence is an attempt to assert that he *is* capable of action, or whether it is some strange, sadistic compulsion that creeps over him with certain people, it is difficult to say; perhaps both. The only thing that seems clear is that the violence is connected with the need to be something more than he is.

This same pattern of boastfulness and self-assertion can be

discerned in some of the most widely publicized English murder cases of recent years. The Kray brothers, whose underworld empire extended from Whitechapel to Chelsea, took great delight in the celebrities they knew; their 'opening nights' of new clubs were crowded with film stars and politicians. The two murders with which they (and eight other men) were charged seem oddly motiveless. Jack McVitie had called Ronald Kray 'a great poove', and George Cornell told him to bugger off in front of other people. Kray subsequently walked up to Cornell in a crowded pub – the Blind Beggar in Stepney – and shot him through the head in front of a crowd of people. The killing seems to have been in the nature of a 'dare'. Later, Reginald, the other brother, shot Jack McVitie to prove (to his brother) that he was also tough enough to commit murder.

This same motivation is again apparent in the case of the Richardson brothers (Charles and Eddie) – the Kray's chief rivals in the protection business. Accounts of the events that led to their arrest make it clear that it was an orgy of motiveless violence. The brothers instituted 'underground courts', at which Charles Richardson wore mock judge's robes. But the tortures that were practised were out of all proportion to the offences that their underworld employees were supposed to have committed. One man who told them that he wanted to withdraw from the 'business' was beaten with a knuckleduster, then held down while deep razor cuts were made. The 'trials' opened with the victim being struck with an iron bar or a golf club and whipped with barbed wire. Teeth were pulled out with pliers, and electric wires attached to the genitals of the victim. This kind of torture might last for hours, with the victim being revived with cold water whenever he fainted. This can only be called sadism if sadism is understood to mean an insane, frenzied self-assertion that would explode into violence at the slightest resistance. Both the Richardsons and the Krays were sentenced to life imprisonment. To compare their careers with those of gangsters of an earlier era – Al Capone or Lucky Luciano – is to recognize that they were more interested in sheer self-assertion than in making a fortune illegally. 'The Krays' success in the East End swelled their heads', said Mr. Barry Hudson, a defence counsel at their trial; 'They moved into the West End and began to get hold of gentlemen with high titles, peers of the realm, baronets; and gradually they tried to get into this world.' A belted earl was actually employed in one of their clubs.

Arthur Hosein, convicted in 1970 of the kidnapping and murder of Mrs. Muriel McKay (whose body was never found), is altogether closer to Van Vogt's picture of the violent man. His German wife (ten years his senior) described how he 'came and went as he pleased', and said that she was not allowed to ask where he had been, although she was fairly certain that he was having affairs with other women. In local pubs, Hosein was known as a boaster who talked about his plans for becoming a millionaire. In a BBC television programme about the case, a relative in Trinidad (which Hosein left in 1954) said that his family expected him to become highly successful, and that on a return visit home a few years later he gave the impression that he was already rich. In fact, he was an excellent tailor, and his business in the East End of London prospered to such an extent that he was able to buy a £6,000 house in Chipping Ongar. This was not enough; in 1968 he sold it, and moved into Rooks Farm at Stocking Pelham, for which he paid £16,000. The picture he now set out to create was of the gentleman farmer, always immaculately manicured and barbered (his hair was dressed weekly by a private hairdresser), strolling around his estate or drinking in pubs with local businessmen. In fact, the money he earned as a tailor and farmer was inadequate; the result seems to have been the decision to kidnap the wife of a newspaper owner, Rupert Murdoch. The wrong woman was accidently kidnapped – Mrs. McKay's husband had borrowed Murdoch's car while the latter was out of the country – and a huge ransom was demanded. Police hiding near the scene where the ransom money was left managed to get the number of a Volvo car, belonging to Hosein. Although no trace of Mrs. McKay was found, other evidence pointed conclusively to the guilt of Arthur Hosein and his younger brother Nizam, and both were found guilty of murder. It is typical of the 'right man' that there was no breakdown, no confession. And pub acquaintances who saw Hosein on the night of the murder found it hard to believe that he had anything on his mind. Relatives in Trinidad also said that it was hard to believe that Hosein could plot a murder; he was not the criminal type. This is undoubtedly true. Crime was only the means to an end: becoming a millionaire, achieving the success he felt to be his right. The 'right man' is seldom a 'criminal type'; on the contrary, he is usually above average intelligence, and strikes people as charming and sensitive.

Raymond Morris, who was sentenced to life imprisonment for the murder of seven-year-old Christine Darby, also fits the pattern described by Van Vogt. Morris was also the chief suspect in the murder of Diana Tift, five, and Margaret Reynolds, six, who disappeared separately in 1965, but whose bodies were found together near Cannock Chase, Staffordshire. In November 1968, Morris tried to drag a ten-year-old girl into his car, and his licence number was taken by a woman who observed the attempt. He had already been among those questioned about the murder of Christine Darby in August 1967 (because his car was of the same type as the car in which the child had taken a lift), but his wife supported his false alibi. When police searched Morris's home, they found a number of blue films and pornographic photographs. Two of these showed a man's hand fondling the genitals of a five-year-old girl: the child turned out to belong to a cousin of Morris's wife, and a wristwatch in the picture identified the man as Morris. He had been photographing the child for a soap advertisement competition, and she had thought that it was all a game.

The picture that emerged after Morris's conviction was of a man of considerable charm and intelligence (I.Q. 120) whose fantasy life seems to have been as elaborate as van Zon's. He was a foreman engineer who could earn high wages, and his employers all described him as completely satisfactory. On the other hand, his workmates said that he was cold, without emotion, and that no one ever had a sense of getting to know him.

In 1951, Morris had married 'the girl next door', two years his junior, a slim, slightly built girl. She spoke of his gaiety and charm, and of his sudden moods of violence. 'Life with Ray was ferocious, and often frightening. I always had the feeling that if I didn't submit to him immediately the way he wanted me to, he'd kill me. Often when we were watching television together he'd suddenly say "Strip!" And if I didn't obey at once, his eyes would go cold and expressionless, and his cheeks would go very white.' Morris had the curious habit of play-acting his favourite characters: pop stars, Humphrey Bogart, the 'Saint', Winifred Atwell, and this apparently triggered some craving for instant satisfaction of the urge to dominate. 'Sex wasn't a thing he could take or leave. It was an overpowering maniacal urge which took complete control of his mind and body. One minute I'd be laughing at his attempt to impersonate the latest pop singer, the next I'd be in a cold sweat as he quietly commanded me to strip.' His self-esteem fantasies were obviously closely connected to his sex life.

After eight years of marriage, Morris decided he had had enough of his wife. He told her he intended to start his own business, and there would be no room for her in his new life. 'It was his calmness that hit me. There was just no emotion at all. He said: "You must go to your mother tomorrow. Leave the key in the dustbin for me to get in." I sent our two little boys to my mother but I waited for him.' She tried hard to persuade him to change his mind but he refused and ordered her to leave. (Note: there was no question of his leaving *her* in the house.) 'A week later I had a letter from him asking me to go to the house to see him. I thought he wanted me back. That day I went to town, bought myself a new skirt and blouse, and had my hair done ... But when I walked into the house ... the first thing he said to me was: "I've asked you to come round because I've decided to kill you." I started to sweat with fear ... Suddenly he changed his tune. "I'll give you five minutes to get undressed," he said, "or I'll kill you." I was so frightened I could hardly get my clothes off. Ray, icily calm, went into the kitchen and made coffee. That night he took me over the table. Then he said: "I don't want to live with you but I'll see you twice a week, Tuesday and Thursday evening. If you visit me on those two evenings I'll pay you £5 a week maintenance." This may sound incredible, but for the next few weeks, I visited him on those two evenings ... Each evening he'd make coffee first, then order me to make love. Then he'd turn me out.' When she stopped going, he stopped paying her, and she had to go on national assistance. Later, when she had someone else's child, he divorced her on grounds of adultery. He then married a girl fourteen years his junior.

At the same time, this highly intelligent man, described by

his second wife as 'so debonair, so much the perfect gentleman', lacked the kind of drive that would have satisfied his dreams of fame and power. He lived in the same working-class area of Walsall all his life, a few streets away from his parents. He made up for the lack of excitement by leading a violent fantasy life, hiring blue films, and reading horror literature and pornography. He had cards printed that described him as 'Midland Representative of Regent Studios, Birmingham'. The need to express violent sexual dominance, which emerges clearly from the statements of his wife, went underground during his second marriage, and erupted in the form of child murder, in which the dominance fantasy could be carried to a new extreme. His first wife found it hard to believe that he had killed a child. 'He always seemed so good and gentle with children.' But this gentleness did not prevent him from walking out on his own children, and later refusing to contribute to their support. Frustration had produced a permanent state of inner tension that blocked all normal feeling.

It would be an over-simplification to say that his frustration was the result of an unsatisfied power-urge. Morris was basically an artistic type. As a photographer, he was close to professional standard. One reporter spoke of his 'fanatical attention to detail' – which was apparent, for example, in the doll's houses he made in his spare time. Blake said: 'When thought is closed in caves Then love shall show its root in deepest hell'; that is, when creation is blocked, the outcome is likely to be cruelty and violence. 'It is only too obvious what she suffered before she died,' said the prosecuting counsel of Christine Darby. Frustration had soured into murderous savagery.

It may also be noted, in passing, that although the case was solved by accident – when a member of the public happened to see the final abduction – Morris was already on a short list of police suspects. An Identikit picture of the killer, put together from accounts of witnesses who saw him on the day of the murder, and comments by a doctor on the temperament of the killer, led a relative of Morris's to tell the police that the description fitted him closely. Only his wife's false alibi saved him from arrest.

In a footnote to *A Casebook of Murder* (1969), I spoke of a rape murder that had been committed in the Ypsilanti area of Michigan, U.S.A., and added: 'It is typical of this area – which has figured in spectacular murder trials since 1931, when three men killed four teenagers in a car and set it on fire – that a second body was found on the same day. This was identified as Mary Fleszar, aged nineteen, who had vanished a week before ... She was naked, and her hands and feet had been removed. At the time this book goes to press, it is clear the murder of Mary Fleszar was the first in the series of a new Ann Arbor Jack the Ripper, who sometimes mutilates, stabs and shoots his victims, as well as sexually assaulting them. There had been five other cases since then ...'

In fact, by the time the book went to press, this murder case had 'broken', and the man who was subsequently convicted was already under arrest.

The body of Mary Fleszar was found on 7th August, 1967, on a farm two miles north of Ypsilanti; she was a student at Eastern Michigan University. Clearly, she had been tortured and raped. It was almost a year later when another body, that of Joan Schell, also a student of Eastern Michigan University, was found not far from the previous site. She had been stabbed twelve times, and the body apparently kept in an earthen cellar for several days.

When, on 21st March, 1969, the fully clothed body of Jane Mixer, twenty-three, a University of Michigan Law School student, was found in the Denton Cemetery, police at first assumed that the three murders were probably unconnected. Jane Mixer had been shot twice through the head with ·22 bullets.

Murders then followed fast. The next victim was a sixteen-year-old girl, Maralynn Skelton. The pattern was here closer to the Mary Fleszar murder; she had been strangled, raped, and also tortured with a knife. Her body was found only four days after Jane Mixer's. Three weeks later, on 16th April, a thirteen-year-old schoolgirl, Dawn Basom, was found; she had been killed in the same manner as Maralynn Skelton.

The sixth murder led police to revise their assumption that the Schell murder was unconnected with the others. On 9th June, 1969, boys crossing a field connected to an abandoned farm discovered a half-nude body: the purple blouse was ripped and cut, and the white mini skirt had been pulled below the knees. Her underclothes lay under the body. She had been shot through the top of the head – with a ·22 bullet, it was later revealed – stabbed twice in the heart, several times in the throat, and the throat was also cut. The body had been slashed and cut, 'like someone in a frenzy,' said a policeman. She had been raped. Now it became possible that all six killings so far were connected. With the exception of Jane Mixer, the connection was the sadism and rape; in the Mixer case, it was the ·22 bullet. Twenty-four hours later, the body was identified as Alice Elizabeth Kalom, a twenty-three-year-old graduate of the University of Michigan. Two days later, the *Ann Arbor News* reported that the murder investigation had 'begun to stall'; police admitted they had no lead.

On 26th July, the seventh – and last – body was discovered in a wooded ravine. It was naked except for a pair of sandals on the feet.

Police decided this might be their opportunity to trap the killer. The body was removed, and replaced with a tailor's dummy. (They had wanted to try this same plan in the case of Alice Kalom, but a local radio station had leaked the story.) In two of the earlier murders, police had found evidence that indicated that the killer had returned to the scene of the murder – perhaps to see if the body had been discovered. The trap was laid; the police waited near the 'body'. It began to rain. Shortly after midnight, the police were startled to see that a man had quietly approached the manikin on the other side from where they were hiding. When the police jumped up, the man ran away; in the rain and darkness, they lost him.

The body was identified as that of Karen Sue Beineman, another co-ed of Eastern Michigan University. The post mortem revealed that she had been stunned with a heavy blow on the side of the head that caused serious brain damage, then strangled. Her wrists and ankles had been tied, and a piece of cloth rammed to the back of her throat to prevent her from screaming – an indication that she was not killed immediately after being knocked unconscious. One breast showed an area of 'burning' as if with a caustic fluid, possibly ammonia. Her torn panties had been jammed into her vagina, where male semen was also discovered.

She had last been seen on 23rd July, three days before the body was discovered. At about 12.30, she had entered a shop called 'Wigs by Joan', to be fitted for a wig. She had remarked jokingly that she had only done two foolish things in her life: one was to buy herself a wig, the other to accept a lift from a stranger. The proprietor of the shop, Mrs. Joan Goshe, and her assistant, both looked out of the window, and saw a good-looking, heavily-built young man sitting on a motorcycle. The girl left the shop and rode off on the pillion seat . . .

On 18th July, five days before the murder, State Police Corporal David Leik took his family on holiday, and asked his nephew, Norman John Collins, twenty-two, to feed the dog while they were away. Collins was a student at Eastern Michigan University. They returned from the holiday on 29th July, and Leik called at a police post; there he was told that his nephew fitted the description of the man wanted for Karen Beineman's murder. The man on the motor cycle had been wearing an orange, green and yellow polo shirt and dark trousers, a distinctive costume. Leik went home and discovered, in the laundry room in the basement, signs of black paint that seemed to have been recently sprayed. Black paint could be used to hide something . . . Leik scraped some of it up, and discovered on the wood underneath a brown stain that could have been blood. In fact, tests showed that it was blood of the same group as Karen Beineman's. There were no fingerprints in the basement. But there were some clipped hairs, which came from the heads of Corporal Leik's children: he used it as a barber shop. Similar clipped hairs had been found in the panties inside Karen Beineman.

At first it seemed possible that two men might be charged with the Beineman murder. In June, Norman Collins had taken a trip to California with his room mate, Andrew Manuel, twenty-five, in a rented caravan. Manuel had moved out of their room the day after the murder; it seemed possible that he might be an accomplice – particularly since they had stayed near Salinas, California, where the naked, mutilated body of Roxie Ann Phillips, seventeen, had been found in Mid-July. When last seen alive, she had told a friend that she was going off to date a Michigan University student. However, when Manuel was located, it was decided that he had played no part in the murders. Collins was also charged with the murder of Roxie Ann Phillips.

Collins, it was revealed, possessed two motor-cycles, as well as a car. Girls had seen no objection to accepting lifts from the good-looking boy, who did not remotely resemble a sex killer. Apart from a brooding, morose sort of temperament (which became apparent in court, where he sat silent and impassive throughout an exhausting trial), there seemed to be nothing abnormal about him. He even had a regular girlfriend, with whom he went motor-cycling. My friend Roger Staples, an assistant professor at Eastern Michigan, taught Collins, and never noticed the slightest abnormality – although he mentions that he once suspected Collins of some fairly ambitious cheating.

The trial lasted a month, beginning 20th July, 1970. It had been due to start in June; but the defence tried to have its location changed, on the grounds that the case had inflamed public opinion too much in Ann Arbor; when this was overruled, the defence took full advantage of its privilege of challenging jurymen who might be prejudiced. Most of them – apparently – were, and it took a month to select the eighteen-member jury. The evidence was largely circumstantial: the bloodstains in the basement (although there were no fingerprints), the ends of hair found in the panties. Various people, including the two women from the wig shop, identified Collins as the man with whom Karen Beineman had left that day. He was found guilty and sentenced to life – a minimum of twenty years. He did not speak throughout the trial, except at the end, to state that he was not guilty.

It may seem that Collins should be classified with straightforward sex killers – like Christie and 'Jack the Stripper' – rather than with killers in whom the self-esteem motivation can be traced. But when we compare him with Christie or the Thames nude murderer, an immediate difference can be sensed. Collins is colder, more self-sufficient. There was no attempt by the defence to suggest mental unbalance; neither was it suggested in any of the reports devoted to the case in Ann Arbor and Detroit newspapers; Collins gave the impression of knowing exactly what he was about. In the *Ann Arbor News* for 4th August, 1969, there appeared the following item:

> Collins is known to have been acquainted with Richard C. Robison Jnr, eldest son of the Lathrup Village family of six

found slain one year ago in their summer home near Good Hart, north of Petoskey. The two young men met at Eastern Michigan University in 1966 when they were going through orientation for new students ... The Robisons were all shot with ·22 caliber slugs in a grisly 'execution style' series of killings. These murders have never been solved.

There has been no evidence to link Collins with these killings: but they would be typical of the image he presented: controlled, precise, vengeful, capable of incredible violence. I have remarked earlier that most sex killers are of low I.Q., and seldom noted for a high level of self-esteem. Many of them are petty criminals; confidence swindlers (like Neville Heath), burglars (like Kürten); some are simply mentally deranged, like Ed Gein. By comparison, Collins seems as cool and deadly as a Murder Incorporated executioner. Even the sadism is puzzling, giving the impression of savage but controlled violence. This is a case that would seem out of place in an earlier decade; the only comparison that comes to mind is with the Leopold and Loeb case of 1924. The two Chicago University students, sons of wealthy parents, kidnapped and murdered fourteen-year-old Bobby Franks because they wanted to prove themselves capable of an act of calculated lawlessness. They were fascinated by the Nietzschean concept of the superman. (And, in fact, Nathan Leopold had the I.Q. of a man of genius, 210. His parole lawyer, Elmer Gertz, said 'All knowledge seemed to be his sphere – whether of languages, of which he knew 27, of medical research in leprosy and malaria, of bird lore.') But the students were trying to prove their courage and nerve *to one another*. Collins was alone; his crimes have the air of a one-man war against society; this is why he seems to demand classification with 'Zodiac' and van Zon as a 'violent man'.

1. *The Assassins*, London 1956.
2. For example, as contained in Paul de River's books *The Sexual Criminal* and *Crime and the Sexual Psychopath*.
3. *The Violent Man*, Farrar, Straus, New York, 1962. I have also

discussed it in the introduction to my novel *The Killer*, 1970.

4. For example, in London in 1967, offences against the person rose by 13·2 per cent; sex crimes by 18·1 per cent; offences against property by only 0·7 per cent; there was a 1·2 per cent *decrease* in indictable offences compared to 1965.
5. I owe the following account to the kindness of Henk Van Gelre of Nijmegen, Holland.

CHAPTER SIX

Murder and Romanticism

In *The Outsider*, I tried to show the connection between creative frustration and violence. In a state of mental strain – which sprang from frustration of his creative needs – Nijinsky pushed his wife downstairs, Van Gogh attempted to murder Gauguin, then cut off his own ear; other 'outsiders'[1] went insane, like Nietzsche, or behaved with 'calculated irrationality', as when T. E. Lawrence joined the army as a private. Philip O'Connor, an ex-tramp, put his finger on the problem in his book on vagrancy: 'My [tramping] excursions were motivated by what psychiatrists would call neurosis. But in truth it was a sane attempt . . . to get out of a positively neurotic convention of living "respectably".'[2]

Industrial society treats men as numbers, cells in the social body. But intelligent men have a need to evolve, and as our society slowly evolves, an increasing number of intelligent individuals find themselves in this position of frustration and revolt. Hence the increasing number of 'outsider' criminals, 'in betweeners' who are too intelligent to accept a feeling of being nonentities, but not intelligent – or tough – enough to assert themselves at an acceptable level of self-esteem.

A century ago – as I have already noted – most murders were 'economic' – committed for money. The majority of people were living below the subsistence level; and for a hungry man, sex is a secondary consideration. By the mid-twenties, sex crime was on the increase in most civilized countries, although this was more obvious in America than in Europe, where the older patterns tended to persist. And even in America, the sex motive and the economic motive tended to get mixed. In the Ypsilanti 'burning car' case of 1931 – memorable because the killers only just escaped lynching – the original motive was robbery. Three ex-convicts held up four sixteen-year-olds in a lover's lane, and robbed them (of two dollars). One of the girls was then raped – perhaps because the robbers were disappointed with their haul; when the others resisted, all four were battered to death or shot. There is a 1920s atmosphere about the murder, even to the moonshine whiskey the convicts were drinking before they decided to go out and rob somebody.

In England during the 'thirties, the older patterns remained unchanged: Sidney Fox, William Herbert Wallace, Rouse (the Burning Car murderer), Mancini (the Brighton Trunk murderer), Buck Ruxton; any of these murders might have been used as the basis for a novel – like Ernest Raymond's *We the Accused*, which is based on Crippen. They have an air of belonging to an earlier decade; you could imagine Sherlock Holmes being called in to solve any of them.

In America, on the other hand, the violent and illogical pattern of sex crime becomes increasingly prevalent – although in many cases, the murder was accidental, or for the purposes of avoiding recognition. The Jerry Thompson case may be taken as typical. Thompson, twenty-five, was an engineer of Peoria, Illinois, who was charged in 1935 with the murder of Mildred Hallmark. The girl's half-naked body was found in a cemetery. When police appealed for information, promising anonymity to any woman who came forward, more than twenty-five women admitted they had been raped during the past eighteen months. The rapist, a good-looking, well-spoken young man, usually approached them as they waited at bus stops, and offered them a lift. He would drive to a lonely place, and assault them; if they resisted, he beat them or knocked them unconscious. In several cases, he took photographs of the naked girl in the headlights of the car, and told her he would send them to her relatives if she made any complaint. Mildred Hallmark was the daughter of a man he worked with, and willingly accepted a lift. When she struggled, he knocked her unconscious and raped her. He may have decided to kill her because he was afraid of recognition; his own story is that he realized she was dead after the assault. One of Thompson's victims, a girl he had raped and photographed six months earlier, later met him at a dance and recognized him. When the police appealed for information, she was one of the women who came forward. Thompson's diary, with details of the rapes, and photographs of naked girls, were found in his room. He told the police he had been committing rape since he was sixteen, and had raped more than fifty women.

The unsolved Cleveland Torso murders also began in 1935. This killer was almost certainly a sadist, of the same type as Jack the Ripper.[1] Between September 1935 and August 1938, the 'mad butcher of Kingsbury Run' (as the newspapers called him) killed a dozen men and women. Most of them were derelicts or prostitutes. In most cases, the head was removed (and in six of the cases these were never found) in two cases, he killed two victims at the same time, and dismembered the bodies. Elliot Ness, who became Cleveland's Public Safety Director in 1935 (after 'cleaning up' Chicago), reasoned that the killer was large and powerful, probably homosexual, and that he possessed a car and probably had a house of his own (in which he could dismember the bodies undisturbed). Inquiries in Cleveland's social set revealed a man who fitted this description; and according to Ness's chronicler, Oscar Fraley,[2] Ness confronted the man and told him he was the chief suspect. But while Ness's men were still trying to build up a case against him, the man had himself confined in a private lunatic asylum, and the murders ceased.

In England, there were a number of sex murders during the forties – mostly frustrated soldiers on leave – but nothing to parallel these American cases until the early 'fifties, the era of Heath and Christie. The case of Alfred Whiteway (1953) recalls the Peoria case in certain details. Whiteway, twenty-two, was also an experienced rapist, and his decision to kill two teenage girls on the towpath near Teddington may have been made because one of the girls recognized him as he attacked them.

Meanwhile, in America, the trend of sadism and gruesome violence continued. The Arkansas 'moonlight murders' took place in 1946. In 1947, the 'Black Dahlia case'[3] shocked the whole country. The body of Elizabeth Short, a would-be film actress, was found on a piece of waste ground. It had been cut in two at the waist, and badly mutilated with a knife. The pathologist established that the killer had suspended her upside down by her feet and inflicted many of the injuries while she was still alive. The body had then been cut in half and carefully washed. In spite of an enormous manhunt, the killer was never found. (And it is probably a safe guess that he committed suicide not long after the murder.) There were dozens of confessions to this murder – all false – and several imitative crimes.

In December 1953, a courting couple were reported missing near Pamplico, South Carolina. The half-naked body of Betty Cain, sixteen, was found in a newly dug grave, but her head was missing. The head was found later in the grave that contained her fiancé, Henry Allen. An escaped convict, Raymond Carney, thirty-seven, was convicted of the crime; he insisted that his motive was robbery; but examination of the girl's body revealed that she had been raped. It is not clear why the convict decapitated the girl, or whether this was before or after the sexual assault; but the motive was probably sadistic.

The Ed Gein case, which has already been discussed, occurred in 1957. Two years later there occurred in Miami, Florida, a murder that in many respects recalls the case of Elizabeth Short, the 'Black Dahlia'. The victim was a fifty-three-year-old spinster who worked as a secretary. On the night of 14th December 1959, Ethel Ione Little returned home and undressed for bed. Then a man who had been hiding in a closet knocked her to the floor, lifted her to the bed and tied her wrists and ankles to the four bedposts. The full details of what happened during the next four to six hours have never been published; all that is clear is that she was tortured by a sexual deviate until she died of shock and loss of blood. No male semen was found, but the nature of the injuries – including bite-marks – make it clear that the attack was sexual. In spite of a widespread police search and mass fingerprinting, the killer was never found.

In England, during the same month, there was a case similar in many respects to the double murder in South Carolina; an Irish labourer, Patrick Byrne, twenty-eight, got drunk on Christmas Eve, and crept into the grounds of a hostel for women in Edgbaston, Birmingham, hoping to spy on women undressing. As he peered through the skylight of a door, the girl in the room came to the door – and was immediately attacked by Byrne, who strangled her, raped her, then cut off her head with a breadknife, after which he raped her again. All this excited him so much that he went off looking for another girl to attack; but a girl screamed when he struck her on the head, and he fled. Byrne was not a suspect in the murder; but when questioned – in a routine investigation – seven weeks later, he immediately confessed. He admitted to indulging in sadistic fantasies about women, and said that he had killed Stephanie Baird as a revenge against all women, 'to get my own back on them for causing my nervous tension through sex'.

These cases, taken almost at random, show clearly the changing patterns of violent crime in the past twenty or thirty years. The Cleveland Torso murders stand out, like Jack the Ripper's murders, as the exception to the rule, the harbinger of things to come. We can see the slow change from murders that are basically economic to murders that are basically sexual, and finally, to the type of murder that seems typical of the second half of the twentieth century: what might be called 'resentment murders'. All that these murders have in common is that the basic motivation seems to be a rage against society that expresses itself as cruelty. It is difficult to discern a 'pattern' because the pattern continues to change so fast.

An increasing number of cases are 'first evers'. Richard Speck's murder of eight nurses in Chicago in 1966 was obviously a sex killing; and yet only one of the girls was actually raped. Eleven-year-old Mary Bell, of Newcastle-on-Tyne, strangled two small boys (aged three and four) 'for fun' in 1968; because of her influence over a thirteen-year-old girl (accused with her) she is described by the prosecuting counsel as 'an evil Svengali'. On 14th July, 1970, a California police patrolman arrested two men who were driving a stolen car; one of them, Dean Baker, a bearded hippy type, told the police: 'I have a problem. I'm a cannibal,' and then described how he had shot a man who had given him a lift near the Yellowstone Park, then cut out the heart and ate it. In his pockets were found the fingers of the dead man, which he had decided to keep as souvenirs. Dismembered pieces of the body were recovered from the river; but not the heart.

The resentment motif can be seen in crimes of pointless violence, particularly in America. 'Sniping' has become an increasing problem; the sniper usually shoots from a slightly opened window or from behind the parapet of a roof, where his chances of being seen are minimal. New York has an increasing problem as snipers from Harlem rooftops fire at passing trains. Twenty years ago, psychologists declared unhesitatingly that the sniper is driven by sexual aggression; the gun is a substitute for the penis. Nowadays, the aggression is more often social. On 3rd July, 1968, a man climbed on to the roof of the lavatory in the children's playground in Central Park, New York, and began firing at random; an eighty-year-old man and a twenty-four-year-old girl were killed before the sniper was shot by police; he turned out to be a Bulgarian immigrant 'with a deep-seated hatred of communism' that seems to have turned into a deep-seated hatred of American society.

Readers who admire the macabre writings of H. P. Lovecraft may be reminded by the above remarks of a passage in his best known story *The Call of Cthulhu*. Cthulhu is chief of the 'ancient old ones', monstrous creatures who once inhabited the earth, but who destroyed their civilization through the practise of black magic; Cthulhu lies in a trance at the bottom of the Atlantic ocean, but the time for his return is approaching, and artists all over the world have horrifying dreams of great alien cities. And a professor who suspects what is going on has collected press cuttings that reveal the eruption of strange psychic influences:

> Here was a nocturnal suicide in London, where a lone sleeper had leaped from a window after a shocking cry. Here likewise a rambling letter to the editor of a paper in South America, where a fanatic deduces a dire future from visions he has seen. A dispatch from California describes a theosophist colony as donning white robes en masse for some 'glorious fulfilment' which never arrives, whilst items from India speak guardedly of serious native unrest toward the end of March. Voodoo orgies multiply in Haiti, and African outposts report ominous mutterings. American officers in the Philippines find certain tribes bothersome about this time, and New York policemen are mobbed by hysterical Levantines on the night of March 22–23rd. The west of Ireland too, is full of wild rumour and legendry, and a fantastic painter named Ardois-Bonnot hangs a blasphemous *Dream Landscape* in the Paris spring salon of 1926. And so numerous are the recorded troubles in insane asylums that only a miracle can have stopped the medical fraternity from noting strange parallelisms . . .

One feels that if this had been written in 1971 instead of 1928, Lovecraft might have added the Manson murders, the killing of the Ohta family, Dean Baker's cannibalism, the Zodiac killer.

The literary parallel is more significant than it appears on the surface. Lovecraft's work is far more than grotesque escapism. When he talks about a 'blasphemous' dream landscape, he does not mean that it contains indecent mockery of the Christian religion, but something horrible, frightening, nauseating, something like those odd fungus-like creatures in the paintings of Hieronymus Bosch. His work is romanticism gone sour and bitter; instead of turning away, like Shelley and Keats, to visionary dream-worlds, he creates nightmares that help to relieve his loathing of modern western civilization. He is fond of the word 'loathing', with its suggestion of revulsion from something slimy and slug-like. He writes in one letter of 'loathsome Asiatic hordes who trail their dirty carcases over streets where white men once moved', and in another of his 'mad physical loathing' of the semitic types who jam the New York subway, and says that he has often felt capable of murdering a few of them. The feeling is reminiscent of certain passages about Jews in *Mein Kampf*. But it would be a mistake to label Lovecraft a cranky racialist. The hatred is curdled romanticism, a frustrated appetite for beauty. (In the case of Hitler, the anti-semitism orginated in Vienna in the years when he was an unsuccessful young artist living in doss houses.) It is 'love showing its root in deepest hell' again.

Hitler was inspired by a vast, strange work called *Foundations of the Nineteenth Century* by an Englishman, Houston Stewart Chamberlain; the book was published (in German) in Vienna in 1899. It speaks of two 'pure' races, the Jews and the Aryans, and the impure mixed breeds of the Mediterranean. It casts a long, nostalgic backward look at the legacy of Greece and Rome, and concludes that the Germans are the true heirs to all this glory. (He says that Jesus was almost certainly an Aryan.) Chamberlain argues – very convincingly – that German culture is the greatest in Europe, that its music, literature and philosophy surpass those of any other European country. The future of the west, says Chamberlain, lies in the hands of this nation that produced Bach, Beethoven, Goethe, Kant, Hegel, Wagner . . .

Hitler was deeply influenced by all this, and also by the music of Wagner and the philosophy of Nietzsche. (He had seen all Wagner's operas many times.) Wagner himself is another idealizer of the German past – the Mastersingers of Nuremberg, the Teutonic knights; while Nietzsche's spiritual homeland was classical Greece. And so Nazism must be seen as an idealistic revolt against the aspects of the modern world that Lovecraft also hated: the materialism and cultural debasement. Lovecraft's 'loathing' expressed itself in visions of a remote, nightmarish past that can still make incursions into our modern world; Hitler's, in Buchenwald and Belsen. Hitler once remarked (to Hermann Rauschning) that although he did not greatly enjoy Goethe, he had to admire him for his line: 'In the beginning was *action*.'[3] 'To desire and act not breeds a pestilence,' said William blake, expressing the same idea. Hitler desired and acted; Lovecraft desired and acted not. But once we understand the underlying spirit of his writing, with its 'blasphemous' horrors and monstrosities, we also understand something important about Norman John Collins and the Zodiac killer and Charles Manson and Ian Brady. The basic spirit of Lovecraft's writing is the basic spirit of Sade's. There is a desire to shock, to shake his fist in the face of modern civlization. And the use of horror is central to his aim. In fact, many of Lovecraft's stories could be regarded as science fiction rather than horror stories. Great underground cities built a million years ago, creatures from outer space: these themes are not necessarily horrifying. Lovecraft preferred to treat them in a context of horror because the horror story expresses aggressions, and science fiction doesn't. In a story called 'The Unnamable', the narrator, a writer of horror stories, mentions that one of his stories had appeared in a magazine in 1922, but that many shops 'took the magazine off their stands at the complaints of silly milksops'. In fact, something of the sort had happened, in 1924; but the story that caused the furore was not by Lovecraft, but by C. M. Eddy, and 'The Loved Dead' caused *Weird Tales* to be attacked for obscenity rather than frightening the milksops. It is a story about a necrophiliac who becomes a sex murderer. The narrator says of his childhood: 'Strictly ascetic, wan, pallid, undersized, and subject to protracted spells of morbid moroseness, I was ostracized by the healthy, normal youngsters of my own age ...' At the age of sixteen he sees his dead grandfather: 'A baleful, malignant influence that seemed to emanate from the corpse itself held me with magnetic fascination'. But after two weeks of this morbid excitement, he reverts to his 'old time languor' (which sounds like van Zon's 'infantile autism'). After the death of his parents he becomes apprenticed to an undertaker, and each corpse brought 'a return of that rapturous tumult of the arteries which transformed my grisly task into one of beloved devotion'. He adds unambiguously: 'But every carnal satisfaction exacted its toll.' He becomes a kind of Jack the Ripper, perpetrating (unspecified) 'abominable atrocities' – occasionally the corpses of his victims were even sent to him to embalm ('O rare and delicious memory!'). After being caught embracing a corpse, he is dismissed, but luckily, the 1914 War begins, and gives him four years of 'transcendent satisfaction'. Back in America he returns to Jack-the-Ripper-type crimes, until the murder of a family sets the police on his trail; he writes his story as he crouches in a graveyard, listening to the barking of the bloodhounds as they draw closer ...

This story catches, more boldly than any by Lovecraft, the basic emotion of the horror story, and what lies behind it. The lonely, sickly boy, shunned by healthy, normal boys, who feels a stranger in the world of ordinary people – until he discovers that he belongs to another world, the world of the dead. But on closer examination, this turns out to mean sex crime. He is drawn to the dead for the same reason as Sergeant Bertrand. He is also, he says, a sadistic killer. In fact, necrophilia and cruelty are completely unrelated. The necrophile is interested in the corpse because it is passive; an anaesthetized woman would probably do just as well. With fully conscious women – even willing ones – he has inhibitions; he need have none with a corpse. The sadist's urge has nothing to do with inhibitions; it is a desire to exercise power. In the published annals of sex crime, few necrophiles have been sadists and few sadists have been necrophiles. The narrator of 'The Loved Dead' – and presumably its author – is ignorant of this. He is thinking vaguely in terms of total sexual gratification. So the story jumps unexpectedly from necrophilia to murder; in fact, it is really a story about a sex maniac who defies every social code, whose whole life is a scream of defiance at society. (Hence the family murder at the end.)

Lovecraft himself was too much a puritan ever to allow a

sexual element to intrude into his stories. Perhaps the nearest he comes to it is a story called 'The Picture in the House', which describes an old man who has become increasingly fascinated by a book on cannibalism, full of gruesome pictures. 'That feller bein' chopped up gives me a tickle every time I look at 'im – I hev ta keep lookin' at 'im – see whar the butcher cut off his feet?' Lovecraft uses the word perversion to describe the old man's obsession. When drops of blood being to fall on the book the narrator notices a red stain spreading across the ceiling . . .

Nearly four decades after his death (in 1937) Lovecraft's work is enjoying an unexpected revival; like Borges (a writer to whom he is related in spirit) he has become a cult among the young. Paperbacks of his weird tales can be found on every seaside bookstall. There is even a pop group that calls itself The H. P. Lovecraft by way of homage. What makes the appeal is not the gothic machinery of the horror tale; otherwise there would be a similar revival of all those old writers out of *Weird Tales* – William Hope Hodgson, Robert W. Chambers, Zealia Bishop, Clark Ashton Smith. It is the underlying spirit of Lovecraft, the revolt against civilization, the feeling that the material success by which the modern world justifies itself is the shallowest of all standards, that has made him a cult. Lovecraft was not a democrat; like Nietzsche, he felt that democracy is the rise of botchers and bunglers and mediocrities against the superior type of man. He was not a logical philosopher; he did not ask himself what he would like to put in its place; he only knew that he hated the impersonal rush and hurry of the modern city, and all the standards and values of 'industrial man'.

Things are no worse now than they were in Lovecraft's day – or for that matter, in the days of the 'dark satanic mills' of more than a century ago; on the contrary, they have improved. There is more freedom, more leisure, better education, more public subsidy of the arts. But the increased freedom has also increased the number of rebels and misfits. Blake, Nietzsche and Lovecraft were lone 'outsiders' (one of Lovecraft's best stories is called 'The Outsider') solitary rebels in an alien society. As the population increases, and as illiteracy becomes the exception rather than the rule, more and more people come to share their view.

Inevitably, it finds its way into action. Melvin Rees, a jazz musician, told a friend: 'You can't say it's wrong to kill. Only individual standards make it right or wrong.' And one night, when under the stimulus of benzedrine, he told another friend that he wanted to experience everything – love, hate, life, death. That was on Saturday 10th January, 1959, and by that time, Rees had already realized his ambition, having killed and sexually assaulted at least one girl, and possibly five. The following day, Rees tried to force a car to drive into the ditch, but as he got out of his own car, holding a gun, the other driver managed to reverse out and drive away. Rees's intention was to kill him and rape his wife, who was also in the car. Rees's next attempt, later in the day, *was* successful. His old blue Chevrolet forced another car off the road; it contained a family on an afternoon outing. Rees shot the husband, Carrol Jackson, and tossed his body into the ditch, together with their eighteen-month-old girl (who suffocated under her father's body). He then forced the wife and five-year-old daughter to drive off with him. What happened to them during the next hours is not certain; when the two bodies were found some months later, all that was clear was that Mildred Jackson had been strangled and the child beaten to death with a heavy instrument.

It was not until the following year, 1960, that Rees was arrested in a music shop in Arkansas, where he was working. The friend to whom he had made the comments about murder suspected him of the Jackson killings, and told the police. A search of his parents' home revealed the gun that had been used in an earlier murder. A courting couple in a lonely spot had been held up by a man, who shot the woman through the head. The killer allowed the man to run away, and then apparently sexually assaulted the body of the woman – a thirty-six-year-old nurse. Also in his room at home were found press cuttings about the Jackson murder, and an account of the crime. Rees was executed. The Dutch clairvoyant, Peter Hurkos, was called into the case some time before Rees's arrest; he not only gave an accurate description of Rees (left-handed, tattooed, ape-like arms) but stated that he had committed nine murders. Friends of Rees at the University of Maryland – which he had attended – found it difficult to believe he was a murderer; one described him as mild-mannered and intelligent.

Eddy's portrait of a sex killer in 'The Loved Dead' is an

imaginative absurdity; Rees is the real thing. It is doubtful whether he felt any compunction about killing the Jackson family. They were in every way 'bourgeois' and normal; Mildred Jackson was president of the women's missionary society at the local Baptist church; her husband was a bank clerk who was a teetotaller and non-smoker. A man of Rees's views would have felt that such people were his natural prey. The state of mind is like that of a spy in an enemy country. He has to pretend to be something he is not, and to gain the trust of these people. But he is there in order to work towards their destruction. His loyalty is to his own people. And if they knew this, they would destroy him . . .

Why does he feel so alienated? Is it his own fault, or the fault of the society itself? Lovecraft felt that there is something rotten about the whole trend of modern civilization, and that it is this that forces people like himself into the position of outsiders and rebels.

Now it must be remembered that this idea was asserted more than two centuries ago by Jean-Jacques Rousseau. Rousseau's fundamental doctrine is sometimes summarized by the phrase 'Back to nature', as if he advocated living in the treetops; but this is to oversimplify. Man has become alienated from his own basic nature by the artificiality of society, says Rousseau. The chief enemy is social convention, which encourages pride, egoism, ruthlessness, at the cost of the natural virtues of kindness, decency, honesty. Culture – by which Matthew Arnold set so much store – is attacked as a product of vanity and pride. Even science and art are really unnecessary to man; their products encourage idleness, artificiality and shallowness. According to Rousseau, civilization has simply taken a wrong turning. Its values are all wrong, and since these values are successful, and success begets success, they will go on getting more wrong. Mankind is happiest, he said, in tribes, or small, quiet rural communities; the city is an abomination.

The romantics were the direct descendants of Rousseau. Wordsworth's sonnet 'The world is too much with us' expresses the basic Rousseau sentiment: 'Little we see in nature that is ours / We have given our hearts away, a sordid boon . . .' And the complaint echoes down the century. Man is 'out of tune' with the universe, trapped in a sordid world of 'getting and spending'. And the nature of the complaint becomes clearer as industry spreads across Europe. It is *beauty starvation.* According to the romantic poets, beauty is an essential vitamin; without it, the soul shrivels up and becomes dried and brittle. Ruskin tells Yeats's father that as he goes to the British Museum, he sees the faces of the people become daily more corrupt. Yeats himself writes that 'the wrong of unshapely things is a wrong too great to be told'; and unlike Oscar Wilde, he meant it. The 'religion of beauty' of the aesthetes aroused a great deal of mockery, good-natured and otherwise; but the mockery missed the point. The talk of beauty was not 'idle chatter of a transcendental kind'; it was an instinctive recognition that, in the long run, beauty-deficiency is as serious as calcium deficiency, or exposure to radioactivity. It produces a blight of the will, a sickening of the vital forces. For beauty is, in the last analysis, the same thing as a sense of purpose. When you are very hungry, and you contemplate a good dinner, the sensation that arises in you is the same as the sense of beauty; it is also a sense of immediate purpose. And a traveller standing on top of a mountain also experiences hunger and a sense of purpose: the wide horizons produce a feeling of an open future, of important things to be done and important meanings to be grasped. It is the feeling of freedom, of *openness,* that constitutes the sense of beauty. Conversely, ugliness is a sense of being trapped, closed-in, suffocated by dirt and triviality. Man is an evolutionary creature who is at his best when possessed by visions of purpose, and who becomes frustrated and soured and embittered when he is suffocated by the trivial.

But as the nineteenth century drew towards its close, there was no sign of an improvement: everything Wordsworth hated got worse. The romantics wrote sadly about 'beauty that has passed away' and dreamed of a return to the courtly days of the middle ages. The 1914 war was the watershed; the sadness changed to anger and hatred. Ezra Pound stopped writing about the troubadors of Provence and turned to denunciation:

> There died a myriad,
> And of the best, among them,
> For an old bitch gone in the teeth
> For a botched civilization . . .

Pound's *Mauberley* and Eliot's *Waste Land* are in direct line of descent from Rousseau and from Wordsworth's sonnet. They even use the same method: contrasting the moral ugliness of civilization with the world of nature or of the past: 'Sweet Thames run softly till I end my song . . .' There seems to be little enough in common between Proust, D. H. Lawrence, William Faulkner, Ernest Hemingway, Aldous Huxley, Thomas Mann, Robert Musil, Hermann Hesse, Graham Greene. What they share is a feeling of protest, and the protest is about beauty-starvation, the 'botched civilization'. In *Heartbreak House*, Shotover asks Ellie Dunn how much her soul eats, and she answers: 'Oh, a lot. It eats music and pictures and books and mountains and lakes and beautiful things to wear and nice people to be with. In this country you can't have them without lots of money: that is why our souls are so horribly starved.' Lawrence or Mann or Huxley would express it in different terms, but they would mean the same thing: that if civilization is to satisfy the evolutionary appetite as well as the material needs, then it must somehow provide *meaning* as well as security. If the sense of meaning is starved, the result is a feeling of futility that will eventually produce violence.

The Russian writer Valery Briussov expressed this in a remarkable fable called 'The Republic of the Southern Cross', written about 1910. It describes an ideal city at the South Pole, under a great glass dome. The workers earn good wages, and are well fed; they live in identical comfortable houses and wear identical clothes. But one day they begin to develop a curious psychosis called 'contradiction mania', a compulsion to do the exact opposite of what they want to do: they say no instead of yes, are rude instead of polite; eventually the natural urge to live becomes an urge to destroy and commit suicide. Finally the whole city is destroyed by mobs of insane rioters . . . Riot police in every large city of the world understand '*mania contradicens*', the urge of a violent mob to destroy anybody's property – *even their own.* A riot may begin as a protest against a particular injustice, but it ends by becoming a generalized expression of revolt against boredom, the dreary routine of everyday life.

In the Wimbledon 'queer bashing' murder case of September 1969, the gang of boys who battered Michael de Gruchy to death were not embittered slum-dwellers, but the children of working-class parents who lived in an 'architectural showpiece' called the Alton Estate. One of the mothers of the convicted boys remarked: 'We thought we were coming to paradise and it was sending us to hell.' The builders of the Alton Estate had every reason to be proud of their achievement – from the point of view of planning; the huge blocks of glass and concrete flats stood on pillars that raised them above the ground, giving an impression of space and open air; they were surrounded by lawns, and close to the green expanse of Wimbledon Common. But no one had anticipated the psychological effect of transferring families from London slums to this strange, impersonal place in the middle of nowhere, the feeling of boredom and rootlessness. The Common was – and is – a haunt of homosexuals. On 29th September, 1969, a dozen boys whose ages ranged between fifteen and eighteen set out to hunt for queers; they carried wooden palings. On other occasions they had contented themselves with damaging the cars belonging to the 'pooves'; but their victims had got wise, and now parked several streets away. Michael de Gruchy, a twenty-eight-year-old clerk who lived with his mother, parked his Austin 1100 on the Alton Estate and then walked through the subway tunnel leading to the Queensmere – known locally as Queersmere – part of the common. The twelve boys moved forward, and one hit him with a stick. De Gruchy tried to escape, but he was trapped. There was a shout of 'Charge', and de Gruchy received a rain of blows on his back. They were violent blows; the pathologist discovered later that the back of his skull was shattered into fragments like a broken vase. The boys ran away, leaving de Gruchy dying. The next day, Geoffrey Hammond, the ringleader, told his employer what had happened, and his employer took the boys to the police station. Hammond, who was eighteen, received a life sentence; the others rcceived shorter sentences or Borstal training.

But Hammond was not, as might be supposed, an illiterate thug with a chip on his shoulder. He had been a choirboy, and had been in the St John's Ambulance and Royal Marine Cadets; he was a Duke of Edinburgh Bronze Medal winner, and had appeared in life-saving demonstrations on the children's television programme 'Blue Peter'. His father said: 'He loves anything to do with nature. He loves children. He's a sentimental boy. He's a sportsman – climbing, swimming, diving.'[4] But all this could not outweigh the boredom of a model estate, the slow-burning resentment, the desire for excitement and action. (Charge!)

Melvin Rees and Geoffrey Hammond seem to have little in common, but they share a sense of rootlessness, of meaninglessness – as well as an above-average I.Q. And although Hammond hardly qualifies as an intellectual, boredom had much the same effect upon him as on Rees – or as on Norman Smith, the sniper who shot Hazel Woodward 'for something to do'. 'Life being what it is, one dreams of revenge,' said Gauguin, and the Birmingham Y.W.C.A. murderer talks of getting his own back on all women for causing his nervous tension through sex – as if the very existence of women is a dangerous provocation of his sexual appetite.

One of the most interesting things about the human mind is its fundamental craving for newness, and its strange tendency to stagnate.

It is this appetite for newness, for strangeness, for adventure and excitement, that distinguishes man from every other animal on earth. Cows seem to possess very little of it, and even lions are contented with a few square miles of territory. But human beings devour 'newness'. You only have to watch the face of a child setting out on a train journey to the seaside to understand the power of the urge. For most human beings, the word 'travel' is synonymous with pleasure and relaxation. Because the sight of new places, changing scenery, has the power of stimulating delight in all but the most jaded. The more tired we are, the less we notice things; the fresher we feel, the more we notice everything. And 'newness', change, adventure, satisfies a basic *hunger* in all of us; there is no human being so dull and cow-like that he would not agree that 'a change is as good as a rest'. We seem to need change and newness as much as a growing child needs vitamins. This is why the inhabitants of the Republic of the Southern Cross became murderous. Lack of 'newness' produces a kind of sickness which becomes steadily worse.

In that case, why should Melvin Rees become murderous? He had plenty of change; as a jazz musician he was 'on the road' all the time. But it is one thing to be on the deck of a luxury liner, watching the shoreline of Alexandria drawing nearer; quite another to move around like a tramp from town to town, staying in cheap lodgings or sleeping rough. Such a life condemns you to endless preoccupation with the trivial, the physical; the mind has no freedom. 'Newness' depends upon a certain eagerness and openness of the mind. You would not keep an open mouth in a sandstorm because you would get it full of sand; and you cannot keep the mind 'open' when living the life of an itinerant, because triviality is like sawdust. It hands us over to the 'robot', because we don't want to waste good attention on something we feel to be dreary and repetitive.

I have said that one of the oddest things about the human mind is not only its craving for newness, but also its *tendency to stagnate*. A Martian who knew about human beings only from psychological textbooks might well expect us to stagnate when faced with dullness and ugliness, but he would certainly find it very strange that we also stagnate in quite pleasant circumstances, if the pleasantness is *unchanging*. It is the passivity of the human mind that is so baffling. A man who is starving to death struggles frantically to keep alive. But a stockbroker living in the suburbs with an attractive wife and pretty children often becomes so jaded that he has to spend his weekend playing strenuous rounds of golf.

The psychologist John Hughlings Jackson made the discovery that the eye cannot remain focused on an object that does not move. And the same applies, apparently, to human consciousness. No matter how much we have to be grateful for, we stagnate unless change keeps us wide-awake. It is as if something is wrong with consciousness, a kind of tiredness that means that we drop off to sleep unless things keep us interested. What is more, the effects of stagnation build up from mild boredom to frenzied self-loathing in an amazingly short spell of time. This is why 'the black room' – a totally black and silent room – is such a potent instrument for brainwashing. It places people in a boring situation, and waits for their mental pressures to do the rest. It is as cruel as the torture Tiberius was supposed to have practised: tying catgut around the end of a man's penis, then forcing him to drink large quantities of water.

These are basic facts of human nature. Everybody is

vaguely aware of them, but no one has yet seen clearly that they are important because of the danger they represent. A diabetic needs a sugar-free diet, and if he doesn't get it, the results are serious. But this human tendency to passivity and craving for 'newness' is a more serious disease than diabetes – as the cases in this book demonstrate repeatedly. We cannot even begin to understand the strange violence of modern society without recognizing that it is not 'abnormal', a series of 'exceptions to the rule' of peaceful co-existence and non-aggression. If a certain type of aeroplane continues to crash, the experts conclude that there is something basically wrong with its design; it would be blindness to declare that each accident has a different cause. And as irrational, freakish crimes take place with increasing frequency, we should make an attempt to seek the common psychological root of each one, even if this takes us into fields of psychology that seem remote from our everyday motivations. The psychology of 'motiveless' murder cannot be understood without the psychology of mysticism and visionary consciousness.

The Moors murder case may serve as an illustration of most of the themes mentioned so far in this book. The bare facts have a quality of nightmare, like the dreams of a sadistic pornographer: a young man who admires Hitler and de Sade seduces a religious and rather ordinary girl, and persuades her to join with him in kidnapping, torturing and killing a number of children. There have so far been four full length books on the case. Each one presents the facts that emerged at the trial; but there is a curious lack of speculation about the motive. Judge Gerald Sparrow discusses sadism and sexual perversion (*Satan's Children*), but does not attempt to show that Ian Brady *was* a sadist in the textbook sense of the word. Even Emlyn Williams, in a kind of novel about the murders (*Beyond Belief*), fails to give a convincing account of the motivations. Pamela Hansford Johnson, in a short essay on the murders (*On Iniquity*), gets closer to the root of the problem when she talks about boredom and 'the affectless society'; but the book then turns into an attack on pornography and the permissive society. This is to shift the emphasis back to purely external factors, and to move away from the psychological key to it all.

What we know of Brady is this. He was born in a tough slum area, the Clydeside district of Glasgow, in January 1938. He was illegitimate; his mother was a waitress who was nineteen when she became a mother. Her name was Stewart, but Ian adopted the name Sloan from the woman who brought him up. Until the age of seven, he continued to live in an overcrowded Glasgow tenement. He lived on Clydeside throughout the heavy bombing. When the war ended, the Sloan family were re-housed on a new estate on the outskirts of Glasgow. He was a good student at school; after passing the qualifying exam at the age of eleven, he was sent to Shawlands Academy – a 'posh' school that had come down in the world since the new estate was built. There seems to have been a certain amount of ill-feeling between the re-housed slum boys and the sons of well-to-do tradesmen in their blue blazers, and Brady's reaction to it all was a feeling of resentment. His imagination was active, fed on a diet of Superman comics and gangster films. He was not a mixer; he had few friends. There was something sulky and unfriendly about him – it is still there in the photographs taken after the murder, the look of a delinquent Elvis Presley. Emlyn Williams tells a story – gathered from one of Brady's childhood acquaintances – about a cat, which Brady dropped into a deep hole in the graveyard and sealed in with a stone; he wanted to find out how long it would take a cat to starve to death. The acquaintance moved the stone to check on his story and the cat escaped.

His first appearance in court was at the age of thirteen; he was accused of housebreaking, and put on probation for two years. A year later, in July 1952, he was again in a juvenile court on a charge of housebreaking, but got off with a warning. And when the probationary period ended in 1954, he again appeared in court charged with housebreaking, and asked for nine other cases to be taken into consideration. He received another two years' probation. It was in this year – 1954 – that he moved to Manchester to live with his mother, who had now married a man called Brady. If his mother had neglected him in early years, she now tried to make up for it. A next door neighbour remarked that her eyes followed him everywhere. The home life was quiet and dull: films, comedy programmes on the radio, paperback books on gangsters, the *No Orchids for Miss Blandish* type of thing. He found a job as a labourer in a brewery, and a year later was caught stealing lead from the roof. Since he was still on probation, he was sentenced to undergo Borstal training. He spent a year at the Borstal at Hatfield, Yorkshire, and was observed to be moody and unco-operative, but otherwise unremarkable. He told one of the inmates that he had sold himself to homosexuals. After a year in detention, he returned to Manchester, and went on the dole. It was a dull life, alone in the small house with his mother and stepfather out at work, making himself tea, reading the papers. He was twenty-one before he was in regular full-time employment again; he became a stock clerk at Millwards, a chemical firm in Gorton.

And it was there, according to Emlyn Williams, that he became interested in the Nazis and began collecting books about them. It would be interesting to know how it happened, what was the first book on Hitler's Germany that touched his imagination, that convinced him that *here* was something the modern world needed.

It is important to try to see this through Brady's eyes. He is twenty-three years old and reasonably intelligent; and ever since he left school, life has been a succession of trivialities. Yeats said that life is a preparation for something that never happens; but in Brady's case, even the element of preparation was lacking. Life had turned into a succession of wasted days, days and weeks that drift by and leave nothing behind except that you get older. Brady was not literary enough to have read *The Waste Land* or *The Hollow Men;* but if he had, he would have recognized his own feelings. Then he begins to read about the Nazis – through anti-Nazi books like *The Scourge of the Swastika* – and it is like a religious conversion. To ask how he could be converted by anti-Nazi books is to miss the point. The idea of violence itself was emotionally satisfying, a reality in a make-believe world. Any strong imaginative experience produces a sense of reality, a feeling of seriousness, of meaning. This is why our Victorian ancestors read Foxe's *Book of Martyrs* on Sundays, and why one of the chief spiritual exercises of saints is to imagine Christ's suffering on the cross. Until it is touched by some serious aim, the mind's powers are diffused, dispersed. In order to experience a sense of its own force, the mind must *clench*, exactly as one might clench one's fists or teeth. And in order to do that, it must *focus* on something that arouses deep interest or strong feelings. Brady found all this in the Nazis: salvation from mediocrity and boredom, a vision of a society in which people like himself would have something more interesting to do than work as a stock clerk.

The field of his interest expanded to books on torture. This could indicate that Gerald Sparrow is correct in assuming Brady to be a sadist in the technical sense – one for whom the ideas of sex and pain are associated. But not necessarily. De Sade's type of sadism sprang out of a desire for revenge on society, out of a Swiftian detestation of 99 per cent of his fellow human beings. That Brady's sadism was of this nature becomes fairly certain when one considers his attitude to de Sade. Most people who buy Sade read it for the sex and skip the long discussions. Brady was enthusiastic about the ideas. Society is utterly corrupt. Human life is unimportant; nature gives and takes away with total indifference. We live in a meaningless universe, created by chance. Surrounded by emptiness, we delude ourselves with dreams of a benevolent God, when every earthquake and tidal wave proves that such a Being is pure wishful thinking.

This view is not as irreligious as it sounds; it is, in fact, fairly close to Buddhism, and is held by a large proportion of the world's population. To accept it is not the sign of a sick mind, although it is the sign of a pessimistic one. And although Swift went insane, this was not the result of his loathing of his fellow men, but of illness. Shaw also shared Swift's view that man, as he exists at present, is hopelessly inadequate, and Shaw was sane enough. The devil in *Man and Superman* warns Don Juan: 'Beware of the pursuit of the Superhuman; it leads to an indiscriminate contempt for the human,' and he adds: 'To a man, horses and dogs and cats are mere species, outside the moral world. Well, to the Superman, men and women are a mere species too, also outside the moral world.' But Shaw agrees with Don Juan, not with the devil. Brady's views about his fellow human beings, do not prove him to have been insane or possessed by a spirit of evil. They only prove that he belonged to the 'dominant five per cent'. And the violence with which he held them proves that he was a particularly frustrated member of the dominant five per cent.

At this point, Myra Hindley enters the story. She was four

and a half years younger than Brady, a completely normal typical working-class girl, not bad-looking, inclined to go in for blonde hair-do's and bright lipstick, interested in boys and dancing, not particularly bright; rather like Gerty MacDowell in *Ulysses*. She had been born a Catholic, brought up Protestant, and decided to become a Catholic again at sixteen. She liked children and animals, and was fond of her family. She had been engaged, but broke it off, finding the boy 'immature'. This is one of the problems of the working-class girl. Her notion of male attractiveness is formed by the cinema and television, hard-bitten heroes with strong jaws, and the youths she meets at the dance hall are ordinary local boys of no particular ambition.

Brady had been at Millwards for almost two years when Myra Hindley joined the firm as a typist. He glanced at her, decided she was just another working-class moron, and went back to his work. If one is to believe her diary, he had still not even spoken to her six months later. By this time, she was a thoroughly infatuated teenager (she was eighteen at the time). By 1st August, her diary records: 'Ian taking sly looks at me at work.' By the end of the month: 'I hope he loves me and will marry me some day.' Apparently without any encouragement, she fills her diary with declarations of her love for Ian. She went out with other boys, and on 5th November records that she had finished with Eddie because he is courting another girl. During December, she hates Ian because he is rude, uncouth, uses foul language and loses his temper. 'I have seen the other side of him . . .' She called him a big-headed pig and 'he goes out of his way to annoy me'. But just before Christmas, he invited her out. On New Year's Eve, 1962, they were drinking German wine and Scotch whisky. Later they went back to Myra's house where Gran was asleep – Myra lived alone with her 'gran' – and Myra lost her virginity on the divan bed in the front room.

The next day, Brady was apparently indifferent again. No doubt Myra's soupy bliss bored him. A few days later he took her out on his motor-bike and they drank more German wine. (Brady was learning German, and wore black shirts.) At a fairly early stage, he explained that marriage was bourgeois nonsense, and he would have no part of it; but she was willing to wait. He called her Myra Hess, and told her she looked like Irma Grese, the Belsen guard who beat and shot prisoners for fun. He talked to her a great deal about Hitler and the Nazis, and explained that he was a rebel against society. As a love affair, it was never entirely satisfactory; he never told her he loved her – for the simple reason that he didn't. She was a sloppy idiot who didn't mind removing her clothes, and who was good for his ego. She was the slave, he was the master.[5] When he told her that he was planning a series of payroll robberies, she accepted this as another proof of his daring and unpredictable nature.

All this did not happen overnight. She had met him in January 1961, become his mistress in January 1962, persuaded her grandmother to allow him to spend occasional nights at the house by the following autumn. By April 1963 he had persuaded her to buy a gun for him. In England it is against the law to possess a hand gun unless you are a member of a pistol club. Myra accordingly joined the Cheadle Rifle Club, and managed to buy two pistols from members. She also began to take driving lessons – Brady suggested they ought to buy a car. Brady took up photography, and bought a camera with a timing device. He took photographs of Myra in black lace panties and in the nude; she photographed Ian holding his erect penis; then, using the timing device, they photographed themselves in acts of sexual intercourse. In two of the photographs she has whip marks across her buttocks and a whip hangs from the wall.

When the couple committed their first murder cannot be known. When police were investigating the case, they started with the file of Pauline Reade, sixteen, who disappeared in the Gorton district of Manchester – where both Brady and Myra Hindley lived – on 12th July 1963. On the evening of that day she set out alone to go to a dance at a railwaymen's club. She never reached the club and was never seen again. An acquaintance saw her turn into the street leading to the club. It seems likely that she was picked up by a car. A sixteen-year-old girl would not get into a car with a strange man, particularly on her way to a dance; nor is it likely that she was dragged into a car on a summer evening in a crowded area. If she got into a car, then it contained someone she knew – either a man or a woman, or both. Myra had bought a car two months before, and she lived only a few hundred yards away from Wiles Street, Pauline Reade's home. The body has never been found –

which again suggests that it was concealed, perhaps buried. But a casual rapist seldom goes to the trouble of burying the body.

Myra was becoming more like Brady. A neighbour who knew her in her teens described her as 'fun loving', but the manager at Millwards described her as surly and aggressive. A bookmaker who took Brady's bets said of him: 'In four years he came into my shop every day. I never saw him smile.'

By November 1963 they had got rid of the second hand green Morris. On Saturday, 23rd November, they hired a car and drove out to Ashton-under-Lyne, a small market town not far from Gorton. A twelve-year-old boy, John Kilbride, had spent Saturday afternoon at the cinema, and afterwards hung around the market-place hoping to make a few pence by doing odd jobs for the stall holders. It began to get dark and a fog came down from the Pennines. And at this moment, a friendly lady leaned out of a car and asked him if he wanted a lift. It seemed safe enough; he climbed in. It was the last time he was seen alive.

Nearly two years later, when the body of John Kilbride was dug up on Saddleworth Moor, his trousers and underpants were pulled down around his knees. The body was badly decomposed, but there was no obvious sign of injury; the brain was undamaged and the hyoid bone unbroken; he could have been smothered to death. Only Brady and Myra Hindley know precisely how he died, or what happened before death. The only thing that is certain is that this murder was fully planned, and that they experienced no regret later – Myra Hindley allowed Brady to take a photograph of her kneeling on the grave. It is difficult to believe that this was their first murder. In October 1965, not long after their arrest, Superintendent Arthur Benfield, in charge of the case, told pressmen that the police were considering eight disappearances over the past three or four years (i.e. back to about 1961–62). But only five names are usually mentioned in connection with the case. The names of the other suspected victims have never been published.

Brady had moved in to Bannock Street – Myra's address – in June 1963. In early '64, Gran was informed that Bannock Street was due for demolition, and that she had been assigned a house on a new estate out at Hattersley, altogether closer to the moor ... They eventually moved in the following September. In the meantime, another twelve-year-old boy had vanished. On 16th June, 1964, Keith Bennett set out to spend the night at his grandmother's house, in the Longsight district of Manchester. This was where Brady had lived until he moved in with Myra; he still visited his mother regularly. It was eight o'clock when Keith waved good-bye to his mother, who was on her way to a bingo game. The following morning, his mother called at the grandmother's to collect him (and his brother), but he had not arrived. His grandmother had not been worried; she assumed he had stayed at home. There were eight children in the family, and some of them stayed at their grandmother's every night. Keith Bennett vanished, like Pauline Reade.

In May, Myra's younger sister Maureen discovered she was pregnant; the father was a sixteen-year-old boy, David Smith, who had been in trouble with the police on a number of occasions. He married Maureen in August. On the eve of the wedding, he called at Bannock Street and met Ian Brady. Brady took to the sixteen-year-old, and talked about Hitler as they drank wine. The following day, Myra and Brady drove the newly weds to the Lake District for the day, and the relationship between the men developed. Brady saw the chance of another admirer. After all, a born leader needs more than one follower. During the next month, the Smiths saw a great deal of Brady and Myra. They had moved into Wiles Street – where Pauline Reade had lived. Brady provided large amounts of cheap red wine – he had discovered that Spanish wine is cheaper than German – and gradually took David Smith into his confidence. He expounded the ideas of de Sade, and found Smith an intelligent pupil. It was not difficult to convince Smith that everyone would commit crimes if they were not afraid – or enslaved by false morality. Smith started to keep a diary, in which he wrote: 'Every man and woman is one of two things, a sadist or a masochist. Only a few practise what they feel.' 'Rape is not a crime, it is a state of mind. Murder is a hobby, and a supreme pleasure.' 'God is a disease, a plague, a weight round a man's neck ... God is a superstition, a cancer that eats into the brain.' 'Sadism is a supreme pleasure.' 'People are like maggots, small, blind and worthless.' David Smith was an apt pupil; in fact, the excerpts suggest that he had made the philosophy his own.

Later still, Brady talked about robbing banks, of setting up their own small crime syndicate. It is difficult to know whether this was intended seriously, or whether Brady was only repeating the tactics he had used to 'convert' Myra. He showed Smith his two guns, and they 'cased' banks and drew up detailed plans. But all this came to nothing.

In September 1964, Brady, Myra Hindley and 'Gran' moved to 16 Wardle Brook Avenue, Hattersley, the end house of a block of four on a raised terrace. It was small, but large enough for the three of them. The Smiths continued to visit, and bank robberies were discussed without real conviction.

On Boxing Day, 1964, Brady and Myra Hindley murdered a ten-year-old girl, Lesley Ann Downey, whom they picked up at a fairground in the Ancoats district of central Manchester. For anyone who has followed the case chronologically, and found its motivation baffling, this murder is like a flash of lightning that suddenly makes everything clear. On that day, Myra drove her grandmother to visit an uncle in Dukinfield – as she usually did on a Saturday afternoon. But instead of returning at nine o'clock, she returned two hours late, explaining that a snowstorm was on the way, and that it would be better if the grandmother spent the night where she was. Gran protested, pointed out that she would have to sleep on the floor, but Myra was oddly stubborn, and drove off back to Hattersley at 11.30.

Lesley Ann Downey had gone to the fair in Hulme Lane early in the afternoon; on her way home with a friend, she decided to go back for one more look. Brady and Myra Hindley must have picked her up at about six o'clock. Their intention was to take pornographic photographs of the child, then dispose of her as they had disposed of the others. They recorded what took place – at least, during the first seventeen minutes – on tape. Brady asked her name. For some reason, she gave a false surname. 'I have to get home before eight o'clock, honest to god . . .' Against a background of music by the Ray Conniff singers – intended to drown the child's voice – Brady and Myra Hindley keep ordering her to 'put it in, put it in tighter . . .' The child screams, cries, and asks to be released. Myra Hindley says: 'Hush, shut up or I'll forget myself and hit you one.' Presumably what is happening, then, is not actual torture, but something that frightens the child rather than intentionally hurting her. And this is the only thing that can be said in favour of the couple. Emlyn Williams remarks: 'I purposely emphasize that compared with the rumoured atrocities, the real thing is comparatively mild.' They took nine photographs of the child in various poses, which Emlyn Williams described as looking like ballet exercises; she is naked, with a scarf tied round her mouth, and she raised her arms or legs at the orders of the photographer; in the ninth, she faces the camera with her hands raised in an attitude of prayer. The couple were still amateur pornographers, not yet sadistic maniacs with an urge to torment. But murder *was* a part of the plan, because it was the thought of a body, buried on the moors, that justified the whole thing. It confirmed their feeling that they were not merely two low paid office workers, trapped in working-class lives, but Enemies of Society, dangerous revolutionaries. In order to indulge this feeling, they even went up to the moors in freezing weather and slept out on the graves, covered with a few blankets. To sleep out like that was a kind of ascetic exercise – but given meaning by their *own* mythology; by the lives and acts of Brady and Hindley, not of the saints and apostles. The saint sits in his cave and meditates on the crucifixion. They meditated on the gospel of de Sade, and the corpses underneath them. David Smith remarked that after the last murder, they looked exhausted and replete, as if sexually satisfied. But there are other things besides sex that can produce emotional catharsis: art and religion, for example. At the time when the bodies were being dug up on the moors, a BBC commentator remarked that there were rumours that the whole case was mixed up with witchcraft and black magic. And in a certain sense, it was. They were like a black magic cult, performing their own blasphemous ceremony. In effect, they had created their own religion, a religion with something in common with the Hindu sect called Thugee, which treats murder as a religious duty as well as a pleasure.

The starting point of this religion was sex. This is no doubt why David Smith was so easy to convert. Among the quotations from Sade in his notebook there are long extracts copied out from novels like *The Carpetbaggers* and *Eternal Fire*. Now neither of these novels is pornographic in the technical sense. They simply share the assumption that modern man is sexually frustrated and needs books as aids to masturbation: that no twentieth-century city dweller ever 'eats his fill' of sex. How can he when he is perpetually being reminded of it by mini-skirted girls and underwear advertisements? In Shaw's *Major Barbara,* Undershaft says: 'I moralized and starved until one day I swore that I would be a full-fed free man at all costs; that nothing should stop me except a bullet . . .' Brady made the same decision about sex, fortified by Sade. All it needed was the belief that there is nothing wrong in treating other people as objects, as we treat the animals we eat for dinner.

The odd thing is that Myra Hindley remained, in many ways, a quite ordinary girl of normal affections. Her kindness to dogs was exceptional; when, later on, she heard that her own dog had died while in the hands of the police, she burst out: 'They're just a lot of bloody murderers.' This in itself would seem to indicate that no actual physical cruelty was practised on the children – at least, for its own sake. The children were intended as 'props' in a sexual orgy, like the whip and the black lace panties. In *A Casebook of Murder* I cited two recent cases in which a couple had offered lifts to young girls, and the woman helped to subdue the girl while the man raped her. And in a case that took place in Chatham, Kent, in 1968, Mrs. Joyce Ballard, thirty, admitted that she had enticed a twelve-year-old girl into her flat so that her husband, Robert Ballard, could assault her. Ballard, who was obsessed by books on torture and witchcraft, tied up the girl, cut open her veins and stabbed her, then committed suicide. The wife was sentenced to three years in prison. In these cases, the woman shared the man's sexual fantasies and derived sexual pleasure from observing the assault. This was the basis of the Brady-Hindley relation.

On 25th September, 1965, nine months after the disappearance of Lesley Ann Downey, David Smith called on Brady, and during the course of a drinking session, was taken into Brady's confidence. Brady asked him if he had ever killed anybody, then said: 'I have – three or four. The bodies are buried up on the moors.' He also told Smith that he had once stopped the car on a deserted street (Myra Hindley must have been driving, since Brady couldn't) and shot a passer-by. Whether Smith believed him is not quite clear. But having committed himself, Brady believed that it was time Smith became involved in the murders. He may have regretted telling Smith; on the other hand, it may have been simply that he wanted to enrol another member in their murder sect, and perhaps involve Maureen Smith too. (By this time, their baby had died, and the Smiths had also moved out to Hattersley.)

Then days later, on 6th October, the plan to involve Smith was put into effect. They had decided that the victim this time was to be a homosexual, who would be picked up in one of the queer bars in the Oxford Street area. Some time between 9 and 11 that evening, they became friendly with a seventeen-year-old youth, Edward Evans, a homosexual.

At 11.30 that night, Myra Hindley rang the doorbell of the Smiths' flat. She said she had a message from her mother for Maureen. A few minutes later, she asked David Smith to walk her back home. As they approached the Wardle Brook house, she asked him to come in to collect some miniature wine bottles. Smith went into the kitchen, where Brady handed him some bottles, then went out 'to get the rest'. A moment later there was a loud scream, and Myra yelled: 'Dave, help him.' Smith rushed into the sitting-room, and found Brady hitting Edward Evans with an axe. It seemed to take a long time for the youth to collapse. When he finally lay, face downward, on the floor, Brady gave him a final blow with the axe – he had been striking with the back of the blade, to avoid blood. There was a noise like gargling – the death rattle. After that, Brady took a cord and strangled the body that still twitched. He was swearing all the time. Myra's two barking dogs were soothed. Brady held out the hatchet to David Smith; 'Feel the weight of it.' The idea was to get Smith's fingerprints on the handle: Smith took it, then handed it back. The room was covered with spots of blood. And at this moment, Gran called down to ask what all the noise was about. Myra shouted back that she had dropped a tape-recorder on her foot. Brady, seeing that Smith looked sick, handed him a glass of wine. Then, while the body lay there, all three of them cleaned the room with a mop and bucket. After this, the corpse was wrapped in a polythene sheet. Smith observed that the fly was undone. The body was carried upstairs – Brady joking: 'Eddie's a dead weight' – into Myra's room. Brady was limping; he had been kicked on the ankle as Evans thrashed about on the floor. After this, they all drank tea, and Myra reminisced about a time when a policeman had stopped to talk to her while Brady was burying a body. After this, Smith agreed to return the next day with an old pram, to transport the body to the car. Shortly after three, David Smith left. When he arrived home, he was violently sick, then told Maureen what had happened. It was Maureen who decided they were going to the police. They waited until dawn – Smith was afraid that Brady might be watching the flat, prepared to attack him if he made a move towards a phone. Then, hiding a bread-knife and a screwdriver under his coat, Smith crept down the stairs, followed by Maureen.

At 8.40 the next morning – 7th October – a man dressed as a baker's roundsman knocked at the door of 16 Wardle Brook Avenue. When Myra Hindley, rubbing the sleep out of her eyes, came to the door, the man identified himself as a police officer, and said they had reason to believe there was a body in the house. Brady was on the divan bed in the living-room, writing a note to explain why he would not be going to work that day. He was wearing only a vest. Superintendent Talbot – dressed as a roundsman, in case Brady had his guns ready – was joined by a detective sergeant. They demanded to be taken round the house. When they came to the locked bedroom, they asked for the key. Myra said it was at work, and the policemen offered to take her there to collect it. At this, Brady said: 'You'd better tell him . . . There was a row here last night. It's in there . . .' Under the window in the bedroom there was a plastic wrapped bundle, obviously a body. The two loaded revolvers were found in a shoe box in the same room.

Enough evidence was found in the house to charge Brady with the premeditated murder of Edward Evans, including a notebook with plans for the disposal of the body. The book also contained the name 'John Kilbride'. Myra Hindley was allowed to go free, and she went to stay with her mother. Four days later, she was charged with being an accessory.

In a careful search of the house, the police discovered a cloakroom ticket in the spine of a prayer book. It led them to Manchester Central Station, where they discovered two suitcases. These proved to contain pornographic photos, tapes, books on sex and torture, coshes, wigs, masks and notes on robbing banks. The photographs included the nine of Lesley Ann Downey, and her voice was heard on the tape.

But there was no breakdown or confession. Brady maintained that Lesley had been brought to the house by two men, and had been taken away by them after they had taken the photographs. He knew he stood no chance of escaping a life sentence, but he was determined not to give an inch.

Two doors away, there lived a twelve-year-old girl, Patricia Hodges, who had been friendly with the couple. She told the police that she had been up on the moors with them, and had been given wine to drink. She took the police to the spot where Myra Hindley had parked. It was close to a place called Hollin Brown Knoll. The search began. The method was to look for any patch that might have been dug over, and then to drive a long stick down through the turf and sniff the end for the smell of physical decomposition. Six days later, a policeman noticed a bone sticking up from a bare patch of ground. Three feet down, they found the naked body of Lesley Ann Downey, her clothes at her feet. The spot where John Kilbride was buried was discovered through a photograph that showed Myra Hindley kneeling with a dog; she proved to have been posing on the grave.

The trial provided no surprises. The couple were charged with three murders. The most horrifying moment was when the tape of Lesley Ann Downey was played in court. Myra Hindley hung her head and said: 'I am ashamed,' but Brady opened a packet of peppermints and popped one into his mouth. Brady showed a disposition to get his own back on Smith by doing his best to drag him into the murder of Lesley Ann Downey and Evans. He also tended to answer questions with a pedantic, schoolmasterly manner, as if insisting on his status as an intellectual. Maurice Richardson in *The Observer* described Myra: 'Her hair, naturally brown, has been changing colour from week to week [of the trial]. First silver-lilac, then bright canary blonde. She is a big girl with a striking face; fine straight nose, thinnish curved lips, rather hefty chin, blue eyes. Full face she is almost a beauty. The Victorians would have admired her.' Richardson's view was that it was a case of a hysteric falling in love with a psychotic and coming to share his delusions.

On 6th May, 1966, both were sentenced to life imprisonment. Since that time, there have been occasional news stories about them: of Myra being put into solitary confinement for her own safety (child killers are notoriously unpopular in prisons), of Brady quarrelling violently with Raymond Morris, the Cannock Chase murderer, in the maximum security wing of Durham jail. Brady has also been on hunger strike several times because the authorities have refused to allow him to see Myra Hindley. (This is a curious feature; during the trial, Myra declared that she had loved him, and was still in love with him; she watched Brady intently much of the time; Brady, on the other hand, showed no sign of a similar attachment to Myra.) Lord Longford, who has corresponded with Brady in prison, has put it on record that Brady has matured and become altogether less anti-social; in fact, has shown a disposition to work for the good of his fellow prisoners. But, in July 1971, a newspaper report stated that Brady was showing signs of severe mental disturbance, and may be transferred to Broadmoor. Maurice Richardson quotes someone as commenting, at the time of the trial: 'If those two were sane, they'd have gone mad long ago.'[5]

1. My novel *The Glass Cage* was based on these crimes, and on the Thames nude murders.
2. *Four Against the Mob*, 1961.
3. *'I'm anfang war die Tat'*. *Faust*, line 1237.
4. *The Sunday Times*, 7th February, 1971.
5. Maslow's paper on Dominance Feeling in Women (1939), which I quote in *New Pathways in Psychology*, seems to throw an interesting light on this relationship. Maslow's researches suggested that all men and women may be classed as high-dominance, medium-dominance or low-dominance. High-dominance men and women are highly sexed and tend to promiscuity; the medium-dominance range tends to be 'romantics' about sex; low-dominance men and women are scared of sex, and tend to regard it as indecent. The most interesting point to emerge was that women prefer a man in their own dominance group – low and medium-dominance women are frightened by high-dominance males – but not by one of *slightly* higher dominance than themselves. (This seems to suggest that couples could be tested for suitability by checking their dominance rating.) What may happen if the 'dominance gap' is too great may be seen in the case of Brady and

Myra Hindley. Myra was clearly of medium-dominance; Brady was high-dominance. The result – the total, slave-like domination of Myra by Brady.

This view is interestingly supported by Dr. Rachel Pinney, the devisor of 'Creative Listening', who was able to talk to Myra in gaol. She became convinced of Myra's innocence, writing to me in a letter: 'I still think Myra had no part in the killings or torture, and the end result of my work will be a fuller study of the psychology of being "hooked" – e.g. Rasputin and the Tsarina, Loeb and Leopold, Hitler and his "worshippers".' She holds the view that Myra was 'framed' – much as David Smith was almost framed when Brady induced him to hold the axe.

CHAPTER SEVEN

The Dostoevskian Synthesis

All healthy creatures require a field for the expression of their energies. The most important difference between the socially privileged and the underprivileged is that the sons of the rich can choose a wider range of methods of getting rid of their energies: skiing, mountain climbing, big-game hunting, exploring, driving racing cars. By comparison, the son of working-class parents has few energy outlets; his freedom is circumscribed by the need to keep a roof over his head and to eat at least once a day. He might spend his two weeks' annual holiday pot-holing or rock climbing; he might join the navy 'to see the world'; he might become a hippie and hitch-hike to warmer climes. But whatever he does, his lack of money will restrict his freedom.

Fortunately – for the stability of society – a relatively small number of people experience a strong need to seek out adventurous ways of energy dissipation. 'Civilization cannot survive without adventure,' said Whitehead; but that is because the progress of civilization depends upon a small minority of enterprising individuals, the 'adventure seekers'. Most people are unwilling to pay the price of adventure: the discomfort and danger. But this enterprising minority *need* challenges if they are to maintain their mental health; without challenge, they begin to suffocate. Energies that ought to be flowing stagnate, and stagnant energy turns into poison, or into fat, like the muscles of a retired athlete.

Now when my mind is healthy and relaxed, nearly everthing I do gives me a small 'feedback' of pleasure; stroking a cat, drinking a glass of water, opening a newspaper and smelling printer's ink. It may be such a small feedback that I do not even recognize it as pleasure: I am simply aware that I am *noticing* things. If I become tired or frustrated or tense, this sensitivity vanishes. I cease to respond to things. I am thirsty and I drink a glass of water; but it gives me no particular pleasure. I begin to look on the negative side of things. If the cat rubs itself against my leg and purrs, I experience irritable rejection, and the thought that cats are sneaky, ingratiating animals that care for nothing but themselves ...

A man who has spent a long time in this state ceases to experience normal feelings. His self-image fades. He is like someone who has become partly deaf: he gets used to never hearing sounds below a certain level. It takes very strong stimuli – of either pleasure or pain to produce an ordinary 'feedback', and he longs for an earthquake of feeling to shake him out of his indifference. Camus describes a man in this state in his novel *L'Etranger*, and he is only shaken out of it by the prospect of his execution for murder.

The thoughts of such a man turn naturally towards crime (although this is not to say that he puts his daydreams into practice). Obeying the same rules as everybody else fails to satisfy him; he would like to do everything more violently: hit that man with a superior voice, beat that whining child, smash that shop window, rape that girl ... If he crosses the borderline between thought and action, the crime is likely to be sexual. For sex *is* an earthquake of feeling, and the male sexual drive has its impersonal, aggressive component.

Dostoevsky was the first novelist to make a full-length, clinical study of this type of personality, the man who has ceased to feel. He was also obsessed throughout his life by the theme of irrational violence. He writes in his prison memoirs, *The House of the Dead:*

> The entire meaning of the word convict is of a man without freedom ... The authorities are sometimes surprised when a convict, having lived ... quietly for several years, suddenly *á propos* of nothing, as if some devil had got into him, misbehaves, goes on a binge, starts a brawl, and sometimes even takes the risk of committing a criminal offence – showing gross disrespect for senior authority, killing or raping ... They see this and are astonished. In fact, perhaps the sole reason for this sudden explosion from a man from whom one might least expect it, is an anguished, fevered expression of his own individuality ... a wish to assert himself and his humiliated personality.

That is, to restore the self-image. Since Dostoevsky himself was something of a humiliated personality, he is fascinated by the concept of brutal characters who exercise a powerful will for its own sake. It is a Sadeian theme: the notion of someone being willing to hurt or injure a weaker person out of pure self-assertion. Significantly enough, Dostoevsky was also obsessed by the idea of the rape or seduction of under-age girls. His first novel, *Poor Folk*, written at the age of twenty-four (in 1844), excited Russian critics because it seemed to be full of pity for the unfortunate young girl Varenka, seduced and betrayed, and moral condemnation of the villain, who triumphs in the end. In fact, Dostoevsky was morbidly fascinated by the idea of seduction and the triumph of the seducer. Versilov, the Sadeian hero-villain of *A Raw Youth*, has a penchant for seducing under-age girls, and Svidrigailov in *Crime and Punishment* and Stavrogin in *The Possessed* actually commit rape on children.

The most characteristic feature of Dostoevsky is his ambivalence, his tendency to be torn between two conflicting emotions, usually love and hate. In the early *Netochka Nezvanova*, the imperious child Katya showers kisses on her playmate Netochka, and tells her: 'I used to want to love you very much, and then I'd suddenly take it into my heart to hate you ...' And this is typical. Versilov, in *A Raw Youth*, advances the theory that he possesses a 'double' who stands beside him and urges him to do the opposite of what he wants to do. 'I am split mentally and horribly afraid of it. It is as if you have your own double standing next to you. You yourself are intelligent and rational, but the double at your side insists on wanting to commit some absurdity ...' This is what Poe called 'the imp of the perverse', which makes a murderer who is no longer in danger of discovery suddenly shout his guilt aloud in the street. The psychologist Viktor Frankl calls it 'The Law of Reversed Effort'.

But the significance of this split becomes clearer in less violent situations. In *A Raw Youth*, Arkady describes how, when he was at boarding school, he was visited by his mother, a simple peasant woman, who brought him some food. He makes her cry by refusing to accept it, remarking coldly that the school food is good enough, and cuts short her tearful farewell by pointing out that other boys are watching; then, when she is gone, he sobs with remorse and clutches the handkerchief she has given him. Again, the narrator of *The Insulted and the Injured* remarks: 'How many times in the old days I used to walk up and down my room with an unconscious wish for someone to do me an injury or say a word that could be taken as an insult, so I could then vent my anger on something.' When Dostoevsky himself discovered that the woman he was in love with had transferred her affections to a penniless school-teacher, he immediately became the teacher's best friend, ('he is dearer to me than my own brother . . .') and urged him to pass an examination that would qualify him for a well-paid job.

The real problem here is lack of imagination – in a precise and clinical sense. Children have an appetite for violent emotions – ghosts and horrors – because their lives are relatively uneventful. Tom Sawyer indulges in daydreams of how Aunt Polly would feel if he were dead . . . All this is simply an attempt to warm-up tepid emotions, and it is a legitimate use of the imagination. If you imagine losing someone you love, the effect is to re-focus that love, to arouse gratitude. It is like waking from a nightmare to the familiar room. For precisely the same reason, we enjoy listening to the patter of rain on the windows when we feel warm and secure; it has the effect of transforming an ordinary room – of no particular interest – into a haven of delight. Lovers may quarrel for the same reason: because they have discovered that the pleasure of making up is intenser than the pleasure of a placid and uneventful courtship.

And here we can see clearly that the real problem is *boredom*, our tendency to 'take for granted' and lose the meaning of an experience. 'Where is the life we have lost in living?' If you stare at an unmoving object, your gaze *blurs*; if you want to prevent this blurring, you have to keep re-focusing. This is what is fundamentally wrong with human beings, what the Catholics call original sin: this tendency of our values to blur into boredom. Crisis causes them to re-focus. Dostoevsky knew this from experience, having been sentenced to death by firing squad and reprieved at the last moment. Such an experience ought to last a man a lifetime, rescue him permanently from trivial emotions. But Dostoevsky was a highly emotional man; self-discipline was never his strong point. In fact, without the experience of his trial and subsequent imprisonment in Siberia, he would probably never have become a major writer. Hence the attempts to *make himself* feel by exposing himself to humiliation. Hence the need to burst out of any situation that threatened him with stability. To the end of his life he remained a cantankerous man who enjoyed quarrelling and provoking insults, and hurting people he loved and then rushing to extremes of penitence and self-abasement.

All this amounts to a failure of imagination. Imagination is the power of anticipation. I do not jump into the sea with all my clothes on – no matter how hot I feel – because I can foresee the inconvenience. The imagination could be considered a kind of *regulator* of my psychological health, something like a thermostat. If the thermostat is not working, a man may do absurd things to try to adjust the balance. Van Gogh cut off one of his ears. T. E. Lawrence hired someone to flog him.

In animals, this kind of irrational response is known as 'displacement activity'. The zoologist Tinbergen observed that when sticklebacks have a quarrel about the limits of their 'territory', both suddenly stand on their heads in the sand and dig holes; the anger is taken out on the sand. Herring gulls tear up grass: tits unleash their fury on leaves and buds. Frank Harris claims that Carlyle was seen tearing up flowers on the morning after his honeymoon night – he had made the discovery that he was impotent. This is 'displacement activity'. Nail biting is a typical displacement activity; it can also be seen in the father striding up and down as his wife has a baby. Displacement activity is not, strictly speaking, irrational; it is simply the more-or-less conscious decision to allow frustrated energies to spill-over and find an outlet through another channel. The aim is to restore emotional equilibrium.

In the case of Dostoevsky, it is arguable that the emotional upheavals were largely his own fault, the outcome of a typically Russian laziness and self-indulgence. (Tolstoy thought so; he told his biographer that he thought Dostoevsky weak and vicious.) It should have been unnecessary to engineer situations that would lead to humiliation or remorse. The imagination is an instrument whose efficiency depends upon the force and seriousness with which it is exercised. Dostoevsky's tendency to self-indulgence made him prefer to *act* out his fantasies; he was like a man who has to count on his fingers or move his lips while reading.

But at least this weakness produced a classic – and prophetic – study in the criminal mentality, in the character of Nicholas Stavrogin in *The Possessed*. Stavrogin is the only child of a wealthy woman. He has spent years completing his education in Europe. On his return to his home town he impresses people with his seriousness, and an air of sternness and preoccupation, as well as by his physical beauty and obvious strength; one of the characters nicknames him 'Prince Harry'. But his actions puzzle everybody. He bites the ear of a provincial governor at a party. When he fights a duel, he fires into the air – three times – with the utmost indifference. He allows a man to slap his face, and though he obviously has difficulty mastering himself, his eyes have become cold and calm ten seconds later. Although he is good-looking enough to take his pick of attractive girls, it turns out that he has married a cripple girl who is almost an imbecile.

In a climactic chapter of the novel (often omitted from translations), Stavrogin goes to visit a saintly monk, and hands him his 'confession'. This begins by describing how he had lived in St. Petersburg in 'dissipation in which I found no pleasure'; he was having an affair with a lady's maid and also with her mistress, and was thinking of allowing the two of them to meet in his rooms one day – by way of a 'silly joke'. He has a hysterical landlady who often beats her small daughter, a girl of about ten. One day his penknife disappears, and the landlady whips her daughter for stealing it. Afterwards, Stavrogin finds the knife in his room, and throws it away. 'Immediately I felt I had done something vile. At the same time I experienced a pleasurable sensation . . .' Every vile, exceedingly disgraceful . . . situation in which I happened to be . . . always roused in me, together with measureless anger, incredible delight. I felt the same in moments when I was committing a crime and in moments when my life was in danger. If I were stealing . . . I would feel rapture from the consciousness of the depths of my baseness . . .' He steals money from a poverty-stricken clerk in order to 'savour his baseness'. He also seduces the child when her mother is out, but feels revulsion afterwards and leaves her; later, he allows the child to hang herself without attempting to interfere.

All this follows the pattern of the incident between

Arkady and his mother, but in a grimmer key. The monk goes to the heart of the problem when he says: 'Evil passions *and the habit of idleness* have made you callous and stupid.' But he misses the point when he tells Stavrogin that his confession is born 'of the need of a heart wounded unto death' and out of the need for repentance. For the confession is another attempt to stir himself into feeling by 'focusing' his 'vileness', and he is disappointed that the priest shows no revulsion. The confession, like the crimes, is an attempt to *re-establish contact with reality,* to experience strong feelings instead of inner stagnation. When he commits suicide at the end of the novel, he admits in a letter: 'I have tried my strength everywhere ... As long as I was experimenting for myself and for others, it seemed infinite, as it has all my life ... But *to what to apply my strength* – that is what I have never seen, and do not see now ... My desires are too weak; they are not enough to guide me. On a log one may cross a river, but not a chip ...'

Stavrogin is suffering from an intensified version of the boredom that schoolchildren suffer during overlong holidays. If you become passive for too long, the 'attention muscles' relax; the energies sink; sudden flashes of delight cease to occur. It is the 'blurring effect'. Stavrogin's 'crimes' are an instinctive attempt to re-focus his values. He would like to experience agonizing remorse. In fact, he experiences only faint twinges of repentance. Kierkegaard understood the answer to the problem. There is a passage in *Either/Or* where he claims that the strongest impulse of the human race is the need to escape boredom. But he then points out that a schoolboy can experience intense interest as he plays with a beetle in an inkwell, or listens to the drip of rain from the eaves. For the schoolboy is already *prepared* for boredom; he has fortified himself against it, expecting to sit there for the next hour or so, with nothing to interest him except the master's voice; so any minor distraction fascinates him. Freedom demands that initial effort. It is the opposite of laziness: a state of being prepared to dissipate a great deal of effort without much reward ... Once the mind has braced itself for this effort, it again becomes sensitive to values, to meaning.

Consciousness is basically *a device for registering meaning,* just as a voltmeter is a device for registering volts. But a voltmeter has a needle suspended on a spring, and if the spring becomes too slack, it ceases to work. Consciousness also has its equivalent of the spring: the muscles that are used for concentrating the attention. If these muscles are allowed to become slack and lazy – because it seems there is no worth-while 'object of attention' – then consciousness will perceive reality without registering its meaning. This is Stavrogin's problem. And it is not merely a literary or philosophical problem. It is the problem of the motivation of Raymond Morris and Norman Collins and Ian Brady.

Towards the end of Stavrogin's confession, there occurs a passage that reveals that Dostoevsky has not been entirely honest. Stavrogin describes how he is passing through a small German town. After a good meal, he falls asleep in a hotel bedroom, and has a dream of a 'golden age'. It seems to be inspired by a picture of Claude Lorraine in the Dresden Gallery called *Acis and Galatea:*

> I saw a corner of the Greek archipelago the way it was some three thousand years ago; caressing azure waves, rocks and islands, a shore in blossom, a magic panorama further off, a beckoning sunset ... Here was mankind's early paradise, gods descended from heaven and united with mortals ... Here lived beautiful men and women. They rose, they went to sleep, happy and innocent ... The most improbable of all visions, to which mankind throughout its existence has given its best energies, for which it has sacrificed everything, for which it has pined and been tormented ...

This vision of the golden age is the necessary counterweight to those pictures of stuffy, dirty, overcrowded tenements full of miserable people that can be found in all Dostoevsky's novels. It is significant that this dream should come to Stavrogin in a small German town, when he has missed a train and has half a day to wait for the next – a time when he can relax because there is nothing to do. He mentions that the day is clear, that the hotel has shrubs and flower beds around it. And so again we see that it is not simply a question of man's boredom and lack of purpose, but of beauty-starvation. Dostoevsky appears to be speaking only about the problem of boredom and meaninglessness, for he endows

Stavrogin with qualities he himself did not possess: wealth, good looks, attractiveness to women.

He implies that Stavrogin is satiated with experience, with 'meaning'; a man who has tried everything and discovered that life is basically futile . . . And then he admits that what Stavrogin wants is a vision of meaning. The talk about the meaninglessness of life is a kind of sour grapes, Sartre's 'magic'.

The same thing can be found in the letters of H. P. Lovecraft; in 1924 he wrote to Edwin Baird: 'My daily life is a sort of contemptuous lethargy, devoid alike of virtues or vices. I am not of the world, but an amused and sometimes disgusted spectator to it. I detest the human race and its pretences and swinishnesses – to me life is a fine art, and although I believe the universe is an automatic meaningless chaos devoid of ultimate values or distinctions of right and wrong, I consider it most artistic to take into account the emotional heritage of our civilization and follow the patterns which produce the least pain to delicate sensibilities.' This could almost be a passage from Stavrogin's confession. But in another letter, written at about the same time, he says: 'Books are very feeble things. Neither you nor I, for all the classics we have read, has even a hundredth of the joy of Greece and Rome which comes to the millionaire whose car and yacht enable him to linger indefinitely under Mediterranean skies and drink in through all five senses the glory which we are never likely to know save through the dense filter of the visual imagination.'

But perhaps it is misleading to speak of beauty-starvation, or even of experience-starvation. What Stavrogin and Lovecraft both want is more than beauty. Why does Stavrogin talk about three thousand years ago? He is thinking also of history, the epochs of time that are hidden behind the thick curtain of the present. And in *The Brothers Karamazov*, Alyosha's vision of meaning occurs outdoors at night, when there seem to be threads running between the stars and linking his soul to them, a vision that brings to mind Van Gogh's painting of the Starry Night. No, the basic human craving is for meaning, for 'otherness', for the broad realms of *impersonal* meanings. We are trapped in a small, personal world that stifles us, suffocates us; we go around in this tiny world of personal meaning like a donkey tied to a post. These greater meanings, the 'impersonal', serve the same purpose as the water in a car radiator; they cool the engine. To be trapped in one's personality is like living always in a small room the size of a closet; it soon becomes filthy and untidy. *Anything* that distracts us from the small, personal world is a blessing, even vicious gossip about the neighbours. The advantage of intelligence is that it has a wider field of impersonal interests. The expansion of intelligence costs a certain effort – the same effort, for example, that a music lover has to make to sit through long operas or symphonies. And the reward is in proportion to this effort. A scientist examining crystals through an electron microscope or stars through a reflecting telescope is not necessarily in a state of 'impersonality'. He may be putting no real effort into it, and half-thinking about some quarrel with a colleague. But if he has just got back from a scientific conference where the atmosphere was trivial and personal, he is more likely to plunge into his real work with eagerness and relief because he has become clearly aware of what he *doesn't* want, and this creates a strong sense of what he *does* want. All crisis or inconvenience has this effect of destroying our indifference and re-focusing the sense of values; but we shouldn't need crisis. We should be able to focus the values without it.

Dostoevsky again touches on the human need for 'the impersonal' in his portrait of Svidrigailov in *Crime and Punishment.* Svidrigailov is another Sadeian anti-hero: strong, ruthless, a rake with a taste for under-age girls, a perpetually erect penis eager to deflower the world's maidenhood. Like Stavrogin, he suffers from boredom, and finally commits suicide. But one of his most significant speeches occurs in an earlier conversation with Raskolnikov: 'We always imagine eternity as something beyond our conception, something vast, vast! But why must it be vast? Instead of all that, what if it's one little room, like a bath house in the country, black and grimy and spiders in every corner . . .'[2]

And in a sense, this *is* the ultimate horror: the idea of final non-escape from personality. The greatest thing a human being can experience is the sense of 'otherness'. Our deepest instinct drives us to seek out meaning as a bee seeks out honey, and the sense of 'otherness', of distant horizons of fact, is like a vision of endless fields of wild flowers.

Sartre developed the same insight in *Huis Clos* (*In Camera*)

– hell as an eternity in a single room, in which three mutually antagonistic people bicker and quarrel forever, preventing each other from losing the sense of personal identity for one moment. But Sartre summarized his theme in the words: 'Hell is other people.' It is not. Hell is *personality*, subjectivity; heaven is impersonality, objectivity.

Just before Svidrigailov kills himself, he falls asleep in a cheap hotel room, and has a dream. The wind, Dostoevsky explains, has aroused 'a persistent craving for the fantastic'. There follows a description of a sunny day, a country cottage ('in the English style') surrounded by beds of flowers and lawns; light, cool rooms strewn with freshly cut hay; wide staircases; a light breeze ... Then, in an upstairs room, he discovers a coffin, containing the body of a fourteen-year-old girl who has committed suicide after he had raped her. Svidrigailov wakes up, the paradise gone. So again it is clear that it is not boredom that is at issue. He is bored because he is trapped in his personality, like a narrow room. His perpetual sexual itch is a need to escape from personality. But it never carries him far enough. His lack of self-discipline lands him back in the old listlessness.

The same was true of Dostoevsky himself. An atmosphere of triviality and hysteria pervades even his greatest work, something essentially petty, like two homosexuals having a row. It can be seen in the prose style; characters never walk around to see someone: they run around. They trot, they rush, they exclaim. They are fond of shouting 'What nonsense,' and 'Would you believe it?' Gogol's *Government Inspector* has two fat little squires called Bobchinsky and Dobchinsky, and one gets the feeling that they are just around the corner in all Dostoevsky's novels. Only in his greatest scenes does Dostoevsky succeed in purging his prose of this incongruous touch of Enid Blyton which sprang out of a lack of self-assurance. And this in turn sprang out of self-division, acceptance of his own weakness. So the great criminals in Dostoevsky, the 'ruthless men', are exercises in compensatory imagination – as Sade's criminals are. Dostoevsky likes to portray them as ruthless men, but basically they are weak.

Once this has been recognized, we become aware that Dostoevsky also understood the 'magical' psychology of 'the violent man'. At first sight, Raymond Morris, Arthur Hosein, Ian

Brady, seem to have little enough in common with Svidrigailov and Stavrogin; that is because Dostoevsky has tried to suppress the element of weakness and laziness in his villains. When this is taken into account, Stavrogin suddenly looks more like Morris or Brady.

The central character of *The Possessed* is not Stavrogin, but a nihilistic revolutionary called Peter Verkovensky, based on an actual nihilist, Sergei Netchaev. Netchaev (1847–1883) was perhaps the most violent and thorough revolutionary of his time, a man who was fascinated by destruction for its own sake. He claimed to have 'an entirely negative plan ... total annihilation'. A 'spoiled priest', he slipped away from the divinity school in St. Petersburg, leaving a note claiming that he had been arrested by the secret police and was being transported to some distant place. It was a quick way of making a reputation as a revolutionary; he was twenty-one at the time. In Switzerland, he convinced the old revolutionary Bakunin that he had escaped the Peter and Paul fortress and was an envoy of a revolutionary committee, and Bakunin gave him a paper asserting that he was member number 2771 of the World Revolutionary Alliance. Back in Russia he organized a number of 'groups of five', who were all supposed to obey him without question. (The groups had no contact with one another; they depended on Netachaev to co-ordinate them.) A student named Ivanov, a member of a Moscow group, showed signs of questioning Netchaev's authority; Netchaev immediately ordered his execution, and ordered the other four members to carry it out. In the event, it was Netchaev himself who had to pull the trigger. When Ivanov's body was found in a pond a few days later, Netachaev decided to flee again, and his confederates were arrested and tried; the case caused a tremendous sensation, and for a time Netchaev's notoriety eclipsed that of Bakunin or Herzen.

Back in Geneva, his sheer ruthlessness and violence alienated other Russian expatriate revolutionaries; after a period in London, he returned to Geneva, and the Russian police finally succeeded in getting him extradited – in 1872 – as a common criminal. He spent the remaining nine years of his life in the Peter and Paul fortress, but even in that impregnable jail, he succeeded in converting some of his guards to the cause of revolution, and used them to establish contact with a revolutionary group called The People's Will, which planned to assassinate the Tsar, Alexander II. The group wanted to rescue Netchaev, but did not have the resources to plan two large-scale coups; typically, Netchaev told them to forget him and concentrate on the oppressor. Alexander was murdered (by a bomb, which also killed the assassin) in March 1881. The connection between Netchaev and The People's Will became known; the guards were purged, and Netchaev was thrust into a deeper dungeon, where he died of scurvy two years later, aged thirty-five.

Dostoevsky's portrait of Netchaev lacks the savagery and complexity of the original. Verkovensky is 'Stavrogin's ape' and worships him slavishly; Netchaev admired no one. Verkovensky is weak, vain, stupid and boorish, and lacks the insane drive that characterized Netchaev. Netchaev was very definitely a member of the 'dominant five per cent'; Verkovensky is a clownish mediocrity. On the other hand, Dostoevsky's sketch of the 'revolutionary circle' is brilliant: young and enthusiastic students, neglected by their parents, looking for something to believe in, and older men suffering from wounded self-esteem. The account of the murder follows Netchaev's murder of Ivanov fairly closely.

The parallels between Russia of the 1860s and '70s, and America of the 1960s and '70s, are too obvious to miss: the revolutionary unrest centring around emancipation and civil rights, the assassination of public men, the young looking for a cause, the extremes of rigid conservatism and nihilistic radicalism. The murder of Ivanov took place in 1869. Exactly one hundred years later, its American equivalent took place in Benedict Canyon, Southern California. Before the end of that year, Charles Manson had achieved the same dubious celebrity as Netchaev, and his face, with hypnotic eyes, glared from the cover of *Life*.

In August 1969 I wrote an essay on the philosophy of Herbert Marcuse for an American academic publication. Speaking of Marcuse's *Essay on Liberation*, I wrote:

> Could anyone be sincere in encouraging hippies not to wash, to cultivate 'the methodical use of obscenity', to refer to President X and Governor Y as 'pig X' and 'pig Y' and to address them as mother-fuckers because they have

'perpetrated the unspeakable Oedipal crime', to take drug-trips to escape 'the ego shaped by the established society' and to seize every opportunity for social sabotage? . . . [A few days ago] came the news of two Hollywood murder cases in which the multiple killer scrawled 'death to pigs' in blood on refrigerator doors. At the time I write this, the killer is still at large, so there is no way of knowing whether he has been influenced by Marcuse, or is an illiterate psychotic who detests bacon.

In fact, there is no evidence that Manson had ever read Marcuse, or even heard of him, although two of the girls charged with him were college graduates, one an ex-librarian.

Although Manson lacked the savagery and drive – and perhaps the exhibitionism – of Netchaev, the key to his personality certainly lay in dominance and self-esteem.

And this is, perhaps, the place to reiterate the point that Shaw made in discussing the explorer Stanley and his discovery of the dominant five per cent: that although one person in every twenty may be dominant, a Julius Caesar, a Shakespeare, a Leonardo, is born only once in ten generations. The dominant five per cent is not composed entirely of geniuses and leaders; it includes businessmen, politicians, ministers of religion, pop singers, army officers, professors, protest marchers, members of women's lib . . . The men of genius are probably 0·005 per cent of the five per cent. Genuine leaders are less rare; but they still constitute a very small proportion of the five per cent. Manson, Netchaev, Brady, belonged to this small proportion.

According to the *Los Angeles Times*, Manson's mother was a teenage prostitute. Manson himself later denied this: 'They call her a whore, a prostitute, but that's not true. She was what the flower children were . . .' But he confirmed that his mother became pregnant at fifteen, by a boyfriend of seventeen. His mother went to prison shortly after he was born; Manson moved from home to home, living mostly with an aunt and uncle in Charleston, West Virginia. He was sent to his first reform school at the age of nine – in 1943 – and was there for a year. He was later in the Federal Reformatory at Chilicothe, Ohio. He hated all the schools; he ran away repeatedly – twenty-seven times from one of them. An Indianapolis newspaper printed a photograph of Manson in 1949

– looking very young and neatly dressed – and a story saying that he was being taken from a 'sinful home' – presumably his mother's – and sent to a local 'Boy's Town'; he stayed there three days. He later talked bitterly about the bullying that went on in these schools – by the authorities as well as other boys. 'You had to be a tough guy. They have to know how tough you are. It's like in here [prison] – *they're* the ones that are scared, the cops.' What is abundantly clear, even from the most hostile accounts of Manson's childhood and teens, is that society was treating him the wrong way. He was intelligent, basically affectionate, but also dominant; from the beginning, he had the feeling that he had to fight, to hold his own against a world that had no use for him and no interest in him. A parole officer later said: 'Charlie was the most hostile parolee I've ever come across.' He was in the reformatory until he was twenty (in 1955). He then married a seventeen-year-old girl named Rosalie, and drove with her in a stolen car to Los Angeles sometime in mid-1955. In March 1956, a son was born; a month later, Manson was sent to prison for three years for car theft. Rosalie divorced him. He was out of jail in October 1958, but after only twenty months of freedom, was back again on a ten-year sentence – this time for a number of offences including car theft, cheque fraud, stealing credit cards, and transporting girls over a state line for immoral purposes. It was during this period, according to Ed Sanders (in his book *The Family**), that Manson began to study magic and hypnotism, and learned to play the guitar from the famous gangster 'Creepy' Karpis. He also became enthusiastic about a science fiction novel called *Stranger in a Strange Land* by Robert Heinlein, which is basically a piece of satirical social criticism. Its hero, Valentine Michael Smith, is a man from Mars, who finds earth and its weird customs totally alien and frightening. He founds a religious cult whose rituals include cannibalism and free love. One of his disciples explains: 'If Mike can show us a better way to run this fouled-up planet, his sex life needs no vindication. Geniuses are justifiably contemptuous of lesser opinion and are always indifferent to the sexual customs of the tribe . . .' Manson apparently found the Messianic Martian so exhilarating that he later named one of his illegitimate children Valentine Michael Manson.

* Rupert Hart-Davies, London, 1972.

Released from prison again in 1967, at the age of thirty-two, Manson drifted to San Francisco. He later admitted: 'I was frightened. I didn't know where to go. I didn't want to leave jail, but they insisted and gave me back my $35 and a suitcase filled with old clothes. For several days I just rode around on buses. I slept on the bus, and drivers woke me when we reached the end of somewhere.' He found his way to the Haight-Ashbury district, San Francisco's equivalent of Soho or Greenwich Village.

In 1966, I had walked down Haight Street with the poet Kenneth Rexroth – the father figure of the 'beat generation'. It struck me as being very much like Soho, except that the flower children were more flamboyant than their London counterparts. Rexroth had been the first critic to describe and analyse the 'beat generation' – which came to prominence in 1957, with the publication of Jack Kerouac's book *On the Road*. But it was Kerouac's next book *The Dharma Bums*, that made clear the affinities of the new type of 'bohemian'. I gathered from various hippies that my own book *The Outsider* (1956) also played its part in creating the ideology of the beats, particularly the chapter analysing the work of Hermann Hesse. Hesse was, at this time, almost unknown in the English speaking world, and the few translations of his books had been out of print for a long time. By 1967, reprints of *Steppenwolf, Siddartha, Demian,* had joined *The Dharma Bums* and Ginsberg's *Howl* as basic texts of this generation. The leaning towards Taoism, Zen Buddhism and Hinduism was strong.

This was, in fact, a revival of nineteenth-century romanticism. What lay behind it went deeper than laziness or the desire to opt out of a materialistic society. Hesse's novels are mostly about heroes who become 'wanderers', seekers after salvation, and they are full of nostalgic longing for the peace of monasteries and the life of religious communities. One of the most unexpected best-sellers of post-war years was Thomas Merton's *Seven Storey Mountain* (1948), describing Merton's increasing dissatisfaction with modern life until he decided to become a Trappist monk. It was not simply the increasing exhausting tempo of our society that was being condemned; there was also a feeling that something important was being *missed*. Kerouac found this missing vitamin in jazz rather than in literature, for the basic jazz legend is also tragic and romantic: the great artist who becomes an alcoholic or drug addict because the world is a dreary, murderous place, but who leaves behind a life-affirming perfection on gramophone records. But what they are affirming is their inner life, the soul's innocence and vitality; what they are mourning is their total failure to find any counterpart of this vision in the actual world. Kerouac's heroes were Charlie Parker, Lester Young, Billie Holiday; by the time Manson came along, it would be Bob Dylan, Pete Seegar, the Beatles.

The 'beat revolt' might have faded as quickly as its English counterpart, the 'Angry Young Man' movement, if it had not been for the discovery of psychedelic drugs. Kerouac had smoked marijuana, and described its effects in *On the Road*, the total relaxation, the feeling that time has stopped. But mescalin and LSD (discovered in Basle in 1948) could produce visions, create strange patterns of colour or intensify perception until every object seemed to *exist more*, to stand out from its background. Aldous Huxley said that the effect of mescalin was to make him aware of the 'is-ness' of things, and advocated that it should be sold as openly as tobacco or alcohol. I had reservations about psychedelics, and these were confirmed in 1963 when I took mescalin. What it did was to remove the usual 'filters' from perception, as if you were to play a gramophone record at top volume, with all the tone controls turned up to maximum. But the filters are there to aid the mind's work of grasping and ordering reality – the kind of ordering that, at its best, produces great art – or philosophy. Mescalin simultaneously weakens the will, the mind's 'ordering power' and strengthens the incoming stimuli. The immediate result is intensified perception of meaning.

But it should also be recognized that our constant relation with the world is a *will*-relation. When something upsets me, I 'retreat', I withdraw; when something delights me, I advance. *Everything* that happens to me during my waking life causes small advances and retreats, almost as if my skin were the skin of a balloon, which swells or contracts according to the outer pressure. But there is an important difference; whatever the outer pressure, it is *I* who decides whether to expand or contract. A jazz trumpeter who suddenly begins to play superbly, a boxer who suddenly turns into the perfect fighting machine, even a philosopher who begins to think with magnificent clarity – all these are *in control* to a degree we rarely achieve. And it is this control, this power of expanding and driving forward, that constitutes real greatness in human beings.

Psychedelics weaken this element of control. So, of course, does alcohol. Even music and poetry can have the same effect; (the theme of Mann's *Buddenbrooks*, for example, is the decline of a commercial family once it begins to produce artistic types.) It is a question of maintaining a balance, of retaining control. But the psychedelic philosophy propagated by Timothy Leary flatly denied the need for any such control. The ultimate aim was self-abandonment, 'to escape the ego shaped by established society'; you might say the prize went to whoever could abandon and forget himself most completely. Alan Watts, another powerful influence on the 'flower generation', declared that man's basic trouble is his aggressiveness towards his environment, his desire to impose his will on everything; he speaks about space rockets being enormous erect penises pointing at the sky. Man should learn that he is a part of nature, says Watts, like the clouds or trees; he should learn to blend into his universe, stop *willing* so much . . . And perhaps this explains why the whole experiment in love and self-abandonment was petering out by the late sixties. Kerouac was dead, his talent destroyed by manic drinking sessions. The drug peddlers in Haight-Ashbury became professional racketeers, who ended by throwing out the hippies. Manson and his disciples moved out to Death Valley.

But when Manson came to Haight-Ashbury in 1967, it looked as if the flower culture had come to stay. The hippies had occasional clashes with police, but they had come to a kind of working agreement by which they agreed not to obstruct traffic so long as they were left alone.

It is understandable that all this should have hit Manson as a revelation. He had spent his life being slapped and kicked around – taught that you either joined society as a hard-working, fully paid-up member, or declared yourself a bum and took the consequences. To discover a whole *way of life* that allowed maximum freedom must have seemed an impossible piece of luck, rather like Rousseau discovering that his community of 'noble savages' actually existed in some remote Swiss valley. Here was not only immediate acceptance by a community that didn't care about his past; it was also a field for the operation of his natural dominance.

It must be borne in mind that although Manson was thirty-three years old, in another sense he was a teenager. He had spent practically all his adult life behind bars or in reformatories. According to Manson, when he came out of jail at the age of twenty-one, 'I'd never been with a woman, never made love to one in my life. I'd never had a drink of beer.' And his period of freedom was short. In a sense, then, he was learning to live for the first time when he came to Haight-Ashbury.

It must also be recognized that the majority of hippies, like the majority of any other group, do not belong to the dominant five per cent. They are not Nietzschean free spirits, living like characters out of *La Bohème,* roaring with laughter as they burn their manuscripts to keep warm. Most of them are little more than mirrors that reflect their environment; their minds are full of one another's doings, ('Where's Tex today?' 'Didn'tcha hear, he got busted . . .') The Beatles, hippie slang, Vietnam protest, Tom and Jerry cartoons, *Easy Rider*. Kerouac's later books (*Big Sur, Desolation Angels*) are a free-associating jumble of basic hippie preoccupations. Tom Wolfe's *Electric Kool-Acid Test,* an attempt to catch the hippie life-style in straight reportage, ends by producing a sense of bewilderment and sheer futility. But above all, of the basic mediocrity of most of these drop-outs.

It was inevitable that Manson should soon become an important character among San Francisco's hippies, and also that he should make up for years of lost sexual opportunity. His view of women was definitely Nietzschean. ('Goest thou to woman? Don't forget thy whip . . .') A girl who had hitchhiked across the country with him described how Manson ordered her to carry both rucksacks, and when she refused, made her walk several paces behind him. After his arrest, this kind of story was cited by newspapers to prove Manson's paranoid tendencies, but this is hardly fair: it is like accusing Casanova of spending his life trying to prove his masculinity. Manson's dominance, like his gentleness and persuasiveness, was a natural part of his personality.

On first moving to San Francisco, Manson stayed with friends in Berkeley. There he met a girl named Mary Brunner, with whom he 'shacked up'. (She was later described as 'his favourite wife'.) In Venice, California, he found a girl named Lynn Fromme crying by the kerbside – she had been thrown out of home after a quarrel; she also joined the Manson menage, which now moved to the Haight district. There he continued to collect runaways; the place seemed to be full of girls who were emotionally deprived, obsessed with the need to be loved, looking for a father figure. One of these was Susan Atkins. 'Self-confidence, that's what Charlie did for me,' she explained. 'He gave my faith in myself back to me.' The *Life* magazine portrait of Manson as manic messiah, the wild-eyed seducer, seems to have no basis in fact. On the contrary, his extraordinary influence was due to his 'Christ-like' appearance and personality. He was small and unformidable, played the guitar and sang protest songs in the manner of Bob Dylan, and had a sympathetic and affectionate manner. He had obviously suffered, and looked as though he had. (Many of the photographs catch this sad-eyed look, the man of sorrows on his way to Calvary.) He was interested in mysticism, scientology and magic; he was full of deep convictions about the rottenness of society and the need for a revolution. If he had not read Marcuse, this is only another proof of the extent to which he had become a vessel for the *zeitgeist*. Marcuse argues that technical civilization *ought* to mean more leisure for everyone; instead, it has produced 'the repressive society'. In *Eros and Civilization* (1951) he asserts that our sexuality has become sick. Sex ought to produce 'unrepressive sublimation', an unfolding of our higher human possibilities; instead of that, it has become commercialized, and becomes another instrument of repression by the people who run society. His *One Dimensional Man* (1964) continues the argument, and makes the startling assertion that modern democratic societies – America in particular – are really as totalitarian and repressive as Stalin's Russia or Hitler's Germany. Marcuse has been violently attacked for emotionalism and woolly thinking; but in order to do justice to his thought, he must be seen as a poetic idealist, a kind of twentieth-century Rousseau, with a strong imaginative vision of how delightful society *could* be if it could be cured of its materialism.

Manson instinctively practised the 'unrepressive sublimation' advocated in *Eros and Civilization*; he taught a kind of D. H. Lawrentian vision of sex as total release, a religious communion. Susan Atkins' 'Confession' describes going to Manson's room for the first time. 'I want to make love to you – with you,' he said. He then told her to take off her clothes and to look at herself naked in a full-length mirror. 'Look how beautiful you are . . . Look, you're perfect.' She adds: 'And while he was making love with me he told me to imagine I was making love with my father to get me through that particular hang-up.' (Earlier she mentions that her father wanted to have an affair with her – after her mother's death – and that she would have been perfectly willing.) Manson understood that most girls want a father figure; this explains his remarkable success. 'I really felt privileged walking with Charlie because all the girls in the house I was sharing were just in love with him . . .' His peculiar charm and gentleness worked with men as well as with girls – he is quoted as saying that he had 3,000 friends.

By October 1967, Manson had had enough of Haight-Ashbury. Ever since leaving jail, his chief obsession had been the idea of breaking into the field of pop music; he was convinced he could become as famous as the Beatles or Bob Dylan. He traded a grand piano (a present from a friend) for a Volkswagen bus, and later changed this for an old yellow school bus. In October, the 'family' moved south; after a trip through Nevada, New Mexico and Alabama, they returned to Los Angeles, and rented a place near Malibu. Manson began to play his guitar in a Topanga Canyon club known as the Spiral Staircase. It was there that Manson met a twenty-year-old musician named Bobby Beausoleil. Beausoleil was a student of magic and an admirer of Aleister Crowley; he had played the role of Lucifer in the film *Lucifer Rising*, made by the 'undergound' film maker, Kenneth Anger. Manson and Beausoleil discussed how to break into the field of pop music, and Beausoleil introduced Manson to another musician and music teacher, Gary Hinman, who owned a house in Topanga Canyon. When Manson was evicted from the Malibu place in February 1968, Beausoleil suggested they might move in with him in a small house he shared with a girlfriend in Horseshoe Lane, Topanga. He was shocked when the crowded school bus arrived. 'I didn't expect that many people.' The family camped on the hillside behind the house. It now included thirteen-year-old Didi Lansbury, daughter of the film actress Angela Lansbury, and a fourteen-year-old named Diana Lake, nicknamed The Snake – according to Ed Sanders, 'in tribute to the transverse ophidian wiggles she made during intercourse'. They stayed there for six weeks. Bobby Beausoleil had decided to leave before that; he did not see Manson for several months.

In March, the family moved to a house on the other side of the canyon. Mary Brunner's baby, Valentine Michael, was born in April; the family delivered the baby. At this time there were about sixteen girls in the group, and four men; these included Bruce Davis, a disciple Manson had encountered on a trip through Oregon, and Phil Kaufman, a friend from prison days. Sandy Good, the daughter of a wealthy stockbroker, also became one of Manson's mistresses at this time. It was she who told Manson about a ranch owned by a man named George Spahn – eighty years old and almost blind – situated at Chatsworth, thirty miles from the centre of Los Angeles. In May, Manson and the family went to look at the Spahn movie ranch (so called because it had once belonged to the cowboy star William S. Hart and had been used in film sets); it was now a riding stable, and there was some vague suggestion that the family might take it over, in exchange for running the stable. On this occasion, they stayed for only a few days.

It was after this visit that Manson's luck seemed to improve suddenly. He somehow became acquainted with Dennis Wilson, the drummer of an immensely successful pop group, the Beach Boys. Wilson actually allowed the family – now numbering about twenty-five – to move into his luxury home on Sunset Boulevard. Manson was taken to parties and met film stars. (Many were on drugs, and it is possible that Manson did some 'pushing'.) When Beausoleil returned to Los Angeles, he met Manson in a supermarket, and was invited back to swim in Dennis Wilson's swimming pool.

It was also at the Sunset Boulevard house that Manson met a well-dressed young college dropout named Charles Watson, who owned a wig shop, and seemed set for a respectable middle-class career. It may have been Manson's girls who converted him to the hippie way of life, or it may have been admiration for Manson; at all events, he became another of the regular male disciples.

Manson met Terry Melcher, son of the film star Doris Day, who was in the record business, and there was talk of a $20,000 contract. Manson also sold two of his songs to the Beach Boys for $5,000 – at least, according to his own account. (He was angry they changed his title 'Cease to Exist' to 'Cease to Resist'.) Manson also recorded some of his own songs in the studio of Dennis Wilson's brother.

When the family had to move out of the Sunset Boulevard house – leaving it barer than when they arrived – they stayed for a while at the house of Gary Hinman in Topanga Canyon. In August, the family moved back to the Spahn ranch, and persuaded George Spahn to allow them to take care of the stables in exchange for accommodation (in 'outlaw shack' at the back of the ranch). For a few months it seems to have been an ideal situation, a realization of the Haight-Ashbury dream of perfect harmony. One girl who lived there for a time said of Manson 'He was very beautiful in many ways and gave out lots of love.' It began to be spoiled by the sheer number of hippies who came to share the fun, and Manson began to get 'uptight' about some of these new arrivals. Someone brought venereal disease to the ranch, and it spread so fast that Manson had to call in a doctor to stamp it out. (Manson always accused Susan Atkins of being the carrier.) Much of their spare time was spent 'jamming' with drums and guitar – with pot or psychedelics to create a mood – and Manson continued to dream of fame as a singer and composer. (His former prison friend Phil Kaufman arranged three recording sessions during this period, but Manson was becoming increasingly disillusioned about the commercial side of the business.) Manson disliked Negro jazz, and Jimi Hendrix records were banned. Books were also banned, although Manson liked to have his girls reading aloud from Hermann Hesse's *Siddartha.*

There were more spectacular successes for Manson at this period. The owner of a ranch behind the Spahn ranch, Richard Kaplan, was persuaded to give it to the family in exchange for a painted tent. (Kaplan was under the influence of a drug at the time.) A female schoolteacher who gave a lift to members of the family and returned to the ranch was so enslaved by Manson that she gave him her savings – $11,000.

Not far from the ranch there was the headquarters of a

religious cult called The Fountain of the World; its founder, Krishna Venta, had been blown up by dynamite, probably by a disgruntled follower, in 1958. Manson attended many of the Fountain's ceremonies, and it may have been these that inspired him to hold a sort of symbolic crucifixion ceremony in a glade near the ranch; Manson was strapped to a cross, and the crucifixion scene was enacted like a morality play – except that it ended with ritual sex.

There seems to be no doubt that Manson was becoming increasingly obsessive, increasingly embittered, during the three months at the Spahn ranch. He wanted to retreat further away from civilization. One of his followers told him about Death Valley, the national park on the other side of the Mojave desert, three hundred miles away. In October 1968, the family drove their bus across the desert, abandoned it when the brakes burned out, and finally arrived at the derelict Barker Ranch. Here they established themselves, in the sun-baked solitude. Manson now dreamed of an even remoter retreat from the world; he heard of a legend about a great underground hole from which the Hopi Indians emerged, and he decided that this hole was somewhere under Death Valley; according to Ed Sanders, he actually went looking for his hole, perhaps hoping to use it as a vast air raid shelter when the Bomb dropped. He was convinced that civilization would destroy itself.

In November 1968, Dennis Wilson and a friend drove to Death Valley to collect a jeep Manson had borrowed, and they took Manson back with them to Los Angeles. He returned the following January. But the winter cold made them decide to return to civilization. In February, Manson rented a house in Gresham Street, Canoga Park, in Los Angeles. Manson's next door neighbour told a reporter: 'We were on very good terms, but he was very opinionated, and very anti-establishment ... His whole thing [philosophy] was that sooner or later everyone would kill each other off'. It seemed obvious to Manson that in a world with so much hatred, mass killing of blacks by whites would break out sooner or later. He was very fond of quoting the Bible, said his neighbour; (it is, after all, the only book available in many prisons). The Book of Revelation, with its prophecies of doom, appealed particularly. Manson presided over his family of women – ranging in age from thirteen to nineteen

– like some Jewish patriarch. 'They seemed quite happy. They were not being held against their will. On many occasions they said they would give their lives for Charlie . . .' There were also some children. 'Charlie blew up when anyone tried to punish children. He got real mad when the kids in his family tried to spank their kids . . .' The girls stole food from supermarkets. Patricia Krenwinkel, who joined the group at this time, had the job of foraging in waste bins behind stores. (In her court testimony, she also described a 'long idyll' with Manson, when they travelled up and down the California coast, living in woods. 'We were like wood nymphs . . . we would run through the woods with flowers in our hair, and Charlie would play a little pipe.')

But a fourteen-year-old boy who ran away from home and joined the family for a short period soon left, declaring that all Manson wanted was servants. There is undoubtedly an element of truth in this; any born leader wants followers. On the other hand, the reporter of the *National Tatler* who declared; 'It's obvious that Charlie Manson had an enormous sexual appetite and that this was the chief reason he tempted young girls to enter his cult' was completely missing the point. Manson did not need to be a Rasputin or Svengali-figure to get young girls; the girls came to him because he was a father-figure offering love and protection. The same reporter describes Manson as a 'harem keeper [who] treated his women as underlings' out of a neurotic mother-hatred. But Susan Atkins described the attitude of the family towards Manson. 'Man is man. He is the king, and I am his queen. And the queen does what the king says. This is the right way. Charlie is man. The king? Look at his name, Manson. "Man's son" . . . And now I have visible proof of God, the proof the church never gave me. There are reflections all around me. Charlie has brought me this truth.' But in spite of this adoration, Susan Atkins was the one female member of the family who gave Manson any trouble; she felt impelled to defy him on several occasions, although she usually came to heel when challenged.

Manson was becoming increasingly obsessed with the idea of universal destruction. A new Beatles album contained a song called 'Helter Skelter'; Manson, apparently unaware that this is a spiral slide down which children swoop on doormats, decided that it should be the code name for the great day of reckoning, when the Pigs would be slaughtered. (There was another Beatles song called 'Piggies' on the same album.) It is tempting to believe that Manson began to go insane at this period, although there is no definite evidence to support it. It is possible that psychedelic trips made him unable to distinguish between dream and reality. He began to keep a death list of people who would have to die when the time came; it included various film stars – Warren Beatty and Julie Christie among them – and Terry Melcher. Also on the list – which ran to eleven names – were various disciples who had defected. One of these was Paul Watkins, who had heard about Manson's family in 1968, and called on him in Topanga Canyon. 'When I walked in I was knocked off my feet by six naked girls . . . His first words to me were "Take any of these girls. They're all yours".[2] Understandably, the sixteen-year-old Watkins moved in. Watkins also mentioned Manson's love of animals, and said that Manson had some 'weird power over animals'. They came upon a rattlesnake when walking in the desert. 'Charlie told me not to be afraid of it, and to sit in front of it. I did just that. I must have been crazy, but that's the kind of effect he had on me. Anyway the damn thing rattled a few times while I nearly died of fright, then it scuttled away. It was only a coincidence, but at that time I believed Charlie had some weird power . . .' (He seems to have been unaware that snakes, given a chance, will avoid an encounter.) And during this final year – from August 1968 to August 1969 – Manson seems to have cultivated this belief in his magical powers among his followers. Patricia Krenwinkel asserted that she had seen him change a man into a skeleton – obviously a psychedelic hallucination. She also declared that 'thirty or forty times Manson made old people regain their youth. But the effect did not last because they did not have faith in the miracle.' A legend about the Canoga period – mentioned by Sanders – declares that a girl named Bo was on her knees sucking Manson's penis when, in a burst of enthusiasm, she bit it in half; Manson miraculously healed himself immediately. Patricia Krenwinkel also seems to suggest that she saw him as a Christ figure: 'All he ever does is to give, and if you watched him you could see the love he suggests with everything he does – with his motions, with his infinite gentleness.' And this infinitely gentle guru was thinking out a plan for starting the great

Revolution: to get his followers to commit a series of murders, which the whites would blame on the Black Panthers – so the slaughter would begin.

According to Sanders, it was during the Canoga Park period that Manson began to cultivate the acquaintance of members of motor cycle gangs, although it is not clear whether he hoped to make use of them when 'Helter Skelter' arrived. His method of assuring their loyalty was to order his girls to strip off their clothes and 'blow' them – kneel and perform an act of fellatio. One of the motor cyclists, Danny De Carlo, gained the nickname Donkey Dick Dan, due to his unusual endowment.

It is curious that Manson seemed to be colour prejudiced. When a motor-cyclist brought a half-Indian male to the house, Manson refused to allow the guest to 'make it' with the girls.

The family now began full scale preparations for Helter Skelter. They purchased guns and knives, and began acquiring 'dune buggies' – cars or jeeps that would run in the desert. Manson paid for one of these with a forged cheque: another was bought with money stolen by Linda Kasabian. They bought detailed maps of the Death Valley area.

It is difficult to tell how serious all this was supposed to be. Manson was not a hard-headed realist, brooding on the future; he was a kind of sleepwalker, a fantasist whose wild leaps into the irrational often paid off. The adoration of his family gave him the sensation of being infallible; the pot and LSD kept them all in a semi-dream world. What had happened to Manson resembles, on a smaller scale, what happened to Hitler. He acted according to a kind of inner inspiration that ought to have brought a head-on clash with reality followed by disaster; instead, everything he did seemed to come out right. People gave him money and cars and even ranches; his followers trusted him completely and never seemed to come to any serious harm. His success story seemed a proof that what the world needs is inspiration, not calculation. There can be no doubt that, if it had not been for the murders, Manson *would* have ended up as an enormous success in the world of folk music or underground films; the sleepwalking technique would have paid off. The talk about murder and bloody revolution may have been part of a creative fantasy – his own way of writing *The War of the Worlds,* so to speak.

This seems to be borne out by the increasingly wild and confused scene when the family returned to the Spahn ranch, sometime around March or April 1969. The motorcycle gangs were constant visitors. (One was called Satan's Slaves, the name that was later – mistakenly – stuck on the family.) Some of these were associated with 'black magic' groups in the Los Angeles area. All kinds of people turned up at the ranch and slept on mattresses; Sanders quotes one film starlet as complaining that the moment she arrived, someone dragged her into the bushes and raped her. (Since she continued to come, she presumably had no real objection.) Manson continued to negotiate with Terry Melcher and Dennis Wilson about recording contracts, and some songs were actually recorded. Melcher, Wilson and another associate called Gregg Jakobsen seriously considered making a movie about the family. The immense success of low budget films like *Easy Rider* made it a real possibility. Melcher's idea was a film that would capture the gentle, love-pervaded atmosphere of the ranch, with mothers breast feeding their babies, hippies crooning to guitars and Manson sermonizing on universal love. (This *was* the impression most people had of the commune.) Manson wanted something with a more violent impact, conveying some of the ideas of Helter Skelter, with black magic and murder thrown in for good measure; he probably had a keener nose for what the public wanted.

The family income seems to have been large but irregular. Manson was undoubtedly a dope trader. Quantities of stolen goods passed through the ranch, including an NBC Television truck with thousands of dollars' worth of filming equipment. At one point there was a scheme to get the girls to work as topless showgirls in Los Angeles, but this was abandoned when they found that they would need silicone injections to enlarge their breasts. Sanders says that Manson was considering turning some of the girls into prostitutes.

There was considerable police harassment at various times. A seventeen-year-old girl who was taken to the ranch complained that Manson raped her in a car, and he spent a few days in jail before being released on bail. Manson apparently provoked the police by deliberately driving at ninety miles an hour when he passed a police car, and spent three days in jail for this. Then there were various questions of auto thefts, forged cheques and stolen credit cards. The police pressed George Spahn to get rid of the hippies, but he apparently liked being surrounded by girls.

As the summer wore on, there is evidence that Manson's fantasies of violence were becoming more frequent. One male follower later declared that Manson asked him if he would be willing to commit a murder in exchange for money; he finally decided against it. Another described how Manson would park outside middle-class homes, and suggest that they went in and slaughtered everyone. But then, Manson was a 'manipulator'. A small, lightly-built man, surrounded by beefy hippies, many of whom were capable of violence, he may have used the talk of violence and suggestions of murder as a weapon for dominance.

In early July the game began to turn into reality. A Negro dope-dealer named Bernard Crowe became violently angry when Tex Watson vanished with $2,400 of his money and failed to deliver pot to that value. He called at the home of another family associate who had been mixed up in the deal – Rosina Kroner – and talked about killing somebody. Miss Kroner rang Manson, who drove to her house, together with a disciple called T.J. the Terrible. Manson was carrying a wild-Western type revolver. Crowe told Manson that he had no quarrel with him, but wanted his money back. Manson – probably high – performed some kind of dance, then pointed the revolver at Crowe's stomach and pulled the trigger. There was a click, and Manson laughed; it looked like another of his dominance games. He pulled the trigger again; this time the gun fired, and Crowe collapsed with a bullet in his torso. Manson told another of the men present that he liked his leather shirt, and the man hastened to remove it and give it to him. Then Manson and T.J. the Terrible drove back to the Spahn ranch. Both were convinced that Crowe was dead. At one point on the drive, Manson told T.J. he didn't like the way T.J. was looking at him, because it made him question himself ... In fact, Crowe was not dead; he was taken to hospital, and there was an unsuccessful operation to remove the bullet; he left hospital – with the bullet still in him – about two weeks later. No one seems to have pressed the matter; presumably Crowe decided that he would prefer not to be associated with the police.

Why did Manson do this? It brings to mind the two Kray

murders – of George Cornell and Jack McVitie – committed as a sort of 'dare'. Manson was leader; he had to prove it, even though it threw the rest of the family into a panic. It was a question of asserting dominance.

As the days passed, and no police – or Black Panthers – turned up to avenge Crowe, the panic died; no doubt it seemed a further proof that whatever Charlie did came out right.

A few days later, the girl called Gypsy called on an acquaintance, Charles Melton, in Topanga Canyon, and there met a young New Englander, Linda Kasabian, who had a sixteen-month-old baby. Gypsy told Linda about the Spahn ranch, where children were given all the love they needed and everyone shared their possessions. Linda returned to the ranch, and had soon – according to her own account – made love with just about every male in the place, and a few females too. (She was soon pregnant again, by Bobby Beausoleil.) An orgasm with Tex Watson was so violent that she regarded it as a mystic experience. She also mentioned to Watson that her friend and late host, Charles Melton, had money in his trailer; the next day, they returned for her belongings, and left with $5,000 of Melton's money, which was given to Manson. When Melton arrived in search of his money, Manson got rid of him by a method he had used before. He told Melton that if he had any quarrel with the family, he was welcome to kill him – Charlie; with which he handed Melton a knife. Melton said he didn't want to kill him. In that case, said Manson, perhaps he should kill Melton, to prove that there is no such thing as death ... Melton decided that argument was useless, and left hastily. More dune buggies were bought with some of the money.

Life at the ranch was never boring. The police came in and out, looking for stolen cars. On 20th July, Manson flew into such a rage that everyone fled; he beat Gypsy, and smashed everything that came to hand. But not long after this, the family held an orgy. A fifteen-year-old girl who helped with the horses was tied down, and ceremonially deflowered by Beausoleil, after which the watching couples plunged into a love-in; Linda Kasabian made up a threesome with Tex Watson and Leslie Van Houten.

A few days later, the slaughter began. On 25th July, Manson sent Bobby Beausoleil to Gary Hinman's house to ask him for $20,000 to finance the move to Death Valley. Relations with Hinman had been deteriorating for some time. Hinman had become a convert to a Japanese sect called Nichiren Shoshu Buddhism and was eager for converts. A friend of Hinman's – who helped him in the manufacture of mescalin – overheard a telephone argument with Manson during which Hinman categorically refused to sell everything he had and join the family. The argument also seemed to be about the question of leadership; Hinman was convinced people needed leading to salvation; Manson – oddly enough – argued that they should be allowed to do what they liked. It was a few days after this that Manson ordered one of the female members of the sect to go and kill Hinman – according to Sanders; but she refused, and left the ranch with her boyfriend. So Manson persuaded Beausoleil – who was thinking of leaving the ranch – to call on Hinman and try to persuade him to join in the Death Valley exodus. Beausoleil drove over to Hinman's house, together with Susan Atkins and Mary Brunner. They arrived at midnight. Beausoleil explained their scheme, but Hinman was not interested; he was about to leave on a religious pilgrimage to Japan. After a long argument, Beausoleil produced a gun, and told Hinman that he intended to search the house for money – they were convinced that Hinman had $20,000 hidden away. Susan Atkins was left holding the gun; Hinman made a grab for it and it went off; but no one was hurt. Beausoleil came in and grabbed the gun; he gave Hinman a blow on the head with it, which caused bleeding. With Hinman again held at gunpoint, Beausoleil rang Manson at the ranch, and told him that Hinman was being difficult. Whereupon Manson drove over with Bruce Davis. Manson was waving a sword which he seemed to regard as some kind of magical emblem or symbol of power. Manson told Hinman he was determined to have the money; Hinman, in a rage, told him to get out. Whereupon Manson raised the sword and slashed at Hinman's face, cutting deep into the jaw, and half-severing the ear. There was a struggle, in the course of which Manson cut his hand. After this, Manson and Bruce Davis left. Mary Brunner sewed up Hinman's wound, and Beausoleil continued his search.

It was now clear to Beausoleil that Hinman had to be killed – preferably after telling them where he kept the money. (But a police search of the house later revealed that Hinman was telling the truth – there was no money.) Hinman was kept in the house throughout the following day. A couple of people who phoned him were told that his parents had been involved in an accident and he had been called away.

It seems possible that Hinman was tortured, or at least beaten, during the day he spent as a prisoner. Finally Beausoleil rang Manson again, and Manson, according to Beausoleil, told him to kill Hinman. Hinman was forced to sign documents claiming that the ownership of a Volkswagen bus and a Fiat car had passed to Beausoleil. After this, he was stabbed twice in the chest and left; he died of loss of blood. On the wall over his body, Beausoleil wrote 'Political Piggy' in blood, and drew a sign that was supposed to be a panther's paw – the idea being to mislead police into believing that Black Panthers were responsible for the murder.

One of the witnesses, Danny De Carlo, described how Beausoleil came back on the night of the murder, and told him he had tortured Hinman before stabbing him.

With the murder of Hinman, Manson's luck began to turn. Just over a week later, on 6th August, a patrolman saw the Fiat sports car near San Luis Obispo, and checked on the driver. It was Bobby Beausoleil, and he showed the policeman the ownership document signed by Gary Hinman. The decomposing body had been found a week earlier. Beausoleil's story was that he had bought the car from a Negro for $200, which seemed possible – Black Panthers were suspected of the murder. On 7th August, Beausoleil rang the Spahn ranch from the police station; he wanted to talk to Manson. But Manson was in Oceanside, where he was getting a traffic ticket. He came back later to hear the news of Beausoleil's arrest. At the trial, Patricia Krenwinkel asserted that it was at this point that they planned another murder, that of Terry Melcher, with the idea of throwing the blame for the Hinman murder on Melcher. It was not clear how this was to be done; but they were all on LSD at the time, so perhaps the connection was not clear to them either.

The bad luck continued. The police made a swoop on the Spahn ranch, looking for drugs and stolen cars. They found Manson seated in a dune buggy. When they asked him what he was doing Manson explained that he was on guard, looking out for Black Panthers, who were expected to attack the ranch. When the police announced their intention of searching the ranch, Manson solemnly warned them against it. His followers, he said, were armed to the teeth, and might mistake the police for Black Panthers. He should be allowed to go first and prepare the way ... The police let him go ahead; assorted hippies fled out of the rear of the ranch, and the raid was a flop.

It was during the next fortnight that Manson took another trip to Death Valley, and also to the Esalen Institute at Big Sur Hot Springs (where weekend courses and group therapy are held). On the trip, Manson picked up another follower, a seventeen-year-old pregnant girl named Stephanie. While Manson was absent, Beausoleil took the opportunity to leave the ranch. Another young girl, Kitty Lutesinger, also took the opportunity to flee. By this time it was not easy to escape from Manson's ambience; he felt – rightly – that too many of his followers knew too much.

Two days after Beausoleil's arrest, Mary Brunner was arrested for trying to use a stolen credit card. Sandy Good was with her. Their car was found to contain many more credit cards.

When Manson returned to the ranch with Susan Atkins, he heard the various items of bad news, and declared; 'Now is the time for Helter Skelter.'

This raises the question of whether the murders that took place that night were intended as the beginning of the great war against the 'pigs', or were merely part of a plan to get Beausoleil freed. Susan Atkins later testified that they had the idea of committing a 'copycat' murder, that would appear to be by the same killer as the Hinman stabbing. This latter was probably the immediate motive. But there can be no doubt that everybody at the ranch had an 'end of the world' feeling at the time, and Manson's response to being pushed was to erupt into hysterical violence. It is another characteristic in which he resembles Hitler.

The house that had been selected as the murder site was at 10050 Cielo Drive, Benedict Canyon. Terry Melcher had been there until the previous February, then moved out; after this, it was let to the Polish film director Roman Polanski, famous for films like *Repulsion* and *Rosemary's Baby*, and his wife Sharon Tate, the star of *Valley of the Dolls*. Sharon Tate was eight and a half months pregnant.

On the evening of Friday, 8th August, 1969, Sharon Tate had three guests to supper: an ex-lover, Jay Sebring, a men's hair stylist; Voityck Frykowski, a Polish writer and friend of her husband, and Abigail Folger, a coffee heiress, Frykowski's mistress. Both Sebring and Frykowski used drugs. Roman Polanski was in London, working on a film.

It has been argued by Manson supporters that he may have been unaware that Tex Watson intended to lead a murder party that night; but this is unlikely. Manson told Stephanie, the seventeen-year-old girl he had picked up, to sleep in a trailer and wait until he came. Then he ordered Susan Atkins to get a change of clothes. Patricia Krenwinkel – who had been on an LSD trip – was awakened and ordered to get dressed. Some time before midnight, the Ford containing Tex Watson and three girls – Susan Atkins, Patricia Krenwinkel and Linda Kasabian – left the Spahn ranch. About 12.15, it pulled up near the house in Benedict Canyon. It has been suggested that Manson thought Melcher was still in the house, but this is untrue; he had called there in March, looking for Melcher, and was told Melcher had moved. The house was chosen only because Manson knew it.

Tex Watson climbed a telephone pole and cut two wires. Then they all climbed the fence into the garden. At this moment, a car with its headlights on approached them down the drive. A young man named Stephen Parent, who had been visiting the house-boy, William Garretson, was on his way home. He saw the dark figures and called to ask what they were doing. Without hesitation, Watson placed the barrel of a revolver against his head, and shot him five times. Then Watson turned off the car engine, and they went towards the house. They were wearing dark clothes which they had brought with them for the occasion.

Watson cut a screen from a window – a nursery that was being prepared for the expected arrival – and climbed in. He opened the front door, and let in Susan Atkins and Patricia Krenwinkel. Linda Kasabian stayed outside as a lookout.

Frykowski had fallen asleep on the settee, under the influence of a mild psychedelic drug called MDA. Abigail Folger had retired to bed, also under its influence, and was reading. Jay Sebring was in Sharon Tate's bedroom, talking to her as she lay in bed; he was fully dressed.

Frykowski woke up and found Tex Watson standing over him with a revolver. He asked him who he was. Watson said, 'The devil,' and ordered Susan Atkins to get a towel to tie up Frykowski's hands. After bringing the towel, Susan Atkins looked into a bedroom and saw Abigail Folger. She waved, and Abigail Folger waved back. (Susan Atkins said later that they were all on acid, which explains the casualness on both sides.) She looked into Sharon Tate's bedroom, and saw her sitting up in bed talking to Sebring. They did not see her. She went back to the sitting-room and told Watson that there were people in the bedrooms. Watson ordered her to go and bring them. She walked into each bedroom, waving a knife, and told them to go into the sitting-room. Sebring strode in angrily, asking what was happening. When Watson ordered him to lie on the floor, he made a grab for the gun. Watson shot him in the lung. They demanded money, and Abigail Folger led Susan Atkins to the bedroom, where her money was handed over.

Watson had brought a length of nylon rope with them – it seems to have been part of the scenario, planned in advance. One end was tied around Sebring's neck, and the rope was thrown over a beam. It was then tied around the necks of Abigail Folger and Sharon Tate, who had to stand upright to avoid being choked.

Someone asked, 'What are you going to do to us?' and Watson replied, 'You are all going to die.' Watson told Susan Atkins to stab Frykowski. She tried to, but he managed to jump up; she stabbed him in the back as he ran. Then Watson shot him twice with the revolver; it jammed a third time, and Watson clubbed him with it.

Sharon Tate and Abigail Folger struggled to get free; Abigail managed to run for the door, chased by Patricia Krenwinkel. Sebring now began to struggle, so Watson ran up to him and stabbed him several times. After this, he overtook Abigail Folger, who had been stabbed by Patricia Krenwinkel; he battered her with the butt of the gun, and stabbed her several times.

Meanwhile Frykowski, badly wounded, had managed to get out on to the lawn and was shouting for help. Linda Kasabian was horrified to realize what was going on, and shouted to Susan Atkins to stop it; Susan replied it was too late. Watson bounded into the garden and stabbed Frykowski again and again. Linda Kasabian fled.

Back in the house, Watson ordered Susan Atkins to stab Sharon Tate. Sharon begged for her life for the sake of the baby; Susan Atkins said: 'Look bitch, I don't care . . .' But she couldn't bring herself to stab. Tex Watson stabbed her in the left breast, killing her, and then the other two joined in the stabbing. Susan Atkins said she began to enjoy it at this point, and wanted to gouge out her eyeballs and crush them against the wall – after all, the aim was to excite horror. But it was getting late. Watson said they had to leave. He stabbed Abigail Folger a few more times. Susan Atkins dipped a towel in blood from Sharon Tate, and wrote 'Pig' on the hall door – an important point, to link this murder to that of Hinman.

Back in the car, they changed their bloodstained clothing. Linda Kasabian had climbed into the car. The clothes were dumped down a steep embankment (where they were later found by reporters). After this, they found a house with a hose on the lawn, and turned on the water to wash off the blood. The occupants of the house, an old man and woman, heard the noise, and challenged them angrily. The killers drove off, and the irritated householder noted down the number of the Ford.

Back at the ranch, Manson asked why they were back so early, but was pleased when they told him they had left everybody dead. Susan Atkins made love with somebody – she wasn't sure who – then went to sleep.

What Manson did for the rest of the night is not certain; he did not join Stephanie in the trailer until morning. It seems most likely that he drove over to the Polanski house, either alone or with other family members, to make sure his executioners had done their work efficiently. There were signs that someone came back to the house in the night; there was blood on the front porch, and signs that someone had tried to drag the bodies out there. Sander's theory is that Manson wanted to arrange a tableau on the porch with suspended bodies, found there was nothing to bear their weight, and rearranged the scene as Watson and the girls had left it.

The bodies were discovered early the next morning by the housekeeper who came in daily. The Manson family watched the television next morning, and for the first time learned the names of their victims. 'It really blew my mind,' said Susan Atkins, who was delighted that they had murdered such a celebrity as Sharon Tate. Someone commented that The Soul (Manson) had picked a good one this time, and someone else remarked that the aim of the murders was to instil fear in Man himself, Man, the Establishment. 'That's what it was done for. To instil fear, to cause paranoia. To also show the black how to go about taking over the white man.'

It succeeded in its purpose. The murders caused panic in the Los Angeles area, and every gun and guard dog in town was bought before nightfall. The house-boy, Garretson, was arrested, but he claimed he had been playing a record at the time of the murders, and had heard nothing. He was soon released.

That evening, Manson announced they were going to instil further terror into the 'pigs'. This time, he would lead them himself. He took six helpers with him: Tex Watson, Linda Kasabian, Patricia Krenwinkel, Susan Atkins, Gary Tufts (known as Clem) and Leslie Van Houten. All were high on acid.

To begin with, Manson seemed to have no definite direction; they considered a number of houses and decided against them. When they saw a white sports car ahead, halted at traffic lights, Manson prepared for action. As they drew up alongside the car, Manson started to get out; but the lights changed, and it drove away. The young man at the wheel never knew how lucky he was.

Manson now seemed to have decided where to go. He ordered Susan Atkins to drive to the affluent Los Feliz district of Los Angeles. At some point on the drive, Manson looked into the window of a lighted house, but decided not to break in because there were pictures of children on the wall. The Ford finally pulled up in front of a house belonging to a supermarket owner, Leno LaBianca. Susan Atkins recognized the house next door; she and Manson had taken an acid trip there during the Topanga Canyon period, and Manson had some reason for resenting the owner of the house. But it was the LaBianca's home that Manson chose for their second murder rampage.

Leno LaBianca, forty-four, and his wife Rosemary, thirty-eight, had spent the afternoon water-skiing. They returned to their home at 3301 Waverly Drive at some time after 1 a.m.

on Sunday morning, 10th August, and removed the water-skis from the top of the Thunderbird. They had bought a newspaper that carried the story of the Tate murders, and had been discussing it. They got into their night clothes and got into bed. And shortly afterwards, Charles Manson walked into their bedroom with a gun. In a calm voice, he ordered them to get up, and said no harm would come to them; then he tied them up. Then he went back to the car, and told Watson, Patricia Krenwinkel and Leslie Van Houten to go into the house and kill them. After that, they were to hitch-hike back to the ranch. He and others would find another house and kill somebody else. Manson drove off.

Watson and his two helpers went into the house and found the LaBiancas tied up. Mrs. LaBianca was led to the bedroom, where she was tied with an electric light flex, and a pillow case was placed over her head. Then the homicidal Watson pushed Leno LaBianca back on the settee and slashed at his throat four times with his knife. He also stabbed him four times. LaBianca bled to death. His screams caused Rosemary LaBianca to yell 'What are you doing to my husband?' Patricia Krenwinkel began to stab her in the back, severing her spine; Watson joined them in the bed-room, and he helped with the stabbing – forty times in all, mostly in the back. Leslie Van Houten had not joined in, so they asked her to do some stabbing. Hesitantly, she started to stab the buttocks, then became more enthusiastic, and stabbed sixteen times.

Watson slashed the word 'War' on LaBianca's chest, while Patricia Krenwinkel stabbed both bodies with a carving fork – although both were now probably dead – and left it embedded near the navel of Leno LaBianca. After this, they wrote several words in blood in different rooms: 'Death to Pigs', 'Rise' and 'Healter skelter' (a misprint for Helter Skelter). After this they took a shower and changed their clothes, ate some food and fed the three dogs (who had watched the murders without barking, and even licked the killers' hands). Then they walked out of the house, and hitch-hiked back to the Spahn ranch without any problems. There they found Manson, who had decided not to do any killing after all. He had taken his group to a beach south of Venice, and asked the girls if there was not some 'pig' they could kill in a nearby apartment; Linda and Sandy Good had been picked up by an actor some weeks before, and had returned to his apartment near the beach. Linda Kasabian showed Manson the building; they went inside, and she pointed out what she claimed to be the flat of Saladin Nader, a film actor. (It was, she claims, the wrong apartment; she had already decided not to kill him.) Manson told his three assassins to knock on the door and overpower Nader when he opened it; then he left them and went off in the Ford. Linda knocked on a door – the wrong one – and when someone opened it a fraction, apologized, said she had the wrong place, and left. They hitch-hiked back to the Spahn ranch. The bodies of the LaBiancas were found the next morning by their sixteen-year-old son, who had fortunately been elsewhere for the night.

Manson was arrested six days after the LaBianca murder – but not for murder. The local police had decided it was time to clamp down on the hippie commune because of its car-thieving activities. There was a swoop on the ranch, and twenty-five people were arrested. The police seized a number of guns and other weapons, and took down the numbers of the cars – including the Ford that had been used in both murders. Unfortunately, the man who had chased Tex Watson off his lawn after the Sharon Tate murder had not informed the police; otherwise, the case might have been solved forthwith. They were all released three days later, when a judge decided that there was insufficient evidence to charge them. Three days later, Manson was again arrested when two policemen walked into a hut where he was lying naked with Stephanie. The police found what they took to be a reefer in Manson's shirt pocket – Susan Atkins had placed it there – but upon laboratory analysis, it turned out not to be pot, and Manson was released.

On 26th August, 1969, the family murdered a ranch hand, 'Shorty' O'Shea. Manson had various things against him. He had married a negro woman; he knew about the shooting of Bernard Crowe (who was still believed to be dead); and he disliked having the family on the Spahn ranch. Details of his murder are not known. No body was ever found, although his car was discovered in a Canoga parking lot. Sanders says the whole family were involved in the murder, and that he was tortured beforehand. After this, his body was chopped up and partly burned.

In early September, the family once more moved to Death

Valley. Little is known of their activities during this final period; Ed Sanders describes the attempted murder of a prospector named Crockett – which came to nothing – and the hi-jacking of a frozen food truck by Susan Atkins and Leslie Van Houten; he also reports a story that there were further murders there – two boys and a girl, but gives no details.

Manson's major mistake seems to have been the wanton burning of a Michigan skip-loader – a kind of bulldozer – which had dug large holes in a dirt road. It belonged to the rangers at the Death Valley National Monument, and they were enraged at this destruction of an expensive piece of equipment. They found tyre tracks leading from the scene, and some miles further along the road, a wrecked Ford car – which the family had driven into a tree – with more identifiable tyre tracks nearby. These tracks belonged to a stolen car, a Toyota. And two days later, rangers saw the Toyota in a canyon near Ballarat; a check on its licence plates revealed that they were false. Eventually, they discovered the stolen Toyota, without licence plates, not far from the hut of the miner Paul Crockett. He talked to the police about the family, and the search for them now began. But the police were still unaware that the hippies were hiding out at the Barker ranch. (In the hundreds of square miles of desert, locating an army would be slow work.) It took them until 9th October to track down the family. Just before dawn, two teams of police officers closed in on the ranch. Manson was not there, but the police arrested a number of his followers, mostly girls, who tried to disconcert the officers by urinating in front of them and taking off their clothes.

Manson returned to Death Valley three days later, on 12th October. A few of the girls who had escaped the raid told him what had happened. A few hours later, they were all eating in the kitchen when more police burst in. Manson dived for a tiny cupboard under the kitchen sink, and was almost overlooked. As the hippies were marched off to jail, police noticed that Manson said something in a low voice, and the others murmured 'Amen, amen'.

Kitty Lutesinger – the girl who had earlier run away from the Spahn ranch – was in police custody. She had returned to the family, but decided to desert again in Death Valley; she and another young girl had run away one night, and bumped into the police who were on their way to raid the Barker ranch. Kitty was wanted for questioning in connection with the Hinman murder – since she had been Bobby Beausoleil's girlfriend. She now told the police that she had nothing to do with the murder: it was 'Sadie' and Mary. And the police now had Sadie – Susan Atkins – in custody. She was handed over to the Los Angeles police. She soon admitted being present at Hinman's house, but denied having any part in the killing.

Boredom, and perhaps radio news bulletins about the progress of the Tate murder investigation, led her to drop hints to fellow prisoners about her part in the Sharon Tate killing. She told one cell-mate about it, but the woman kept the secret. Later, she told another cell-mate, Virginia Graham, in considerable detail. Virginia Graham let another friend – Ronni Howard – in on the secret. It was Ronni Howard who finally talked to the police about Susan Atkins' detailed confessions. On 1st December, the Chief of Police of Los Angeles told a Press conference that three people had been charged with the Tate-LaBianca murders: Tex Watson, Linda Kasabian and Patricia Krenwinkel. Later, Manson, Susan Atkins and Leslie Van Houten were also charged.

The trial, one of the longest and most expensive in Los Angeles history (by October 1970 it had already passed the quarter million dollar mark, and would continue until late the following March) was noisy and confused. Manson and the four girls were charged with the Tate and LaBianca murders.[1] (Beausoleil was convicted of the Hinman murder.) Predictably, Manson tried to turn it into an indictment of the judges and modern society. 'You make your children what they are.' 'You people put importance on your lives. My life has never been important to anyone . . . The parents kicked them out and I did the best I could and took them up on my garbage dump . . .' 'These children – everything they have done, they have done for the love of their brothers . . .'

There was a slightly insane air about the whole trial, as if everyone were talking at cross purposes. Observers in other countries found it difficult to understand – as, no doubt, did many Americans. Manson's general indictment of society could well have some foundation. But if he had really ordered the murder of so many people then he was a mad dog, a paranoiac, and was guilty. But Manson and thousands of young followers did not, apparently, agree. To begin with, this was perhaps understandable. In effect, Manson was condemned from the moment of his arrest. America's middle classes, said one reporter, had gone into convulsions of delight that the hippies had at last got what was coming to them. This was what they had always suspected lay behind the movement. Photographs of Manson made him look insane, a manic Rasputin. When the reporter of the *Los Angles Free Press* got in to see him shortly after his arrest, he was surprised to find a calm, quiet-spoken little man who talked reasonably and without any sign of paranoia, and who complained that he was not being allowed to see anyone. The newspapers splashed stories about Satan's Slaves, about orgies of sex and drugs, sadism and murder. The 'Confession' of Susan Atkins, edited by Lawrence Schiller, was released to the world's newspapers (in full) on 14th December, 1969, and the paperback book appeared the following January. (On 9th December, the judge had imposed a 'gag' on all media, ordering that the case should not be discussed publicly; ten days later, *Life* carried the full story of the 'love and terror cult'.) And in August 1970, before the trial was half over, President Nixon referred to Manson's guilt in a speech. All this indicated that justice was not getting done in an ideal manner. But in the long run, it got done.

It was the weird logic of Manson's supporters that created the mad atmosphere. Asked if she thought the killing of eight people was unimportant, Susan Atkins countered by asking if the killing of thousands of people with napalm was important. By the rules of ordinary logic, this is nothing more than an attempt at smart repartee. Had Sharon Tate or the LaBiancas killed anybody with napalm? Or did she mean that eight more people made no difference? But when so many young people made a hero of Manson, the older generation began to wonder if it was not somehow missing the point. Were the murders really their fault, as Manson seemed to imply? And when Manson, Susan Atkins, Leslie Van Houten and Patricia Krenwinkel were found guilty and sentenced to death on 30th March, 1970. (Linda Kasabian escaped by turning State's evidence) the question was still unanswered. The murders had caused a certain revulsion among the young, and a 'Jesus cult' had sprung up among the hippies, old-fashioned Billy Graham-type evangelism, but many still regarded Manson as some kind of a symbol. In a TV programme about the Jesus cult, one girl, asked if she believed in Christianity, said: 'No, I believe in black magic and Charles Manson and all that.' The interviewer did not bother to ask her to explain herself; apparently he understood exactly what she meant.

And what is the significance of the Manson case?

As one of the most sensational murder cases of the late 1960s, it certainly has its importance. But this importance has been exaggerated by the social commentators. Kerouac was an archetypal hippie; Manson was not. Manson became a hippie by chance; but fundamentally he was no more a hippie than Netchaev or Hitler or Stalin. The puzzling and paradoxical nature of the case is the result of Manson's own divided personality. To a large extent, he seems to have been genuinely compassionate and well-meaning person. He was also a Violent Man, in Van Vogt's sense, and this aspect of him developed swiftly after his first acceptance as a kind of messiah in Haight-Ashbury. As he became accustomed to absolute obedience, he also came to feel that people who crossed him – or double-crossed him – were insects who should be stamped out. This tendency must have been encouraged by the slavish admiration he received from his admiring family. Teen-aged girls can be hysterical creatures – as anyone who has ever watched a pop concert knows. They are prone to adoration, and a mentally balanced male, while he might take temporary advantage of such adoration, would end by fleeing from it as a spiritual corrosive. Fools are always a bore, whether they are adoring fools or hostile fools. Manson lacked the self-critical faculty to maintain a balanced view of himself. Encouraged by his women, he became increasingly a 'right man'.

He was also, for the first time in his life, the leader, the tribal chieftain. And the leader is under an obligation to show himself in a good light; to appear, if possible, as the conqueror. But in practical terms, Manson was not a conqueror. He had achieved nothing. No doubt he would assert that he had no desire to achieve anything in a corrupt society; but his attempts to become a record star contradict this.

But in another sense, Manson achieved overnight success.

He went to Haight-Ashbury an unknown little ex-jailbird, a kind of Charlie Chaplin figure, strumming a guitar and singing in a voice as undistinguished as Bob Dylan's. A year later, he had become a sort of Jewish patriarch, surrounded by his tribe, the undisputed leader, the dictator in power. He handed out reefers and acid to his girls; he handed out girls to his male followers. Quite indisputably, he had become Someone.

But success brings its obligations. When the dictator is in power, he has to do something to prove that his followers made the right choice. Hitler started a European war for the same reason. And Manson also thought in terms of war, war against the 'pigs'.

The resentment he felt about society is understandable enough. One of the most interesting features of the case is that, in spite of this hatred, Manson was not a violent type. Netchaev killed the student Ivanov himself. Brady murdered Edward Evans and joked about it afterwards. Manson does not seem to have been personally violent – except in the case of Hinman, when he slashed at his ear with a sword. He directed his followers to commit the violence: at least, in the cases where evidence is available. One suspects that his remarkable capacity for inspiring love was due to his non-violence.

This in turn raises the speculation: how far were his women followers – particularly Susan Atkins – responsible for what happened? Manson may have had natural leader qualities; but to some extent, he was *chosen* by his women. It was they who elevated him into his position, a combination of Elvis Presley and Jesus. But Susan Atkins' attitude towards him seems to have been ambivalent. 'He gave my faith in myself back to me.' Possibly he gave her too much. 'Sadie Mae Glutz' is an ugly name, compared to Susan Denise Atkins; it suggests a prostitute out of a Mickey Spillane novel; but Manson gave her the name while they were still living with Gary Hinman. It was Sadie Mae, according to Beausoleil, who told the ranch hand Shorty O'Shea, that Manson had killed a Black Panther ('and she didn't know who else,' added Beausoleil.) It was Sadie Mae who told her cell-mate about the Tate and LaBianca murders, and who implicated Manson. Steve Geller, the American novelist, attended some of the first sessions of the trial, and wrote down his impressions of Susan Atkins (which I quote with his permission):

> In the middle stands Susan Atkins ... wearing a cutesy-pie salmon pink dress with eighteenth century dollymop puffy sleeves, and ten pink buttons down the front ... She is wearing an I.D. plastic band, hospital style, on her left wrist. And I notice that she is hairy, her arms and wrists. With a slight trace of a moustache above her lip ... With her head hanging down slightly, ashamed. The finger girl ...
>
> I begin to realize why I've such a nasty feeling towards her: because she's too composed; in all this, there seems to be a different kind of effect, a super-star, super-cool self-consciousness. Granted, she's been this way before: she's been arrested eight times in three years ... Her testimony has been leaked to the press, her story bought for a reported $175,000. In her own way, she's bigger business than her family father, Charles Manson, could ever be ... It's obvious also that when Judge Keene is addressing the girls collectively, he addresses Miss Atkins as the spokeswoman. He knows the programme. She's one of the stars ...

Lawrence Schiller describes her as 'a sweet-faced young woman with luminous brown eyes', and some reporters described her as pretty. Her photographs contradict this; she is a well-built, sullen-featured girl, and in most of the pictures, her face has a resentful expression. An underground hippie newspaper refers to her as Manson's Judas Iscariot. And it seems a reasonable assumption that she confessed out of some obscure desire for publicity and revenge. Manson built up his hippie empire, his castle in the desert, like Hasan bin Sabbah, the grand master of the Assassins. With a few casual remarks, Susan Atkins made the whole thing topple like a child's sand castle.

But in fairness to Manson, we have to admit that there *was* an element of justice in the counter-charges he brought against his judges. For the real mystery of the case is the psychological mystery. How could a sincere, fairly intelligent, well-meaning little man who gave out an aura of love turn into a dictator obsessed with murder? The answer is that a lifetime in jail, of being pushed around by authority, could destroy the potential of a Saint Francis or Shakespeare. There *must* be psychological tests to enable us to recognize the potentialities of a Manson before his hatred of society becomes the permanent foundation of his consciousness. The sympathy shown for Manson by American youth was basically a recognition that good, creative human potential was here allowed to stagnate and turn rotten: for anyone under twenty, it is too easy to put yourself in his shoes. If Manson is guilty of criminal violence, society is guilty of criminal negligence. And unlike Manson, society is in the position of being able to learn from its mistakes.

1. Watson was later tried separately; at an earlier stage he had been found mentally unfit to plead. Sanders states that his I.Q. had deteriorated by 30 per cent during his period as a family member.

CHAPTER EIGHT

The Passive Fallacy

The Manson case leaves the basic issues clearly exposed. *Is* our society so rotten that nothing but total revolution can improve things? Does the trouble lie in the nature of technical civilization, dragging us into the future faster than we can possibly adjust? As long ago as 1941, H. G. Wells remarked that civilization has changed more in forty years than in the previous four thousand. And the rate of change has increased, producing a feeling of disintegration:

'Things fall apart; the centre cannot hold; Mere anarchy is loosed upon the world . . .'

Moral changes have been as extreme as the physical ones. In an essay called 'Raffles and Miss Blandish' George Orwell pointed out how drastic and total these have been. Raffles, the gentleman cracksman, who burgles the Mayfair homes that he enters as a guest, made his first appearance in 1899, and in spite of his shaky morality, he belongs to the same world as Sherlock Holmes and Rudolph Rassendyl, the 'prisoner of Zenda'. It is a world where honour is the fundamental value, where 'decent chaps' behave well because they couldn't live with themselves otherwise. By comparison, the world of James Hadley Chase's *No Orchids for Miss Blandish* is a world of sharks and piranha fish. The book aims at producing a series of shocks. Miss Blandish, a millionaire's daughter, is kidnapped by a gang who intend to kill her when they have the ransom. They are intercepted by a stronger gang, who kill them and take Miss Blandish. This gang also intends to kill her – as a matter of course – but a gangster called Slim Grisson takes a liking to her. And this is unusual for Slim is sexually impotent, and can only have an orgasm by driving a knife into someone's belly. (As a child, he used to cut up live animals with rusty scissors.) Ma Grisson, the leader of the gang, thinks Miss Blandish might cure her son of his impotence if he can rape her. So Miss Blandish is kept drugged until Slim manages it. ('Now after three months when he had done everything his perverted mind could devise to her, her drugged lack of resistance began to pall.') The police finally wipe out the gang – achieving their object through bribery and brutality. Miss Blandish commits suicide by jumping out of a window. Orwell assumes this is because she has come to enjoy Slim's caresses; in fact, the author makes the reason quite clear in the final speech he puts into her mouth: 'I've never had a sense of value . . . I'm a person without any background, any character, any faith. Some people could cope with this because they believe in God. I haven't believed in anything except having a good time.' This is remarkably subtle psychology. She is saying, in effect, that before this happened she had found life fairly boring, and that now, after her ordeal, she has nothing *to go back to*. Her freedom ought to compensate for the horrors, but it doesn't. She can see no escape from the life-failure that paralyses her.

Orwell notes as a curious paradox that readers of 1940s gangster novels would have rejected descriptions of the London blitz or the struggles of the European resistance movements as 'sissy stuff'. But this proves nothing about the average reader's sense of reality. The purpose of *No Orchids* (and its thousands of imitators – usually written by tough-sounding characters like 'Ben Sarto' and 'Darcy Glinto') was to produce a series of shocks; the reader wanted to be shocked, not edified. So the writer obligingly created a world in which only the lowest human motives are allowed to exist. The police are as corrupt as the gangsters. *No Orchids* was an imitation of Faulkner's *Sanctuary* (as Orwell points out); but in Faulkner, there *is* an 'alternative world' – of the Deep South and its values. In the gangster novel and its derivatives (the James Bond novels, for example) values would be an irrelevance. Even sex has to be hard and violent, and fundamentally unenjoyable. (For example, in Harold Robbins's *The Carpetbaggers*, the hero describes how he finally possesses the girl he has always wanted to marry: 'And with only my devil to guide us, together we plunged into the fiery pleasures of our own particular hell.') E. M. Forster accused James Joyce of trying to cover the universe with mud; this was unfair to Joyce, but it fits Hadley Chase and his successors. And the 'buckets of mud' formula has been a surefire recipe for bestsellers ever since. It is true that in some more recent examples (Mario Puzo's *The Godfather*, for example) some allowance is made for the existence of good guys; but this is only to convince the sophisticated reader of its authenticity, and so increase the shock effect of the cruelty.

But how reprehensible is all this? Orwell condemns *No Orchids* as a disguised fascist daydream, as if all its readers had hankerings to be concentration camp guards, (And Hadley Chase, no doubt inspired by Orwell, then wrote a novel called *More Deadly than the Male* about a Walter Mitty-ish bank clerk who dreams of being a gangster.[1]) But why, in fact, *do* readers want to be shocked? To contrast the gangster novel unfavourably with, say, a true account of the French Resistance is beside the point. The hopes and ideals of the Resistance are unreal to a man whose life follows a boring routine: nothing in him wakes up and responds to them, for his sense of values is anaesthetized by boredom. What shocks him out of his indifference is the thought of mindless cruelty. The thrill it produces is not sadistic (although sadism itself is an attempt to stir an anaesthetized pleasure nerve); it is genuine moral shock. After reading some scene of brutality and torture, he looks at everyday life *with a kind of relief*; these people around him may be small-minded and not over-intelligent, but they are saints in comparison to Slim Grisson ... In fact, Orwell's assumption (about mental sadism) is disproved by the equal popularity of war books and escape books, as well as books about the Nazis and their concentration camps. Political reality *is* acceptable if it produces the shock effect. H. L. Gates's book *Ravished Armenia* appeared in the early 1920s; it is a factual account of the deportation of Armenians by the 'Young Turks' in 1916, and the extraordinary cruelties to which the Armenians were subjected. (It begins with a description of the Turks rounding up all the males in a particular village and burning them alive with petrol.) Under the title *Auction of Souls* it soon achieved wide popularity in a cheap edition. Hemingway's novels – particularly *A Farewell to Arms* and *For Whom the Bell Tolls* – use 'shock tactics' with an identical purpose: not to appeal to sadism, but to try to jar the reader into a sense of the reality of war. They achieved their appeal because readers like to be jarred. The shock has the effect of temporarily lifting them above their everyday lives as a rocket lifts a space satellite.

So the transition from the age of Raffles and Sherlock Holmes to the age of Miss Blandish need not be viewed with total pessimism. Miss Blandish and Harold Robbins are not necessarily a sign of large-scale depravity. Since his first appearance on earth, man has been subject to boredom. The biblical legend of creation should be changed; it was not death the serpent brought into the world, but boredom; for boredom is the real threat to our evolution. Man has always been at his best when fighting battles or facing great challenges; or, failing that, when consuming strong liquor with a girl on his knee. When life becomes calm, he lets himself slide; he experiences a sense of suffocation, and he begins to doubt himself – a thing he never did when hacking at his enemies with a broad-axe. Man is naturally a heroic and tough creature. That is how he became the most dominant creature on earth. He certainly *wants* civilization – as he realizes every time he reads in his newspaper about thousands dying of cholera in some rat-infested city in an underdeveloped country. But it is hard to accept the inactivity that goes with it – for reasons that must now be analysed. So novels in which beautiful heiresses get raped and rival gangs are mowed down with tommy-guns are not a proof of how far man has been demoralized by civilization, but only of how little he has changed in six thousand years.

In 1919, Freud produced a theory that attempted to explain the cruelty and violence of human beings – for example, the mass slaughter of the First World War. He approached the subject in a somewhat roundabout way. He was fascinated by what he called the 'repetition-compulsion' of neurotic patients, the tendency to repeat past patterns of behaviour. This led him to the odd conclusion that the fundamental aim of instinct is to revert to the past, to restore an earlier state. And he was logical enough to see what this entailed: that the aim of life is death. Man's deepest instinct, Freud said, is the death instinct. Various followers pointed out that this was not logical. Repetition – which is certainly a characteristic of all human life – does not point to a desire to return to the past so much as a desire to stay in the same place. And biology can show no evidence of such a desire. But Freud wouldn't have it. Evidently his theory of the death instinct satisfied some emotional craving in him; or perhaps it struck him as an authentic inspiration. In his earlier theory, masochism was an offshoot of sadism; now he began to see sadism as an offshoot of the basic instinct: self-destruction. This theory was propounded in *Beyond the Pleasure Principle*.

The idea of *thanatos*, man's destructive impulse, quickly gained wide acceptance, because it seemed to explain the oddly self-destructive nature of human violence. It was not until Robert Ardrey suggested, in *African Genesis* (1961), that man is basically a killer-ape, that the theory had any serious rival.

At first sight, Freud's theory offers a wholly satisfactory explanation of the Manson case. The life instinct (which includes the sexual drive) is locked in continual struggle with the death instinct, and when the death instinct shows signs of winning, the life instinct tries the device of directing it *outward*, towards other people, as a weak king might try to deflect revolutionary violence by starting a war. (This, as Freud's biographer Ernest Jones points out, is how Austria got into the first world war.) The Freudian view of Manson would be that his long period in gaol had given his self-destructive impulses a chance to gain ascendancy. In Haight-Ashbury, he tried to counteract this with promiscuous sex. But such promiscuity is self-defeating. D. H. Lawrence said; 'What many women cannot give, one woman can,'[1] and conversely, what one woman can give, many women can't. The creation of the 'family' would be seen by a Freudian as an attempt to restrain the psyche bent on self-destruction, but to no avail. The destructive impulses explode, and he even entrusts the killing to lieutenants who cannot be trusted to keep silent . . .

But compared to the Maslovian explanation, all this is unnecessarily complicated. Manson was a self-actualizer whose progress was blocked on every level. From his earliest years, he had no home security[2] – to such an extent that he actually came to enjoy prison and to be afraid of leaving.[3] Until he was twenty he had no chance of normal sexual fulfilment. And then, in a single year, the family provided all the security and sexual fulfilment he needed, while male disciples – like Bruce Davis and Charles Watson – catered for the self-esteem needs. He suddenly developed at an explosive pace; after the years in prison, it was like shaking a bottle of champagne, then taking the cork out. And this kind of forced development can be more harmful than frustration. The best kind is slow and deliberate, allowing for the consolidation of the sense of values and the creation of new self-images. The other kind creates a personality problem that could be compared to the 'bends' suffered by divers who depressurize too fast. The result is 'life failure', a deep-seated psychological exhaustion.

This could have been avoided if Manson's capacity for self-actualization had been greater. But his 'poems' and songs reveal talent of a fairly low order. His various intellectual arguments, cited by witnesses and journalists, sound half-baked; in fact, they are 'magical' justifications of his own emotions. His dislike of books was a self-defensive reaction. Having ascended the 'hierarchy of values' at top speed, Manson was brought up with a bump by lack of training and preparation. He simply had no capacity for inner-direction, for working alone; the crowd of admirers was essential to his well-being. The states of disorientation produced by drugs were no help either. The 'vicious streak' that becomes apparent during the final year is the result of exhaustion and frustration at the creative level – the level of self-actualization. In this state of confusion and emotional fatigue, Manson did what most people do in that situation – reverted to an earlier stage of his development, the prison stage of anti-social resentment.

During that last year, Manson's charisma was his bad luck. What he needed was some kind of equal whom he could like and admire – preferably someone of creative ability. But he had only disciples and slaves – no one to help him maintain a sense of proportion. An image of Gregg Jakobsen's describes what happened to Manson's mind in the final months: 'When Charlie danced . . . he was like fire, a raw explosion, a mechanical toy that suddenly went crazy.' It would be difficult to find a better symbol for the Violent Man.

I have tried to show that no single theory provides a complete insight into the mind of the assassin. Maslow's hierarchy theory is basic, but it is only an outline. Van Vogt and Sartre help to fill in the psychology of self-esteem, while the self-image theory is the essential foundation of a psychology of self-actualization. There is an enoromus amount of work still to be done, and in the remainder of this book, I shall try to suggest possible methods of approach. We are dealing with the psychology of freedom.

The tendency to repetition, which Freud observed, is one of the most curious and least understood characteristics of the human mind. Man is an evolutionary animal. He is at his best when he is going forward with a strong sense of purpose. He *needs and wants* to go forward; it is his deepest impulse. And if he cannot find his way into a new pattern, then he will repeat the old pattern. Anything to keep the wheels turning.

This explains all 'compulsive' behaviour. William James talks of a case of a girl who ate almost non-stop, and of another girl who had to walk all the time, followed by a motor car that contained food, so she could eat while she walked. Joyce mentions in *Ulysses* a professor with a compulsion to tap every lamp post with his cane. Doctor Johnson always tried to avoid walking on the cracks on the pavement. In fact, Johnson's personality was typical of the compulsive: his dislike of the country (because it left him face to face with his own freedom) and his love of London crowds and coffee houses, his need to talk until the early hours of the morning and to keep several 'pensioners' in his house (so as to have company on tap); above all, his morbid fears about death and damnation. (For a long time he was convinced he was damned.) The oddest thing about Johnson is that such a remarkable man should have left behind such unremarkable writings: one short novel modelled on *Candide*, lives of the poets that could have been written by any hack, a dictionary, an edition of Shakespeare, dozens of trivial essays modelled on Addison ... He was an intellectual heavyweight who didn't know what to *do* with his unusual talents. And if a man's creative energies are not allowed to flow, the result is finally as painful as if he cannot urinate.

Maxim Gorky describes a Russian murderer suffering from compulsive neurosis.[4] The judge who told Gorky about the case, L. N. Sviatoukhine, remarked: 'Of all the murderers who have come before me in the last thirteen years, only one, the packhorse driver Merkouloff, ever awoke in me a feeling of terror before man and for man. The ordinary murderer is a hopelessly dull and obtuse creature, half man, half beast, incapable of realizing the significance of his crime; or else a sly, dirty little fellow, a squealing fox caught in a trap; or else a hysterical monomaniac, desperate and bitter. But when Merkouloff stood in front of me in the dock, I instantly scented something weird and unusual about him.’ Merkouloff’s face was thin and intelligent, and the judge’s sympathy led him to try to explain his crimes. A very powerful man, he had one day struck a man who was stealing sugar from his cart. The blow killed the man. And it was this that worried Merkouloff – that it had been so easy to kill. It could happen to anyone; it could happen to him ... The thought became an obsession. Merkouloff was sent to a monastery to do penance. But the words of a kindly priest struck him as meaningless. All this talk about the importance of goodness, about salvation – and yet, this priest could be killed with one violent blow. After being released, the obsession remained, and one day, in a fit of anger, he struck an idiot girl, who was importuning him, with a heavy piece of wood. The blow killed her. Merkouloff became even more obsessed, for this girl seemed to have the good luck of a sleepwalker; she was always falling over and walking into walls, but never got badly hurt. After a prison sentence, Merkouloff killed again, this time his employer. His employer was a good man, and apparently brave as well as cheerful. It was this that tempted Merkouloff to kill him – and to torture him beforehand: a sort of tormented feeling that he *ought* not to be so easily killable. Eventually, Merkouloff strangled himself with his chains in gaol.

The psychology here is easy enough to understand. The ease with which he can kill throws Merkouloff into a permanent state of over-anxiety; when he murders, you might say that he is hoping against hope that the victim will prove unkillable. But the over-anxiety is permanent only because Merkouloff’s mind is stagnant. If he could become deeply interested in something, the obsession would pass away. He is preoccupied with death as a man confined to his bed would become preoccupied by a picture hanging on the opposite wall: because there is nothing else to look at.

This state – of purposelessness and boredom – produces what Sartre has called ‘the vertigo of freedom’. In *Transcendence of the Ego* he describes a case of a young girl newly married, who experiences an odd compulsion to go to the window of her flat – while her husband is at work – and signal to men in the manner of a prostitute. This is not a case of ordinary sexual repression or nymphomania. She has been brought up in a convent; the thought of offering herself to strangers horrifies her; and this is precisely why, with nothing to do for most of the day, she feels the morbid compulsion to do it.

André Gide was the first French writer to explore the psychology of the 'gratuitous act' (in *Les Caves du Vatican*) although (as I have pointed out) Poe and Dostoevsky had already done so. The gratuitous act is not necessarily criminal. In *Le Roi Candaule* it is a gratuitous act of generosity. In *Caves du Vatican* it is a murder – pushing a fellow traveller off a train for no reason. (Lafcadio, the hero, always carries a dice with him to enable him to make 'gratuitous choices'.) In *Le Promethée Mal Enchainé*, the act involves both aggression and generosity; a banker walks down a Paris boulevard every day, and drops his handkerchief. When someone hands it to him, the banker requests the person to write his name and address on an envelope. He then slaps him in the face, and jumps into a cab. Later, he encloses a 500 franc note in the envelope and sends it to his victim. But inevitably, most of the 'gratuitous acts' in Gide's works are acts of cruelty. And they are not really gratuitous; they are performed in the name of freedom and self-development. The hero of *L'Immoralist* protests that a peaceful and happy life with his wife is like resting without being tired; he hungers for experiences that will permit self-development, so he drags his ailing wife around the world until she dies of exhaustion.

Gide's enormous influence over the young sprang from his teaching that one's only duty is to oneself, that one should never be 'encumbered', either by material possessions, memories or other people. Manson had certainly never read Gide; but he preached precisely the same thing. (Patricia Krenwinkel, according to *Life*, quit her job without picking up her pay cheque, and left her car in a parking lot when she went off to become a member of the family.)

Gide died in 1951; by that time, Sartre had taken over the exploration of the psychology of the 'gratuitous act'. Hilbert, the central character in the story *Herostratus*, is sick of feeling a total nonentity, and decides that he will commit a crime that will make him famous; he will shoot five men at random in the street – to demonstrate his dislike of humanity – and then kill himself. He bungles it, of course. But on 12th November, 1966, Robert Benjamin Smith, an eighteen-year-old student, went into a beauty parlour at Mesa, Arizona, made five women and two children lie on the floor face downward, and then shot them all in the back of the head; five died. Smith, known as a quiet, non-violent young man, told the police: 'I wanted to get known – *to get myself a name*.'[1] Since Sartre is himself a non-violent man, his characters never do anything as spectacular as this. His gratuitous acts are an escape from boredom. (A character in *L'Age de Raison* describes human existence as 'drinking oneself without being thirsty'.) The real problem of most of the characters in his trilogy *Chemins de la Liberté* is that they are at a loose end, have no idea of what to do with their lives. The hero, Mathieu, sticks a knife through his hand, simply to demonstrate to a girl that he feels free. His pupil Boris steals books for the same reason (he counts up to five, then takes the book.) Mathieu's friend Daniel, a homosexual, not only refuses to lend Mathieu the money he needs for an abortion, but plots to force Mathieu to marry the girl; he does this because it would be rational and logical to lend Mathieu the money, and he prefers not to act rationally. (Later, he marries the pregnant girl himself, in the same spirit of irrationality.) In the end, Mathieu prefers to die defending a church tower against the advancing Germans – again, for no particular reason, or rather, *because* there is no particular reason. And in the play *Le Diable et le Bon Dieu*, the hero, a general, accepts a wager that he cannot do good as easily as he does evil, and becomes a saint for a while – then goes back to doing evil. Since God is dead, says Sartre, it makes no difference whether he does good or evil. Man is free; he can do a good act in a spirit of wickedness or a wicked act in a spirit of goodness; and the act itself is neither good nor evil.

Clearly, we have returned to the position expounded by Sade based on the will to power. Sade also argues that since God does not exist, no act is good or evil in itself; therefore the only reason for any act is the pleasure it can give. Sartre goes one step further than Sade in elaborating a psychology that justifies this attitude. According to Sartre, every human being is fundamentally alone, living in his own private universe. 'We each think of the key, each in his prison.' I look around me and see a universe of solid, real objects and solid, real people. But when I look inside myself, I find a kind of hollow, like an aching tooth. Man's basic experiences, according to Sartre, are all different ways of feeling this emptiness: shame, embarrassment, uncertainty, lack of self-assurance: in a word, self-consciousness. Everything a man does, says Sartre, is an attempt to escape this feeling of self-consciousness. He tries to *act* in a self-confident way, to give people the idea that he is a force of nature. He seeks love because it makes him feel real – to be loved. But, says Sartre, love can never be satisfactory to a highly self-conscious person, because he is aware that being in love is really a desire to make the other person love you, and that the same goes for the other person. So neither are getting what they want. And this, according to Sartre, explains sadism. When a man inflicts pain on another, he feels real, solid. But again, this cannot satisfy an intelligent person, for he only has to look into the eyes of the other person to see that she *belongs to herself*, that she is permanently 'uninvadable', that even if she wanted to 'give herself completely', she couldn't; she remains in her universe, and he remains in his. (Rupert Brooke expressed a similar view of love three decades earlier: that the lovers remain 'each in his lonely night, each with a ghost'.)

And so, according to Sartre, human relations are fundamentally a matter of conflict, as if each human being were a beast of prey or a cannibal, and others were his food. The destructive instinct, according to Sartre, is man's attempt to experience his freedom as a reality, *to become a do-er instead of a victim*.

This view obviously brings us closer to an understanding of Manson or Brady. But it is not difficult to point out its inadequacies. According to Sartre, man can never escape the feeling of 'toothache'; he may forget it, as you can forget a pain, but he cannot exchange it for its opposite: a feeling of being as solid and real as a material object, of being 'totally yourself'.

But this is untrue. The peak experience is as common to healthy people – as Maslow showed – as depression is to unhealthy people. And in the peak experience, man experiences a sense of freedom and reality.

This brings me to one of the central arguments of this book. The key lies in the word 'depression'. To feel depressed is to experience a sense of low inner-pressure. The peak exprience is a feeling of high inner-pressure. Why is insomnia such an unpleasant experience? After all, lying in a warm, comfortable bed ought to be agreeable enough. Why can it turn into a kind of foretaste of hell? Simply because the relaxed mind is 'de-pressurized', and every minor irritation obtrudes itself inescapably. Molehills become mountains. The Chinese water torture is based on the same principle: so is the 'black room', used in brainwashing. For many insomniacs, W. S. Gilbert's patter song: 'When you're lying awake with a dismal headache' is too real to be funny.

In insomnia or boredom, the mind seems to become *light*, like a balloon. It lacks strength; it is at the mercy of its environment, so that everything that happens blows it off course. A moment's reflection will confirm the truth of this: that all states of depression, misery, boredom, nausea, are moods in which consciousness takes on a ballon-like quality. On the other hand, when a man becomes excited, happy, driven by a strong sense of purpose or expectancy, the mind becomes *heavy*, powerful; the balloon turns into something more like a sledge-hammer. In the Einstein theory, a body in motion actually gains in weight, and this certainly seems to apply to the mind. When it drives towards an important aim, it seems to gain mass.

Because purposeful activity gives the mind this sense of weight, of reality, man *seeks out* purpose instinctively. Casanova discovers that as he is about to penetrate a girl for the first time, he experiences a sense of being real, solid, god-like. When he has made love to her a dozen times, the novelty has gone; so he looks for another girl – in order to induce the god-like sensation, to turn the mind into a sledge-hammer. Sherlock Holmes takes doses of morphine between cases, to dull the ache of boredom. 'I cannot live without brainwork,' he tells Watson: 'What else is there to live for? ... What is the use of having powers, doctor, when one has no field upon which to exert them?'[5] And on another occasion, he tells Watson: 'My mind is like a racing engine, tearing itself to pieces because it is not connected up with the work for which it was built.'[6]

But *what work?* – that is the problem. Edgar Lee Masters expressed the basic human predicament in his poem 'Professor Newcomer' in *The Spoon River Anthology:*

> Everyone laughed at Col. Pritchard
> For buying an engine so powerful
> That it wrecked itself and wrecked the grinder
> He ran it with.
> But here is a joke of cosmic size:
> The urge of nature that made a man
> Evolve from his brain a spiritual life —
> Oh miracle of the world! —
> The very same brain with which the age and wolf
> Get food and shelter and procreate themselves.
> Nature has made man do this,
> In a world where she gives him nothing to do
> After all — (though the strength of his soul
> goes round
> In a futile waste of power.
> To gear itself to the mills of the gods) —
> But get food and shelter and procreate himself!

The mind is a *concentrating machine*.That is the purpose for which it was built: to enable us to focus and concentrate on meanings, in order to be able to pursue them consciously and purposively instead of gropingly and blindly. Whenever we use it for this purpose, the effect is rather like clenching your fist; it gains in hardness and weight, and we experience a sense of reality. If it is left 'unclenched', unconcentrated, for too long, the result is the feeling of 'life failure', of unreality.

This already begins to explain what went wrong with the Manson family. For all their talk about freedom, love, self-expression, they were all drifting. Long sessions with 'acid' and pot would increase this tendency to passivity. According to Manson's doctrines, this way of life should have given them freedom; instead, it produced a feeling of suffocation.

Now the oddest thing about the human mind is this tendency to *seek out objects* that will give it a reason for concentrating. It is an absurd tendency: rather as if, when you itched, you looked around for something to scratch yourself with, unaware that you can do it with your nails. This psychological oddity explains sexual perversion. Sex produces a feeling of being *more alive*, a sense of sharpness and clarity, like a fine autumn afternoon, but it is not the sex itself that produces this clarity. It only causes you to concentrate harder than usual, to make a greater effort of focusing. It is this effort that produces the sharpness and clarity. We totally fail to recognize this causal relation, assuming that the sexual stimulus somehow acts *direct* upon consciousness. So when, on other occasions, we make less effort, and the result is less pleasure, we wonder what went wrong, why the experience has lost its sharpness. Imagining that the stimulus acts direct upon consciousness, the answer would seem to be to increase the stimulus, to add some element of shock, or surprise, to the sex. This might be done, for example, by having a full length mirror beside the bed, or inducing excitement with pornography, or getting the girl to dress in black net underwear, or acting out rape fantasies. The increased stimulus simply causes increased concentration. But we continue to think of this concentration as something that has to be galvanized, like a dead frog's leg, instead of recognizing that it is a *living* muscle, and that a living muscle can be strengthened by effort.

This 'passive fallacy' I am describing is man's most dangerous enemy. For it means that whenever he is comfortable, whenever there is no challenge to keep him on his toes, he tends to sink into a torpor. And after a while, the torpor turns into a sense of suffocation. Everyone knows this feeling – you get it if you watch television for too long, or force yourself to keep on reading a long book, merely to find out what happens at the end. Unless dispersed by action, it turns into a feeling of dyspepsia and general low-spirits, and eventually into a longing for something violent to happen.

The 'passive fallacy' is natural to human beings because our babyhood is so long, compared to other animals. A bird spends only a few weeks of its life sitting with its mouth open, waiting for the mother to drop in a worm; then it has to fend for itself. In primitive or harsh conditions, human babies also have to develop a degree of independence fairly early. But since man's central concern is comfort and security, and he directs all his energy and ingenuity to achieving them, most human beings can reckon on at least five years of parental protection. Then the infant school takes over, then the junior school ... So that in general, modern civilized man can rely upon various forms of protection until he is well into adulthood. Even if he has a taste for independence and adventure, the opportunities for it dwindle from decade to decade. Everything about modern life favours the unchecked growth of the passive attitude to existence, and the frustration and waste of vitality that springs from it.

The frustration needs something to vent itself on; and it finds an ideal scapegoat in that abstraction called 'society'. For Society *is* an abstraction, created by the misuse of language. Society consists of well-meaning *human beings*, all living their own lives and doing their best to make a living. When we say of a criminal 'He is paying his debt to society' we are committing an offence against logic; it is like saying 'He is paying his debt to the atmosphere'. He couldn't possibly owe 'society' a debt unless he had robbed every one of its members individually.

And the criminal also believes that 'society' exists, and that 'it' has put him in gaol. And if he is badly treated in gaol, he may develop an obsession about getting his 'revenge on society' – again an impossibility, since he can only rob or shoot individuals. Kürten the Düsseldorf sadist, managed to convince himself that his murders were not committed out of sexual desire, but out of a determination to make society 'pay' for what he had suffered in prison. When people opened their newspapers and read that another child had been found murdered, he was punishing them for putting him in gaol ...

The attitude of the political assassin is slightly more defensible on grounds of logic. Sometimes the victim *is* a tyrant, and his death changes the course of history in a relatively bloodless way. But a glance down a list of kings and rulers who have been assassinated since 1870 reveals that few of their murders served this purpose. Alexander II of Russia was a liberal Tsar, and his death did no one any good. Umberto I of Italy, killed by an anarchist named Bresci in 1900, was a harmless if somewhat conservative old gentleman. So was the French president, Sadi Carnot, stabbed by an anarchist in 1894. (Edward Hyams, who argues in favour of assassination in his book *Killing No Murder*, admits that Sadi Carnot was no more than a 'scapegoat'.) The Empress Elizabeth of Austria, stabbed in 1898 by a 'socialist' named

Lucheni, was killed solely because she was an empress. ('But it must be someone important, so it gets into the papers . . .') The death of two American presidents, Garfield and McKinley, served no observable purpose except to make their cranky assassins (Guiteau and Czolgosz) famous. The Archduke Franz Ferdinand, killed by Slav patriots, was himself a champion of the Slavs in the Austro-Hungarian empire.[7] There is an air of absurdity about most of these murders, as if they were cases of accident or mistaken identity. The assassin kills because he is bored and frustrated, and his head is full of some confused idea of justice, and anyone who is 'privileged' is a suitable target, whether or not he has any real connection with injustice.

'Between the revolutionary and society there is a war to the death' said Netchaev in the *Revolutionary Catechism* he concocted with Bakunin – an odd assertion that leads one to ask what he intended to replace society *with*. This is typical of the muddled and 'magical' thinking of the 'assassin'. He lacks the insight to recognize self-dissatisfaction for what it is, and directs it against 'society', as a bad-tempered man 'takes it out' on his family.

This brings us to the heart of the problem of the 'motiveless murder'. Aldous Huxley, describing his sensations under the drug mescalin, admitted that it could produce a state of paranoid fear: 'If you started in the wrong way, everything that happened would be a proof of the conspiracy against you . . .' Psychedelic drugs undoubtedly increased Manson's paranoic tendencies: But one does not need to take psychedelics to become paranoid about the modern world. Huxley explains the problem of the schizophrenic:

'He is like a man permanently under the influence of mescalin, and therefore unable to shut off the experience of a reality which he is not holy enough to live with, which he cannot explain away because it is the most stubborn of primary facts, and which, because it never permits him to look at the world with merely human eyes, scares him into interpreting its unremitting strangeness, its burning intensity of significance, as the manifestations of human or even cosmic malevolence, calling for the most desperate countermeasures, from murderous violence at one end of the scale, to catatonia, or pyschological suicide, at the other.' (*Doors of Perception*.)

That is to say, mescalin, like schizophrenia, produces a 'wide open' state of mind, so that you cannot pull down the shutters against the blazing light of reality that beats in. The mind becomes frightened and fatigued, subjected to this endless harassment; a generalized mistrust develops. In the modern city, this state becomes increasingly common. Life is confused and strange and impersonal. But all human beings, even the most extrovert, reach a point when they want to withdraw inside themselves, roll up in a ball, like a child in a warm bed, and pull the blankets up. Sociologists have often commented that people in big cities do not know their next door neighbour – the usual explanation being that there are too many people to get to know. This is absurd; theoretically it is no more difficult to get to know the people in the next flat than the people in the next cottage in a village. The true explanation is that the strain of city life produces a *revulsion,* a self-protective shrinking, a desire to mind your own business. The inhabitants of a village, soothed into confidence by narrow horizons, are prepared to take an interest in their neighbours. A man brought up in a small village gets used to thinking of people as decent and kindly because he sees them taking an active interest in one another's affairs. The big city deafens its inhabitants with noise and variety; they have to learn to ignore it; and in doing so, they ignore one another. The decision to 'mind your own business' is, in fact, a mild form of schizophrenia, a self-chosen sense of isolation that can easily turn into alienation. A few years ago, an American photographer took a remarkable series of photographs of a man who had collapsed on the stairs of a New York subway; people glanced down at him and walked around him; some did not even glance down. In a recent murder case in England, a woman's screams at midnight led neighbours to switch on their lights and look out into the street; but although she went on screaming, no one went out to investigate; she was dead when the police arrived. And only a few days before I wrote this, a British coroner had harsh comments to make about holiday-makers who watched a ten-year-old girl struggling out of her depth in the sea; she was rescued five minutes later by a lifeguard, but could not be revived; if one of the onlookers had gone in, said the coroner, she would still be alive. In each of these cases, it would be inaccurate to describe the attitude of the onlookers as callous; callousness implies a deliberate *rejection* of human values. This is more like absent-mindedness. People in crowds have to learn to *cut out* 90 per cent of their experience, like wearing dark glasses in the sun. They were watching the drowning child through dark glasses, failing to grasp what was going on.

But the cut-out mechanism is a matter of habit. If a man goes to work on the same train every day, walks through the same crowds to his office, eats lunch in the same over-crowded restaurant, he learns what to expect; the robot will do most of his 'living' for him, and it is only occasionally, by accident, that he swallows more experience than he can handle. But if, like Manson, he has no home and no regular job, then the situation becomes altogether more dangerous – for himself and society. He may, as Huxley says, commit 'mental suicide', become a bum on skid row and drift from moment to moment, turning into a kind of ostrich with his head permanently buried. Or the confusion and impersonality of the 'air conditioned nightmare' may produce increasing fatigue and hostility. The 'waste land' state of mind develops. Everything confirms it. The newspapers are full of international mistrust, air disasters, murders, racial violence, Vietnamese villages destroyed with napalm.

'So you think you know where madness lies?' said the doctor who administered the mescalin to Aldous Huxley.

'Yes.'

'And you couldn't control it?'

'No. I couldn't control it. If one began with fear and hate as the major premises, one would have to go on to the conclusion.'

The problem, as Huxley sees, lies in *the premise*. This is the real difference between our world and the world of a century ago. The London and New York of 1860 were as overcrowded and filled with poverty as the London and New York of today. Even then, traffic jams were a major problem. But the fear-and-hate premise had not yet developed. Religion was losing its hold, but it had been replaced by a belief in progress, and in the importance of ordinary human kindness. A Gustav Doré engraving of 1872 shows homeless women and babies sleeping outdoors in the East End of London. Dickens had often seen the same sight – people crouched in the rain outside a workhouse because there was no room inside – and had been horrified. It never occurred to him to doubt that if this kind of thing could be stamped out, society would be half-way toward the golden age. Half a century later, mothers and babies no longer had to sleep outdoors; yet the golden age had receded further. The Victorian moral certainty had vanished. The optimism of the intellectuals gave way to the 'decadence' of the 1890s, then to mounting distrust of civilization and progress. After the First World War, despair became the cultural premise. The older generation of writers – Shaw, Wells, Chesterton, Bennett – lost favour overnight; their eclipse was sudden and startling. The writers who replaced them had only one thing in common: they started from a premise of a fallen world – or at least, a world in which something had gone badly, fundamentally wrong. Shaw and Chesterton had been men of vision and optimists. Now vision and optimism parted company. The optimists of the post-war period were mostly communists who believed in the coming revolution; their doctrinaire narrowness repelled less dogmatic minds. The writers with a broader, more detached vision – Eliot, Huxley, Toynbee, for example – tended to be pessimistic. Even Shaw and Wells became pessimists in their later years. It is impossible to imagine a work of vision *and* optimism – like Dickens's *Christmas Carol* – being written after 1920. The belief in the *basic goodness of life* had evaporated.

And it is against this background of general pessimism that one must try to understand Manson and Brady and Collins. All three were intelligent enough to be influenced by ideas. They found themselves living in a culture that had no positive ideas to offer them. Two centuries earlier there would have been religion; a century after that, Dickensian humanism. By 1960, the accumulated weight of Darwin, Marx, Freud, Spengler, and two generations of pessimistic intellectuals – whose pessimism seemed justified by the hydrogen bomb – had destroyed every possible reason for optimism about the present or the future. There was no counterforce to resist the 'civilization neurosis' that turned Manson and his followers into self-appointed avengers. 'I didn't relate to Sharon Tate as being anything but a store mannequin,' said Susan Atkins. 'She sounded like an I.B.M. machine. She kept begging and pleading and begging and pleading and I got sick of listening to her, so I stabbed her.' The prosecutor asked her: 'Seven dead bodies are no big thing to you?' 'Well, are they? Are one million dead because of napalm, because of your justice, a big thing?' The illogicality staggers the mind – until one grasps the clue. Sharon Tate was a mannequin, a computer, and therefore to be judged by a different set of standards to members of the 'family'. But how could a living human being appear to be a statue? Because she was a part of the 'conspiracy': a conspiracy of statues and robots against the 'real people'. Susan Atkins was suffering from the twentieth-century equivalent of the delusions that made nuns writhe on the floor, convinced that they were possessed by demons. She was living in a paranoiac's world of universal malevolence.

A more recent case confirms the prevalence of the 'fear and hate' premise. Victor Ohta, a highly successful eye surgeon, had built a luxury home near Soquel, near Santa Cruz, California. On 19th October, 1970, this house was seen to be on fire. Firemen discovered five bodies in the swimming pool: those of Dr. Ohta, forty-seven, his wife Virginia, thirty-nine, their two children, Taggart and Derrick, eleven and twelve, and Dr. Ohta's secretary, Dorothy Cadwallader. Dr. Ohta had been shot three times; the others had been shot once in the back of the head, execution-style. The doctor's Rolls-Royce was parked across the drive, blocking it; under the windscreen wiper was a note that read:

'Hallowe'en 1970.

'Today World War III will begin, as brought to you by the people of the free universe.

'From this day forward, anyone and/or company of persons who misuses the natural environment or destroys same will suffer the penalty of death by the people of the Free Universe.

'I and my comrades from this day forth will fight until death or freedom against anyone who does not support natural life on this planet. Materialism must die or mankind will stop.'

The signature read: 'Knight of Wands – Knight of Pentacles – Knight of Cups – Knight of Swords.'

Mrs. Ohta's stationwagon was found in a railway tunnel near the San Lorenzo river; a slow-travelling goods train ran into it, and pushed it out of the tunnel, where it had obviously been left in the hope of causing a serious accident. The upholstery had been slashed and set on fire.

The murders caused panic and rage in the area. There were large numbers of hippies living in the woods; it looked like another Manson-type killing, a protest against the 'pigs'. Then, as police questioned hippies, it began to emerge that the murders had not been the work of several killers, but of one. The suspect, John Linley Frazier, twenty-four was a car mechanic in Santa Cruz. For some time before the murders, he had been experimenting with drugs. A 'bad trip' on mescalin had convinced him that he had received a revelation. He left his job, separated from his wife, and went to live in a shack near a village called Felton, where a number of hippies lived. There he studied the fortune-telling cards called the Tarot (which contains the four 'knights' mentioned), and read about ecology and preservation of the environment. He worked up a violent resentment about the 'materialistic' society, and one witness described how Frazier had admitted breaking into the Ohtas' house and stealing a pair of binoculars. He had commented that they were 'too materialistic' and should be killed. A check on Frazier revealed that he had a police record – he had been arrested for burglary.

A woman had seen someone of Frazier's description – small and bearded, like Manson – driving Virginia Ohta's stationwagon on the day after the murders. A few days later, Frazier was arrested in a shack near his mother's farm. He made no comments, and remained silent throughout his subsequent trial. His fingerprints on the door of the Rolls-Royce, and on a beer can found in the burnt house, established his guilt beyond reasonable doubt; Frazier was sentenced to death – joining the queue of murderers awaiting execution in San Quentin.[8]

The evidence indicates that Frazier planned the murders some days before committing them. He had given his wife his driving licence with the comment that he wouldn't be needing it again. He told three hippy acquaintances that 'big things would be happening Monday' – the day of the murders.

The police reconstructed the crime as follows. Frazier arrived at the Ohta home sometime before three o'clock on the afternoon of the murders, and held up Mrs. Ohta – who was alone – with a ·38 pistol. He tied Mrs. Ohta's hands behind her with a scarf, and took her own gun, a ·22 pistol. He then 'executed' Mrs. Ohta.

Some time after three, a schoolteacher at the school of the two Ohta boys called Dr. Ohta at his office and told him that Mrs. Ohta had failed to turn up and collect the boys. Ohta was not alarmed; he sent his secretary, Mrs. Cadwallader, to pick up one of the boys; he himself picked up the other, and took him on a visit to his elderly mother in Santa Cruz. Mrs. Cadwallader returned to the Ohta home – and was met by the killer, who tied the hands of the new arrivals, and shot them in the back of the head with Mrs. Ohta's gun. Some time after five, Dr. Ohta arrived with the other boy. He seems to have submitted to being tied, but then decided to put up a fight. Frazier shot him three times with the ·38, and shot the boy with the ·22. After this he set the house on fire, and left. The Rolls-Royce was driven across the drive, and the stationwagon taken away.

The parallel with the Manson murders is close; Frazier's 'World War III' was probably inspired by Manson's Helter Skelter. But the charge of 'destroying the environment' hardly applies to Dr. Ohta, who had taken care to leave the natural surroundings of his $300,000 house untouched. Neither was Frazier's assumption that Ohta was 'materialistic' correct. Ohta's life had been difficult. He was the son of Japanese immigrants who had been interned in 1941, when America went to war. In 1943, when he was twenty, Ohta was allowed to join the American army; his elder brother was killed fighting in Europe. After the war, Ohta studied at Montana State College, and also worked as a track-layer on the railway. Later he worked as a cab driver while studying at medical school. Two more years as an Air Force doctor were followed by a further period of study – to become an eye surgeon – during which he also worked as a doctor to support his family. (There were two elder daughters who were away at college at the time of the murders.) It was at a fairly late stage that he began to work as an eye surgeon, specializing in the removal of cataracts, and became astonishingly successful. He was one of the founders of Dominican Hospital, in the Santa Cruz area – a non-profit making organization – to which he also gave considerable financial support; when patients could not afford his fees, he was known to give free treatment. Frazier's 'materialist' was a generous and hardworking man who deserved his success.

As in the case of the Manson family, psychedelic drugs

seem to have been largely to blame for Frazier's paranoid tendencies. His wife said that he had once been a 'beautiful person' who had turned violent and resentful.

At the same time, the murders showed a lack of planning typical of a disoriented person. He set the house on fire – perhaps to destroy the fingerprints. But he did not take the elementary precaution of wearing gloves, and left prints on the Rolls-Royce. As soon as the police checked these prints against his police file, they had their man.

But to say that Frazier, Manson, Ian Brady, the Zodiac killer, were driven by 'ideas' is not to say that ideas in themselves are dangerous. What makes them dangerous is the 'fear and hate' climate that has replaced religion and humanism as the premise of our culture. Dickens felt about Scrooge that in spite of his meanness and bad temper, he was basically decent and kindly. He is to be pitied rather than hated; the 'narrowness' has attacked him like a disease, like hardening of the arteries, and made him thoroughly miserable. Fortunately, it *is* reversible. He can learn to open himself, to stop seeing the world through sunglasses that filter out most of the colour. And when Scrooge rejoined the human race, the Victorian reader gave a sigh of satisfaction. It confirmed his belief that life was basically good, that no human being is unredeemable.

A Christmas Carol was published in 1843. But although Dickens had more than a quarter of a century to live, the age of Dickensian humanism was drawing to a close. In 1859, *The Origin of Species* appeared; in 1867, the first volume of *Das Kapital*. Darwin asserted that the basic principle of nature is conflict, the struggle for survival. Marx said that the same thing holds true for society. There are two warring classes, the bosses and the workers; and one day, the bosses will die out – destroyed by their own competitiveness – and the workers shall inherit the earth.

The church found these views repugnant, arguing that if they gained general acceptance, society would turn into a jungle. In 1920, Bernard Shaw wrote: 'I had always known that civilization needs a religion as a matter of life and death;'[9] and Shaw was right; for he understood that religion is fundamentally *a tradition about the meaning and purpose of human existence*. Its social purpose becomes clear if we consider the work of de Sade. Sade's feelings about society were pretty close to those of Brady and Manson: that it is corrupt, hypocritical, self-seeking and materialistic. But in order to justify his philosophy of murder and cruelty, Sade had to devote thousands of words to refuting and attacking Christianity, which interposed its enormous bulk between his hatred and its logical conclusion. Manson and Brady had no such mountain to scale. Society was corrupt; human beings were vile; therefore murder was justifiable. (Bobby Beausoleil told Gary Hinman: 'Society doesn't need you. You're a pig. You don't deserve to live. You should thank me. I'm doing you a favour.')

1. And also by D. Streatfield's Jungian critical study of *No Orchids, Persephone* (1959) in which the author argues that the book derives its fascination from its use of the Greek myth of the girl kidnapped by the lord of the underworld. In the second part of his study, Streatfield suggests that Thurber's *Secret Life of Walter Mitty*, the ineffectual daydreamer, is an equally potent and central myth of our time.
2. 'This was the first of twenty addresses Manson would have in this particular year [1958].' Ed Sanders, *The Family*, p. 23.
3. 'He tells about his life inside the institution in such a manner as to indicate that he has gotten most satisfaction from institutions'. Psychiatrist's report on Manson, Sanders, p. 24.
4. *Fragments from my Diary*, London, 1924.
5. *The Sign of Four*, Chapter 1.
6. *Wisteria Lodge*.
7. 'The greatest friend of the Slavs had fallen under the bullets of Slav fanatics'. Hitler, *Mein Kampf*.
8. See note 4 on p. 98.
9. From the preface to *Back to Methuselah*.

CHAPTER NINE

The Way Forward

One century after the publication of *A Christmas Carol,* Maslow formulated his theory of the hierarchy of values, and the wheel had come the full circle. Not that Maslow was the only psychologist who had misgivings about Freud's savagely pessimistic view of human nature. Adler and Jung had both emphasized the importance of man's social impulses; Otto Rank, Freud's closest disciple at one time, based his own later psychology upon the startling notion that man's fundamental drive is a *will to health,* and that man becomes sick only when this basic will is overwhelmed by problems and fears. Other psychologists preferred the 'philosophical' approach of Husserl and Heidegger, with its emphasis upon man's sense of strangeness in an alien universe; Ludwig Binswanger, Medard Boss, Erwin Straus and others founded a school that became known as 'existential psychology'. In a Nazi prison camp during the war, another psychiatrist, Viktor Frankl, observed that men are at their best when they have something to look forward to, and tend to become sick when they lose their forward momentum; his psychology (which he called logotherapy) regarded the craving for *meaning* as man's central appetite.[1] But none of these stated the basic notion – that human nature has 'higher ceilings' – with such force and clarity as Maslow.

The implications of his psychology must be stated clearly. If modern civilization is chaotic, this is not due to the natural wickedness of human beings or to an inbuilt destructiveness. Human nature is basically good and decent; neurosis and destructiveness are due to the blocking of its natural creative flow. A society that is run on the assumption that human beings are narrow, selfish and incapable of making use of freedom, will produce poor results because people are frustrated. And, according to Maslow, a society – or business – that is run on the opposite assumption, that man is an *evolutionary* creature, whose basic need is to seek out fruitful activity, should immediately begin to show positive results. In America, a few far-sighted businessmen decided to put Maslow's theory to the test. The old theory of industrial management was authoritarian, based upon the assumption that the interests of management and workers are opposed: that the worker wants as much money as possible for as little work as he can give, while the management wants as much work as possible for as little money. According to Maslow, what *everybody* wants is fruitful activity, to do a good job as well as possible. As far as possible, the worker should be allowed to keep his own time, to do the jobs he prefers and to devise his own way of doing them. Some workers will prefer more freedom, some less; this must also be allowed for. But the final result should be more job-satisfaction all round, and higher productivity.

Maslow's theory was tried out in a small electronics firm in California, then in the huge Saga Food Corporation. In both cases, it worked triumphantly. When an oil refinery in Rotterdam tried it, productivity per man was nearly doubled. Since most of this has taken place in the past few years, it is too soon to say that Maslow has altered the American approach to industrial management; but his theory has so far proved to be 100 per cent correct.

Again, it must be emphasized that there were many other scientists working along parallel lines, driven by the same dissatisfaction with the narrow and rigid assumptions of nineteenth century science. Sir Karl Popper, a philosopher of science, had been attacking these assumptions since the early 'thirties. Science is not a plodding, logical investigation of the universe that could be carried out by an electronic brain, but a creative process closer to poetry or musical composition. It follows that imagination is as important to the scientist as to the artist, and that the narrow, sceptical frame of mind that used to be called 'scientific' is nothing of the sort. These views achieved a wider celebrity – at least among scientists and philosophers – in 1958 when they were expressed in a book called *Personal Knowledge*, by Michael Polanyi, himself a scientist and Fellow of the Royal Society.

The ordinary reader could be forgiven for feeling that all this has no relevance for people like himself – and certainly not for Charles Manson and Ian Brady. He would be wrong. Our civilization is founded on science, and we have built up an image of the scientist as a detached, impersonal human being who doesn't care whether he is working on a cancer cure or the hydrogen bomb. Science is 'inhuman' and it will probably end by destroying us all . . . No one has the same fear of writers and musicians – although they influence our lives as much as scientists, probably more – because we feel they are 'in with us', a part of society. When it is understood that the scientist is driven by the same motivations as the poet, that his mind works in the same way, another one of our basic insecurities will have vanished, and the human race will be a step closer to feeling itself to be a unity.

What creates killers like Brady, Manson and van Zon is the *atmosphere* of our society, just as the atmosphere of some industrial concerns breeds labour troubles. Willem James, the Dutch industrialist who adopted Maslow's theory at his Rotterdam oil refinery, told Robert Ardrey: 'The figures don't say it and maybe it sounds silly. We have a happy oil refinery. People come to work because they enjoy it.' (Conversely, the atmosphere in British Ford plants seems to breed nothing but trouble, to judge by their strike record between 1967 and 1971.) But if Maslow's principles can be applied to giant industries, they can also be applied to society at large. (In fact, Maslow was working on this problem at the time of his death in 1970 – what he called 'Politics 3'.)

Where the question of crime is concerned, perhaps the most interesting advance of recent years has been made by a group who call themselves the Yonan Codex Foundation, with headquarters in Atlanta, Georgia.[2] Dan MacDougald, a lawyer who ran the foundation, calls his psychology 'attitude therapy', and its success in rehabilitating 'hard core deviates' in prisons has been incredible.

MacDougald is not a psychologist but a lawyer. In a pamphlet called 'Attitude Psychotherapy' he explains how he came to get interested in the question. MacDougald was approached by three farmers with a complaint about the Federal authorities, who were overloading the Buford Dam, north of Atlanta, to such an extent that cattle were often swept into the flooded river and crops were ruined. It took three years – starting in 1956 – and $46,000 to get things changed. What baffled MacDougald was *how* Federal authorities could do this kind of thing. Didn't they see that they were causing needless suffering and damage? The engineers of the dam told MacDougald 'You can't make an omelette without breaking eggs,' but that didn't answer his question. He put the question to a psychiatrist, who said that this kind of wilful disrespect of people is a result of paranoia. This didn't seem to help much either, since the engineers weren't obviously paranoid in any meaningful sense. And it eventually dawned on MacDougald that these engineers were simply 'cutting out' the whole question of the rights of the farmers – wearing dark glasses, so to speak .

MacDougald formulated his conclusion this way. Our lives are controlled by continual acts of judgement, continual choices. And the number of choices that a busy man confronts during a normal day is staggering. He has to find shortcuts, ways to do many things quickly and automatically, because he only has so much energy, so much 'attention', to spend. A lot of choices have to be treated very casually, and sometimes these are fairly big choices – like the affair of the Buford dam.

What surprised MacDougald was to realize *how much* we all have to ignore or 'cut out' from our perceptions. A Harvard psychologist, George Miller, performed experiments that showed that human beings can register about seven 'items of information' at once. I.e. if I walk through a strange room, I might notice the colour of the carpet, the flowers decorating the room, the music being played over the radio, the people, the position of the window, the smell of cigar smoke, the presence of a small dog . . . And I would not notice the design of the furniture, the colour of the curtains, the number of people, the position of the radio, and so on. If I spent half an hour in the room, making a list of all the things I *could* notice, I might end with a hundred items on it. That is to say that I notice less than ten per cent of the things I *could* notice.

This has been known to psychologists for a long time – since before Freud, in fact: that the senses are selective, that they 'filter out' about 90 percent of our perceptions. There are certain things that men habitually notice – a girl in a short mini-skirt, for example. And there are things that they habitually fail to notice. A man who does not really care for children may simply not notice children. We cut-out what does not interest us, *what we do not care for*. And – this is the important point, *we* decide what we do not care for. We work up prejudices and irritations.

MacDougald was interested to discover that this is not simply a matter of 'not noticing', ignoring things we don't like. It is a *physical* mechanism. Dr. Jerome Bruner of Harvard described an experiment with a cat. An electrode was placed on the nerve between the cat's ear and its brain, and a wire run from it to an oscilloscope. When a bell was rung in the cat's ear – or any other sound – it registered as a swing of the needle. A cage with mice was now placed in front of the cat. Naturally, it became absorbed in watching them. And when a sound was made in its ear, the needle of the oscilloscope did not stir.

Now this is odd. After all, the sound entered the cat's ear, even if it did not reach the brain. It ought to have registered. But what actually happens is that the neurons (nerve cells) transmit the sound from one to another, rather as if it was a row of billiard balls, and you knocked the end ball, causing each one to hit the next. If we do not want to hear something, we 'raise the neural threshold', put a kind of damper on each neuron which, in effect, is like moving the billiard balls further apart.

Consider what you do if you are resisting something you do not like – for example, a fingernail scratching on glass. You 'tense up', contracting your muscles, perhaps even pulling a face. This is the way we bring the 'inhibitory system' into action. A man full of resentments – a criminal – may be tensed up all the time. There is an English proverb 'There's none so deaf as those who don't want to hear', which expresses the general attitude towards 'not noticing'. But, as the cat experiment shows, such a man quite literally does not hear and see what he doesn't want to hear and see. To begin with, he may be aware that he is deliberately making himself deaf; but after a while it becomes a habit, and he ceases to be even dimly aware. W. S. Gilbert was totally wrong when he wrote:

> 'When a felon's not engaged in his employment
> Or maturing his felonious little plans
> His capacity for innocent enjoyment
> Is just as great as any honest man's.'

Dan MacDougald established that a felon *is* a felon because his 'capacity for innocent enjoyment' is badly eroded.

In Scrooge, Dickens created a well-observed picture of how this comes about. As a child, Scrooge is portrayed as lonely and imaginative, reading the *Arabian Nights* in the classroom when everybody else has gone. The increasing miserliness springs from insecurity; the girl to whom he is engaged tells him: 'You fear the world too much . . .' But the first of the spirits has him weeping within minutes by showing him scenes of his childbirth. The 'blockages' vanish: 'He was conscious of a thousand odours floating in the air, each one connected with a thousand thoughts . . .' The scenes of the past make him aware that his 'inhibitory mechanisms' have stranded him in a bleak, grey world, as different from the real world as paste jewellery is from the real thing. He only has to be *reminded* that he is living according to a set of false premises, and he instantly ceases to do so. The regenerate Scrooge 'went to church, and walked about the streets, and watched the people hurrying to and fro, and patted children on the head, and questioned beggars, and looked down into the kitchens of houses, and up to the windows; *and found that everything could yield him pleasure*. '[My italics]. It is merely a question of learning to 'open up'.

In effect, MacDougald made the assumption that 'hard core deviates' are suffering from the same problem as Scrooge, 'faulty blocking'. The inhibitory system is not, of course, a villain; it enables us to pay attention. But since man has the power to switch his attention from one thing to another, it follows that it *is* within his control. At least, to begin with. Take the case of a man who hates Negroes, and who can produce a thousand arguments to justify his hatred. There was a time when he didn't hate Negroes. Perhaps he heard someone he respected – his father or a schoolmaster – saying that Negroes are inferior. But since he is a schoolboy and quite likes a number of Negroes, he still keeps an open mind. Until various things that he hears or sees make him *decide* that Negroes are inferior. It is a definite act of decision, like religious conversion. From this point, he experiences a certain 'shrinking' when he has to speak to a Negro; he tends to withdraw, to stand back, almost as if trying to avoid a physical smell; he averts his eyes. Inevitably, he ceases to notice the difference between one Negro and another – this one is kind, this one intelligent, etc. They are 'all the same'. He now notices only those things about them that confirm his prejudices; he literally does not *see* any other aspect.

'Attitudes', then, begin as acts of decision, of choice; they only end as 'faulty blocking'.

MacDougald's next step may baffle many readers who have followed the argument so far. He reasoned that 'faulty blocking' leads to a distorted understanding of words. (A criminal, hearing the word 'copper', may experience a feeling – accompanied by an image – that would puzzle a law abiding citizen: something closer to 'Nazi concentration camp guard' or 'sadistic thug'.) So the way to start 'unblocking' criminals is to get them to understand this. What 'attitudes' need to be altered? 'He found that the best source for this information was in ancient documents in the Aramaic language – the language of most of the prophets of the Old Testament, the language of Jesus, the Koran and of Mohammed. It was in the study of this ancient language that MacDougald found considerable instruction on *koodsha* (proper) attitudes, or good attitudes, as well as the precise meanings for the words which ultimately became the foundation for Attitude Psychotherapy.

'MacDougald found that in Aramaic the word "love" was considered to be an attitude rather than a physical exercise or feeling. He also found the statement that all law hangs on love of God, and love for neighbour as oneself, the studies of the word 'law' indicated its meaning in that instruction to be the rules by which human beings live and think. He reasoned that if this were true, conforming one's attitudes to this instruction should yield a yardstick by which the mind could assess all rules, reasoning, perception, memory, judgements and behaviour.'[3]

All this makes it sound as though the MacDougald method is merely a form of religious revivalism. Before reaching this conclusion, one should consider its amazing success with all types of prisoners. According to C. D. Warren, medical director of the Georgia Institute of Corrections[4], it worked with over 60 per cent of prisoners, and follow-up studies seemed to indicate that the improvement was permanent. According to Dr. Warren, two men from the Yonan Codex Foundation told him that anti-social personalities could be rehabilitated in two or three months, with special instructions for only one day a week. 'To my astonishment, they did just exactly what they anticipated, with results now supported by an eighteen-month follow-up.' The two 'instructors' instructed two prisoners in their methods. At the end of two weeks, the four of them then instructed 22 prisoners in a two hour session every week for two months. Four more prisoners were appointed instructors, and the six new instructors now took on 150 prisoners. It took them eight weeks to 'rehabilitate' 63 per cent of them, and the follow-up study, eighteen months later, showed that every one of these was still unchanged; there had been no backsliding.

Neither Dr. Warren nor Dan MacDougald make an attempt to explain *why* it works; but readers of this book should be in a position to understand precisely why. A large number of criminals belong to the 'dominant five per cent'. *All* men have the same basic need to evolve, to grow, to turn from a chrysalis into a butterfly. In the dominant five per cent, this need is far stronger than in the remainder, and its frustration produces a more violent explosion. In a certain sense, it would not have mattered *what* MacDougald's instructors taught the prisoners. All that mattered was that they were suddenly being treated as intelligent, decent human beings, capable of changing their own lives. They were being treated according to the Maslow view of human nature instead of the Darwin-Freud view. And since the Maslow view corresponds to the facts, it worked.

In the mid-1930s, Maslow had been doing some research into monkeys in the Bronx zoo, and he made a discovery that puzzled him. The monkeys were given various problems to solve, and they got food as a reward for solving them. For example, the banana might be placed in a cage with a complicated trapdoor, and the monkey's problem was to hold the trap open with one hand while taking the banana with the other. After a while, Maslow observed that the monkeys seemed to *enjoy* solving the problems for their own sake; they would accept wooden bananas, or even no banana at all. This ran counter to all the theories of animal behaviour: 'a chimpanzee cannot retain a mental image long enough to reflect upon it,' says Grey Walter in his book on the brain; so how the hell could monkeys enjoy a purely intellectual activity? But they did. It was the first clue that led Maslow to his researches into 'higher reaches of human nature'. Monkeys, like men, *will* evoke to 'higher activities' if you give them the chance.

There is no human being in the world, no matter how stupid, who is less intelligent than a monkey. The startling conclusion is that there is no human being in any gaol who cannot be taught to derive a certain pleasure from using his brain for its own sake. This consequence can be derived direct from Maslow, without taking any of MacDougald's important discoveries into account. *In theory, every prisoner in every gaol can be rehabilitated.* The gaols are full of members of the dominant five per cent whose capabilities are being wasted. The present system takes a defeatist attitude towards them. They are suffering from mental problems that could only be cured by lengthy individual treatment (which our system cannot afford), and in any case, a 'cure' is not likely to be permanent, since they have to go back to the chaotic, ruthless society that made them criminals in the first place . . .

MacDougald has shown these assumptions to be untrue. The present system is partly correct, in its assumption that the criminal is a man who wants a higher degree of reward than society offers him; so he tries to grab the reward without trying to earn it. It is mistaken in assuming that the reward has to be physical or tangible. As soon as the prisoners learn to unblock passages of communication that have been closed for years, the reward is the instant enrichment that Scrooge experiences. Frank Goble cites a remarkable example. One of the inmates, a man called Ronnie, took a violent dislike to another prisoner, who apparently returned the feeling. 'I knew that in the penitentiary here, that when you have to fight somebody, you either have to kill them or get killed . . .'[2] So Ronnie concealed a piece of iron pipe and prepared to attack the man – until he began to think about the concepts he had learned in the Yonan Codex course. Was the other convict his 'neighbour'? Was it really his inhibitory system blinding him to the reality of the situation. He went to the prison store, bought the other convict a sandwich and a coffee, and talked the thing over. The desire to commit violence – and the feeling of the need for it – vanished.

Everyone has known this feeling: indignation about something filling the whole mind, and the more you think about it, the more obvious it is that you ought to *do* something, make someone regret it . . . In this state it seems as *logical* to explode into violence – or rage – as to make for the lavatory when you want to urinate. Nothing else seems of comparable importance. Afterwards, you look back on it as a kind of insanity. Such resentment is, in fact, a perfect example of what is meant by faulty blocking. Ninety per cent of all murders are committed in this state – for most murders are 'crimes of passion', committed within the family. The Yonan Codex method makes the prisoner aware that such responses *are* due to faulty blocking, and that a totally different response is far more logical. If it could be generally taught throughout society, it would eliminate most murders.

Lester Maddox, the son of the governor of Georgia, showed an equally dramatic change under therapy. Dr. Ray Craddick, examining Maddox (who had been arrested for burglary when already on parole for a previous violation) reported that Maddox was '*functioning way below his potential and capacity*', was impulsive, self-centred, hostile, aggressive and prone to depression. A month's training in the Yonan Codex methods, and Craddick stated: 'There is overwhelming evidence of drastic changes in this young man's personality, intelligence and behaviour. All changes are in the direction of maturity . . . For example, his intelligence as reflected on the test was raised on practically all the subtests, with the end result of moving him from functioning on the average level to now being in the superior category.'

That phrase 'functioning way below his potential and capacity' is the real key to Attitude Therapy. A man in that condition is a frustrated man, an angry man, and anger is another name for violent impatience, a desire to achieve an end quickly and without regard to the means. MacDougald's attitude therapy is basically a way of persuading people to *slow down*, to take themselves more seriously, to take a long look at their capacities. According to Maslow, *most* people in a civilization like ours are functioning below their potential and capacity. Religion at least told man that he has an immortal soul that is infinitely valuable, and that he is capable of damnation or salvation. Our modern universal culture tells him that he is an animal with various appetites, living in a competitive world. But the 'third culture' that is coming into being (Maslow calls his work 'third force psychology') again asserts that man is an evolutionary animal, functioning way below his capacities, and that with a certain kind of deliberate effort he can transform himself and the world around him. The presuppositions that created our violent society are being quietly changed.

The basic problem can be expressed very simply. It was man's evolutionary urge that led him to create civilization. Now he has landed himself with a civilization that blocks the creative urge. Quite unconsciously, our civilization has adopted the notion that the aim of life is simply to keep alive and comfortable. So a man who travels to work past factory buildings and office blocks has a feeling that the whole purpose of this vast machine is to put milk into his tea and enable him to buy a colour television. It seems a complicated machine for such a simple purpose, and it is not surprising that he dreams nostalgically of a simpler age when the milk came straight out of the cow and the family made their own music in the evenings. We have lost sight of the obvious fact that the purpose of civilization is to offer man better opportunities to become what he is capable of becoming. We have to learn to think in terms of a new concept: the *creative civilization.*

Undoubtedly, this work of Maslow, MacDougald, and other 'third culture' psychologists and scientists, is only a beginning. MacDougald's approach seems to me to place too much emphasis on religion. If Maslow's evolutionism is true, then it should not be necessary to use religious concepts (like God, Jesus and so on.) While they do no actual harm, they seem to me to convey a false impression that the new therapy is allied to hot gospel evangelism. MacDougald's insights should be as valid for an intellectual atheist like Sartre as for a practising Christian: and indeed are. The personality change in a man like Lester Maddox Jnr. is not caused by divine grace, but by making him recognize himself as an intelligent, potentially creative human being who is living well below his capacities. Even love need not be a key concept; a creative man may find his fellow human beings interesting and likeable enough, but love may be altogether too strong a word to describe his attitude. 'Damn braces; bless relaxes,' says Blake; and talk about 'love' may also be a relaxant, an evasion of responsibility, as in the case of the Manson family. MacDougald's psychotherapy is based upon the recognition that most habitual criminals do not enjoy being criminals; and they certainly do not enjoy being in gaol. But they feel that, society being what it is, and they being what they are, there is no alternative; they are caught in a trap ... Attitude psychotherapy aims to 'show the fly the way out of the fly bottle' (to borrow Wittgenstein's phrase), to show that a non-criminal way of life offers greater rewards – in feeling, perceiving, experiencing – than the criminal way. This *may* be religion, but it is also scientific evolutionism.

The connection between Maslow's psychology and MacDougald's is not at once apparent, but is of considerable importance. The key concept of Maslow's psychology is what he calls the 'peak experience', the sudden flash of intense happiness, the feeling of affirmation about life. Maslow made the discovery that most *extremely healthy* people have peak experiences with a fair frequency, although he believed that the peak experience is essentially an accident – that no one can have them at will. But the reason that healthy people have peak experiences is that extremely healthy people are usually highly *responsible* people. And there is a connection here that Maslow was not fully aware of. A responsible person is one who keeps his will awake. When a man sinks into a state of boredom or depression – 'it's just not worth it ...' – he is disconnecting himself from responsibility, like putting a car into neutral gear. And the simile here points to a truth – that responsibility is our main driving force; pleasure is a by-product. When a man becomes irresponsible – or passive – his will 'runs down', in the way that a car battery becomes flat when it is out of use. He ceases to have 'peak experiences'. So we may say that Maslow's psychology throws an entirely new light on MacDougald's psychotherapy. The central trait of the criminal is a kind of passivity, a feeling that other people are to blame for his troubles; he expresses his resentment by passivity, like a drunk who refuses to be helped to his feet. This passivity means that his 'batteries' run down and he ceases to have 'peak experiences'. So what really happens when a prisoner is induced to start thinking for himself is that he begins to treat himself as a responsible human being; the 'engine' begins to work; he becomes healthier, and begins having peak experiences again – a general feeling of the worthwhileness of being alive. This concept of responsibility explains the startling success of MacDougald's method.

An example will clarify this further. A woman who recovered from the edge of a nervous breakdown told me the circumstances of her recovery. Her husband was going off to some remote place, and her brother somewhere else; the question was: which of them should she accompany? The problem caused her acute anxiety, until it came to her in a flash: 'I can do what I like. I am free. I can choose to go off to yet another place on my own.' This thought brought a sudden feeling of *identity* and a sense of power which lasted for several months. She became happier, and also more efficient: for example, she mentioned that her game of tennis suddenly improved enormously.

To understand exactly why this should be so is to grasp new possibilities in the psychology of Maslow and MacDougald. The purpose of the robot, the automatic part of us, is to take over any act that we *repeat* – breathing, for example, or speaking our own language. But there are certain activities that cannot be handed over to the robot. I have been writing books for twenty years, but I can't leave it to my robot (although reviewers will have to take my word for that). For writing requires that my 'I' – the essential, thinking part of me – should strive to be conscious of its freedom. The robot *helps* me – in the choice of words and phrases, in the actual typing – but he must be kept firmly in his subordinate place. It is too easy for the robot to take over more than his share. (This is what happens to nearly all writers as they get older – Aldous Huxley and Ernest Hemingway spring to mind; the familiar mannerisms *overwhelm* the creative content and the book is like a huge lobster shell with a very small lobster inside.) However, there are moments when the 'I' and the robot reach a new level of collaboration, both of them working at top pressure, and in these moments, everything seems to go right. This is why the girl's tennis improved. The 'I' had wakened up, ceased to be dominated by the robot, and the collaboration brought a new level of efficiency.

It is now possible to see why MacDougald's therapy works so well and so quickly. A bored, resentful man is a man who is dominated by his robot. By appealing to his intelligence, to what Maslow would call his 'higher nature', the Yonan therapist gives the 'I' a purpose, a reason for becoming active.

This brings us back to the importance of the self-image. Before an actor can play a part, he must have a clear idea of the character he is playing. Until he has this clear idea, he is groping in the dark. Once he has understood the person he is playing, he can 'get into' the part, and he no longer has to worry about acting; he simply *becomes* the character while he is on stage.

Now what happens when he 'becomes' the character? We say he 'sees himself' in the part – almost as if he had a mirror in front of him: a mirror that is blank while he is learning the part, but in which the character he is playing gradually begins to appear, like a ghost slowly materializing.

The self-image is necessary to *all* efficient action. The reason why shy teenagers are so clumsy and awkward is that their 'mirror' reflects back a blurry and shadowy self-image. This is why they are so anxious to hear other people's opinions about them: it helps to form the self-image, to create a definite mental picture of who they are. This is also why we hate inactivity, why we prefer to be *involved*, excited, absorbed; action, involvement, creates a clear self-image, gives us a positive feeling of who we are. This is why teenagers form into gangs and roar around on motor-cycles; it is an aid to the all-important business of creating a self-image. This also explains why a man confined in a totally black and silent room slowly goes to pieces; without anything to *do*, without a sense of purpose, his self-image slowly disintegrates. This is why Peter Kürten became a sadistic mass murderer; in prison for minor offences, he was often placed in solitary confinement for insubordination, and to keep sane, he spent the time indulging in sexual fantasies, which had to become increasingly violent as he became increasingly depressed.

Although physical activity is important, it is not absolutely essential for the self-image. Imagine a man staring into a mirror, but seeing no reflection there. Suddenly, through a lighted window, he sees a girl beginning to remove her clothes. His attention concentrates; and immediately, his face appears in the mirror. *It is the act of focusing that makes the image solidify.*

This affords another clue. A man watching a girl undressing focuses in the same way as a cat watching mice. Which brings us back to MacDougald, who used the image of a cat watching mice to explain how the criminal comes to 'block out' various perceptions. And we can see that the basic reason a sex criminal commits rape is that as he is involved in the act, he has a sudden sense of identity; for a moment, he knows 'who he is'; his face appears quite clearly in the mirror. For a few minutes he is a purposive organism, aware of its evolutionary purpose, a forward-flowing stream instead of a stagnant pond. This is true of all criminal acts. Why did Manson keep returning to auto thefts between terms in prison or reformatory? He knew that it would land him back in gaol. But he didn't know *what else* to do, and a man without a purpose has no self-image; the mirror remains blank. He stole to create a self-image, the momentary sense of power and identity. Being the head of the 'family' created a self-image, and for a while he ceased to be a criminal. Then the pointless life of acid-trips and wandering from home to home again blurred the self-image. Ordering executions restored it again.

By treating the prisoners as responsible, intelligent individuals, capable of exercising their minds to *alter* their lives, the Yonan therapists had provided them with a new self-image. MacDougald's concepts – of faulty blocking and so on – were a do-it-yourself kit for making self-images.

What is now beginning to develop is a new concept of the human mind and human society. It can be seen, for example, that the Freudian theory of neurosis – with its guilt complexes, incest-wishes, repressions – is unnecessarily complicated. All that is necessary to understand neurosis is the knowledge that man is an evolutionary animal with an inbuilt *forward drive*. But this forward drive is continually being frustrated by the problems we have been discussing – loss of self-image, the lapse into passivity when the 'I' becomes submerged in the robot. Anyone who has ever owned a car with a faulty gearbox will understand what then happens. When you are grinding uphill, and the gear lever slips into neutral, you start to run backwards. Our evolutionary forward drive is being continually frustrated by this odd habit of lapsing into passivity. When the mirror becomes a blank, it is as if we were suddenly afflicted by amnesia. Our prisons are full of frustrated amnesiacs. The aim of therapy should be to provide some kind of permanent self-image.

But the problem is obviously not confined to prisons and

criminals. If it were, there would be no wars and international monetary crises. The concepts of the 'third culture' suggest ways in which the whole system could be improved beyond recognition. For example, MacDougald uses the phrase 'tuning out' for the process of 'inhibition', and 'tuning in' for the unblocking process; this reminds us that *all* human beings tune out 90 per cent of their experience anyway. The criminal has tuned out slightly more than usual – say 91 per cent. If, by a certain act of insight, he can 'tune in' and reduce that 91 per cent, is there any reason why the rest of us should not also tune in and reduce our 90 per cent to 89 per cent?

Let me express this vital point as clearly as I can, for it is obviously the core of this book. We *all* make a habit of 'tuning out' significances all the time. Everything about our hectic world encourages us to concentrate upon personal problems, personal success, and so on. It is true that I can put a Beethoven symphony on the gramophone, open a volume of Rembrandt etchings, or become absorbed in a book about prehistory, and temporarily forget my personal self; unfortunately, I am not conscious of the precise nature of what I have done. I think I have 'escaped' from my problems for an hour or two, when in fact I have *tuned in* to a range of experience that makes my problems seem infinitely stupid and trivial.

Fortunately, tuning-out is only a *habit* encouraged by the false premises of our culture. And if you really want to break a habit, you can always do so – especially if your reason is positive: anticipation of pleasure. Anybody who feels stifled and dissatisfied with the modern world can be taught to break the habit; for they would not feel stifled if they were not intelligent enough to understand the mechanisms involved. What works on hard-core deviates will also work on stockbrokers or engineers – if they want it to.

What is more, there is no logical limit to how far one might go on 'tuning in'. In Freud's psychology, a neurotic who has been restored to 'normality' has achieved equilibrium; but Maslow knew that there is no upward limit. The appetite for 'significance' increases as it is fed. And it is universal; it exists in everyone. Einstein says accurately that the urge behind science and mathematics is the same urge that make city dwellers long for the open spaces of the countryside at week-ends: the impersonal, the sense of the universe as depth after depth of significance. There is no human being who does not possess it.

Significance is acieved by an act of *inward* focusing. Nietzsche describes how, as a young man, he first read Schopenhauer, and felt he was looking in 'a mirror in which I observed the world, life and my own soul in frightful grandeur', a sense of opening vistas like mountain scenery. We all possess this capacity for focusing meaning; it is the end-product of two million years of evolution; it is the power to focus 'other realities', other times and other places, which I have elsewhere called Faculty X. But our preconceptions, our fixed ideas about ourselves, mean that we remain unaware of this power – an absurdity like Aladdin being unaware of the power of the lamp.

Once this is understood, the prospects for civilization are seen to be immense: not merely a society in which violent crime becomes a rarity, but a genuinely 'creative society'. Nearly half a century ago, Hermann Hesse expressed the basic problem in a novel called *Steppenwolf*. Steppenwolf has an ideal kind of existence: enough money to live fairly comfortably, his own room full of books and gramophone records: the contemplative man's delight. There is only one trouble: he suffers from an unaccountable boredom. Most of his days pass in a trance of dullness. Only occasionally, by accident, does he experience a sudden flash of delight, followed by a feeling like a bursting bubble, and the clear awareness of other times, other places, of 'Mozart and the stars'. And H. G. Wells expressed the same problem when he compared man to the earliest amphibian creatures, who wanted to become land animals and leave the sea behind them, but who only had rudimentary legs, so that an hour on land would exhaust them and force them to return to the supporting medium of the sea. Man desires the mental world, the impersonal world of imagination and meaning; the trivialities of personal existence exhaust him. But, said Wells, he is not yet ready to turn away from them. Which would, if it were true, explain why Steppenwolf feels bored even though he has the world's great books and music at his fingertips.

But the above analysis makes it clear that Wells was not quite correct. Man already possesses the 'mental legs' he needs, the power to focus significance, to enter the mountain landscape of meaning. It is only a question of getting rid of false ideas, false premises. The west has been an 'affluent society' for more than a hundred years now, and it is clearer than ever that man is not a creature who can be contented by affluence and comfort. Every religious revival – from Moody and Sankey to Billy Graham and the 'Jesus cult' – proves that he is a creature whose basic need is for significances *beyond* his everday life.

It may seem strange that I choose to illustrate this thesis by talking about Brady, Manson, van Zon. But we cannot even begin to understand the violence of our society unless we understand that it has its roots in the same urge that produced the Billy Graham movement and the occult revival and the search for messiahs and gurus and führers. If man is deprived of meanings beyond his everyday routine, he becomes disgusted and bitter, and eventually violent. A society that provides no outlet for man's idealist passions is asking to be torn apart by violence. When we understand this, the age of motiveless murder will be at an end.

1. These schools are discussed more fully in my book *New Pathways in Psychology* (1972)
2. On the death of its founder, Mr. Yonan, the name was changed to Emotional Maturity Instruction.
3. Frank Goble, 'The Yonan Codex Story', pamphlet issued by the Thomas Jefferson Research Center, Pasadena, California. July 1970.
4. 'A Promising New Approach to Rehabilitation', pamphlet issued by Jefferson Center. I am indebted to Frank Goble for sending me a copy.

Appendix: The New Ripper Theory

Thomas Stowell, a brain surgeon, died a few weeks ago, after causing something of a scandal with his suggestions about the identity of Jack the Ripper. He didn't actually name his suspect, but he didn't leave much margin for doubt either. His son was apparently so irritated by all the publicity that he burnt all his father's papers on the case. And so, it seems, we shall never know . . .

But I *do* know; in fact, I am probably the only person in England, apart from Mr. Stowell's son, who knows the whole story from beginning to end. In telling it, I am breaking a promise I made to Stowell ten years ago; but I strongly suspect he would have wanted me to break it.

In 1960, I wrote a series for the London *Evening Standard* called *My Search for Jack the Ripper*. I had always been interested in the case. My grandmother had lived in the East End of London at the time (1888), and she told me about the feeling of absolute panic that followed every murder. When I was about ten, I read an article in *Tit Bits*, in which General Booth of the Salvation Army said he suspected his secretary of being the Ripper. The secretary (a male) had awful dreams of blood, and one day told Booth, 'Carroty Nell will be the next to go.' Carroty Nell (her name was Frances Coles) was murdered the same night, and the secretary vanished.[1]

When I moved to London in 1951, I was writing a novel about a sadistic killer, and I decided to use the actual Ripper murder sites. Every Saturday, I spent the day in the British Museum Reading Room, studying books on the case, and the reports in *The Times* for 1888. When the Museum closed at five o'clock, I would cycle off to Whitechapel, and make sketches of the murder sites (four of them looked exactly as they did in the Ripper's day). I also talked to a few old people who remembered the murders, including a man who told me he had delivered newspapers at 26 Dorset Street, the scene of the last and bloodiest of the murders. But although I learned a great deal about the case – all of which went into my novel *Ritual in the Dark* – I never came upon any convincing theory of the identity of Jack the Ripper.

The book came out in 1960, and The *Standard* commissioned the articles. I received dozens of letters about them, but three of them interested me particularly. One came from a lady living at Ascot. The letter was unsigned, but for some reason I knew it was a lady. She said that Jack the Ripper had died in her father's mental home near Ascot. The second letter came from Ireland. It pointed out that the painter, Walter Sickert moved to Whitechapel to paint a series of pictures about them. The old couple who rented him a room told him that their previous tenant had been a young veterinary surgeon who had behaved in a very odd manner. On the morning after one of the murders, he was found burning bloodstained clothing in the grate. The old couple became convinced that he was Jack the Ripper; but before they could make up their minds to tell the police, he had a complete mental breakdown, and was removed to Bournemouth by his family. He died there three months later.

The common factor that seemed to emerge from so many of these stories was the idea that the Ripper was young, and that he had a total mental breakdown after that last horrific murder of 8th November, 1888, when he dismembered the body like a jigsaw puzzle.

The third letter was signed 'T. E. A. Stowell'. The writer explained he was a brain surgeon, and that he had always been interested in the Ripper problem. From my articles, he said, he was pretty sure I knew the identity of Jack the Ripper. Would I like to meet him for lunch and talk about it?

I wrote and told him that I hadn't the faintest idea of the identity of the Ripper, but I would be pleased to meet him for lunch.

I met him at the Athenaeum, which seemed to be full of bishops and retired generals. He was in his early seventies; a friendly, likeable man. He told me he was still practising surgery – although, noting the way his hand shook as he cut his steak, I wondered how much longer that could go on ... He came to the point fairly quickly. He was convinced, he told me, that Jack the Ripper was Edward, the Duke of Clarence, grandson of Queen Victoria, son of Edward the Seventh, heir to the throne of England. If he had not died in 1892, he would have become king of England in 1910 . . . an interesting thought. Stowell was convinced that I guessed the identity of the Ripper from various hints in my articles – comments that the Ripper was a 'gentleman', that he was probably young and had a blond moustache. I explained that all this was to be found in the Inquest reports in *The Times* – various people had described the man they had seen with prostitutes shortly before they were murdered.

When I told him about the letter from the lady near Ascot, he was excited. The Duke of Clarence, he said, had died in a mental home near Sandringham – he had actually visited the place in the mid-thirties.

And how did he come by all this knowledge? He had seen the papers of the late Sir William Gull, Physician in Ordinary to Queen Victoria. When Gull died (in the early thirties, I think he said) his daughter Caroline had asked him – Stowell – to examine these papers, because there were certain 'confidential matters' in them, and they wondered whether it would not be safer to burn them. What the papers revealed, he said, was that the Duke of Clarence had *not* died of 'flu in the epidemic of 1892 – as the history books state – but in a mental home near Sandringham, of 'softening of the brain' due to syphilis. There was also mention of a peculiar scandal in which the Duke had been involved. He had been arrested by the police during a raid on a house of ill repute in Cleveland Row, and one newspaper had actually stated baldly 'Among those arrested was the highest in the land'. (Stowell told me he had this cutting in his possession – he quoted it to me on several subsequent occasions, so he obviously refreshed his memory between-times.) But there was something odd about this brothel – it also catered to homosexual clients, and in the subsequent scandal, there was an odd item about the local telegraph boys being given gold pencils. The Duke of Clarence, as well as being Jack the Ripper, was also a homosexual.

I asked Mr. Stowell what made him sure that the Duke *was* the Ripper? He admitted he was not absolutely convinced, but said that the evidence was strong. In the year of the murders, Queen Victoria invited the medium R. J. Lees to the palace on two occasions. Now there is a famous story –

which has been repeated in many versions – to the effect that Lees was instrumental in catching Jack the Ripper. (This story was actually told to my first wife by Lees's daughter, so I have it almost at first hand.) The story goes that Lees had several vivid dreams of the murders before they happened, and in his dreams he saw the face of the murderer. One day, travelling on a bus along Bayswater Road, he recognized the murderer sitting opposite him – a respectable looking man with a frock coat and top hat. When the man got off the bus, so did Lees – and followed him to a house in Park Lane. It turned out to be the house of a famous physician, with connections with the royal family. When Lees went to the police with his story, their first reaction was incredulity; but they checked with the surgeon's wife, and she admitted that her husband *had* been behaving very oddly recently, and that she was afraid he was going insane. The police kept a watch on the doctor, and actually caught him in the act of leaving the house with his carving knife in a black bag . . . He was interned in a mental home for the rest of his life. (A much fuller version of this story is given by my friend Fred Archer in his book *Ghost Detectives* – he also had it from Eva Lees.)

Queen Victoria was known to be interested in the Ripper murders – she even made suggestions about how he could be caught. And if she came to suspect that her grandson was Jack the Ripper, she would obviously have Lees to the palace . . .

I didn't quite follow this. The Duke of Clarence wasn't a physician living in Park Lane. Stowell explained patiently. Sir William Gull *did* live near Park Lane, at 74 Grosvenor Square. And that house *had* been visited by a detective, accompanied by a medium. Gull's daughter, Caroline Acland (who had been a close friend of Stowell) had told him that her mother had been greatly annoyed by this intrusive visit, and had not been co-operative. Sir William knew that his distinguished patient was Jack the Ripper and did his best to shield him. He even went so far, Stowell told me, as to admit that he occasionally suffered from lapses of memory, and had awakened one day to find blood on his shirt. Either this was an attempt to divert suspicion to himself, or Gull had actually examined the Duke after one of the murders and got blood on himself.

But why did Lees say that the physician was Jack the Ripper? Undoubtedly, because Gull *was* hiding the guilty secret and Lees sensed this by telepathy – or the aid of the spirits.

The story of the Duke of Clarence, according to Stowell, went something like this. He was born in 1864, the eldest son of the Prince of Wales, and named Albert Victor. When he was fifteen years old, he went on a three-year tour of the world with his younger brother George, on H.M.S. *Bacchante*. And it was probably while travelling on this appropriately named ship that he contracted the syphilis that killed him at the age of twenty-eight. 'I think he was seduced in Australia or before his arrival there,' Stowell wrote to me in a letter of 28th March, 1966; 'Health somewhat undermined by an acute attack of typhoid, and his youth made him less resistant to the quaternary sequel [of syphilis]. Five to fifteen years is the usual time. My suspect arrived at this disastrous stage in about ten years. His great grandfather appears to have been a manic depressive, and perhaps he inherited a weakness of the central nervous system that prepared the soil.'

On his return to London, the Duke lived the life of a pleasure loving man-about-town, and became affectionately known to the London working classes as 'Collar and Cuffs'. The journalist Henry Labouchere mocked his 'wayward tendencies' under that nickname in *Truth*. (Was it in this newspaper that the innuendo about the 'highest in the land' appeared?) The telegraph boy scandal occurred sometime in the mid-eighties, and Queen Victoria was much displeased. The Duke was sent on another sea voyage until things quietened down. It was on his return from this voyage, Stowell believed, that 'Eddie's brain began to give way, and he began killing prostitutes in the East End of London. Certainly, some of the descriptions by witnesses of the mysterious stranger in Whitechapel *sounded* like the Duke: the blond moustache, the elegance – even a deerstalker hat. (And this deerstalker was also significant, according to Stowell. He was of the opinion that the Duke had developed some kind of sadistic obsession with blood while hunting deer in Scotland. The Ripper, according to legend, possessed 'medical skill', but the evidence of the inquests contradicts this. He only had a rough-and-ready knowledge of where to find the vital organs of his victims – which could have been picked up when dissecting venison in the field.) And so the Duke progressed from deer to daughters of joy. But at some point, the royal family learned of his anti-social hobby. After the murder of Mary Kelly, on 8th November, 1888, he was interned in the mental home near Ascot. Stowell was even of the opinion that 'Eddie' was caught after the earlier murder of Catherine Eddowes in Mitre Square on 30th September, and interned, but that he managed to escape five weeks later and commit his final murder.

And then, according to Stowell, he was treated by Sir William Gull with such success that he was able to go on a five-month cruise in 1889. A further relapse was again treated by Gull, so that the Duke was able to take part in three major public events in 1890. But the softening of the brain continued, and when he died in 1892, the 'flu epidemic provided him with an excellent alibi.

There was only one thing needed to complete his theory, said Stowell. He hadn't been able to check the Court Circular to find out whether the Duke was actually in London during the murders. If he had been in Scotland, of course, that was the end of it.

When I left Stowell that day, outside the Athenaeum, there was no talk about secrecy. I got the impression that he thoroughly enjoyed telling me about it all. Later that afternoon, I met a German murder expert, Frank Lynder (to whom I dedicated my *Encyclopaedia of Murder*), and told him the theory. Lynder immediately offered to check the Court Circular for me. He was the editor of several German newspapers, and had the facilities for research. And not long after – probably the next day – Lynder rang me in excitement to tell me that the dates *did* check; the Duke was never in Scotland at the times of the murders. He asked me if I would be willing to write the story for his newspapers. I said I would have to check with Stowell first. I did – and he told me he would prefer not to publish it, in case it upset the royal family. So that was the end of it – for the time being.

I could not accept the Clarence theory without reservation. To begin with, my friend Dan Farson had done a TV programme on the Ripper in 1957, and had unearthed some new facts. Sir Melville MacNaghten, who joined the force shortly after the Ripper murders, and later became chief of the C.I.D., had his own theories about the identity of the

Ripper. Dan checked with MacNaghten's daughter, Lady Aberconway, and was allowed to see her father's notes. These mentioned the three chief suspects in the case, an insane Polish Jew, an insane Russian doctor (named Ostrog), and a certain 'M. J. Druitt', who committed suicide immediately after the final murder. Druitt was an unsuccessful barrister who was forced to become a schoolmaster. In March 1889, Albert Backert, head of a committee of Vigilantes in Whitechapel, asked the police for some reassurance that the Ripper would not strike again. He was told, 'The man in question is dead. He was fished out of the Thames two months ago.' Druitt threw himself into the Thames on 3rd December, and his body was taken out of the river on the last day of the year.

An American writer, Tom Cullen, later followed up the Druitt story, and his book *Autumn of Terror* contains a full account of it. In my own opinion, Druitt is the likeliest suspect for the Ripper murders.

Stowell did not think so. When I wrote to him to ask his opinion of Donald McCormick's theory that the Ripper was a mad Russian named Pedachenko (alias Ostrog), and later to ask him about the Druitt theory, he seemed almost offended that I should not be wholly convinced by his own theory. But although he asked me many times not to publish his theory, he was not in the least averse to talking about it – in fact, I got the impression that, like a schoolboy, he could hardly bear to keep such a secret to himself and was longing to tell someone. I had a long 'phone conversation with him about it in 1966, and although he repeated that he wanted it kept secret, he talked for more than half an hour about it, adding several new details (which I have included in the above account).

I told another friend, Nigel Morland, about the Clarence theory, and when Nigel started to edit a small magazine called *The Criminologist*, he wrote to Stowell to ask him if he would write up his Clarence theory. To my astonishment, Stowell agreed. The article, 'Jack the Ripper – A Solution, by T. E. A. Stowell, C.B.E., M.D.', appeared in the issue for last December. In this article, Stowell did not actually name the suspect, but his hints made it pretty obvious – he even mentioned the nickname 'Collar and Cuffs'. Magnus Linklater of the *Sunday Times* immediately reported on the theory at some length, and rang up Donald McCormick, to ask if he knew the identity of Stowell's 'suspect'. McCormick did – I had told him. The following evening, Kenneth Allsop questioned Stowell on the TV programme 'Twenty-Four Hours', together with McCormick. Once again, Stowell declined to name his suspect, but he made no objection when Allsop tacitly assumed it was the Duke.

For the next week, it was something of a scandal. A correspondent in the *Sunday Times* pointed out that the Duke had been on a five-month tour in 1889, and had attended various public events – unaware that Stowell had already dealt with that point in *The Criminologist*. But a more effective broadside against the theory appeared in *The Times*, which referred to 'the mischievous calumny'. The royal family, it said, regarded the theory as too ridiculous for comment. But a 'loyalist' on the staff at the Palace had checked on the Court Circular, and discovered that Prince Eddie was, in fact, in Scotland on the day after the Eddowes murder. It is true that the murder occurred in the very early hours of Sunday morning, and the Duke was in Scotland on the Monday – plenty of time for him to travel there by train. Still, it made a point. The loyalist also believes (but has no definite proof) that the Duke was at Sandringham celebrating his father's birthday on the date of the last murder. But the birthday was 9th November – and the celebration presumably took place in the evening. The murder of Mary Jeanette Kelly took place on the *previous* night. So it cannot be said that the 'loyalist' has really disproved the Stowell theory.

In my own opinion, the strongest evidence against it is circumstantial. It seems, to put it mildly, unlikely that the Duke was interned after the Eddowes murder, escaped to murder Mary Kelly, and was interned again, then was allowed to open a dock in Belfast the following May. In 1889, according to Elizabeth Longford's biography of Queen Victoria, he fell in love with Princess Alix of Hesse (who later became the last Tsarina of Russia), but she wouldn't have him. But not long before his death, he became engaged to Princess May of Teck, who later married his younger brother George, and became Queen Mary. Is it likely that the Queen would have rejoiced when Jack the Ripper got engaged to Princess May?

All that we know about the darker side of Eddie's life is

that he was a homosexual (Michael Harrison confirms this in his book *London By Gaslight*). It is also possible that he was syphilitic, if we accept Stowell's assertion that he read it in Sir William Gull's diary: 'informed Blank that his son was dying of syphilis of the brain' – Blank presumably being the Prince of Wales, who later became Edward VII. Gull told the Prince about this in November 1889, after the Duke had fallen in love with Princess Alix, but before the engagement to Princess May. Again, one wonders whether the future king would have allowed the engagement if he knew his son was dying of syphilis of the brain.

But in spite of all this, the Clarence theory refuses to be laid to rest. When I read the letter from the 'loyalist' to *The Times*, I was inclined to believe that was the end of it – until I checked the dates, and realized that it proved nothing. Lord Annan, writing about it, dismisses the Clarence theory on the grounds that Prince Eddie was known to be about as brainless as Wodehouse's Bertie Wooster. But if he was really suffering from brain decay and some inherited disease of the nervous system, I don't see that this is relevant either.

And in reading an article on Jack the Ripper by Dr. Harold Dearden, in a volume called *Unsolved Crimes*, I came across the following odd story. In November 1918, Dearden was in the trenches on the Somme, and they were celebrating the fortieth birthday of a fellow officer. The officer remarked that his tenth birthday had been spoiled by Jack the Ripper. His father ran a mental home 'on the outskirts of London', and on the evening of 9th November, 1888, he had promised to take his son to the pantomime. But in the evening, a 'violent and noisy patient' was brought to the house, 'amidst a huddle of attendants'. The pantomime was called off. Later, the boy got to know the new patient, who was 'one of his father's oldest friends' – a 'gently demented individual', says Dearden, 'who drew excellent pictures of birds and butterflies.' The boy later decided that this was Jack the Ripper.

'The outskirts of London' *could* be Sandringham. In which case, Dearden's friend was the brother of the lady who wrote to me from Ascot. If she is still alive, and happens to read this, I wish she'd write and tell me whether Jack the Ripper had a blond moustache and wore a deerstalker hat.

I should also mention a Ripper theory that has appeared since this book was completed. It was printed in *City*, the magazine of the City of London Police for February 1972[2]. The author, B. E. Reilly, was intrigued by an incident that is alleged to have taken place at some time after 2 a.m. on the night of 29th-30th September – the night of the double murder. P.C. Robert Spicer had decided that night to do his beat 'backwards', because it had been suggested that the Ripper knew the beats of the local constables, and timed his murders accordingly (a suggestion that is borne out by the Mitre Square killing). In an alley called Henage Court, not far from Mitre Square, he saw a well-dressed man talking to a woman. He arrested both on suspicion, and took them to the Commercial Street Police Station. The man, he declared (in 1931, to the *Daily Express*) had blood on his cuffs, and was carrying a brown leather bag. But eight inspectors who were at the station heard his story with disbelief. The well-dressed man established his identity as a Brixton doctor, and was allowed to go without even being required to open his bag. Constable Spicer was transferred to another beat and resigned from the force five months later.

Mr. Reilly felt that the 'Brixton doctor' was worth investigating, and accordingly checked on the medical register for the period. The number of possible suspects was not enormous, and the most obvious was one whom Mr. Reilly calls 'Dr. Merchant' – presumably to protect his descendants. Dr. Merchant died in December 1888, from a septic abscess of tubercular origin. He died very poor, and may have been unconscious when taken into hospital, since the death certificate has 'unknown to informant' written in the column headed 'occupation of deceased'. Mr. Reilly also infers from this that the doctor must have been separated from his wife at the time. (Four years later, when letters of administration were granted to her, she was matron of a mental institution near Salisbury.) Further research revealed that 'Dr. Merchant' had been born in India in 1851, and that his father's regiment had been responsible for executing a number of the mutineers of the 1875 mutiny. Some of these were dispatched in a particularly vengeful manner, being blown out of cannons or sewn into the hides of pigs and cows. (This was in revenge for Indian atrocities committed against British women and children, particularly at Cawnpore.) Mr. Reilly suggests that reports of these executions may have made a permanent impression on the boy's mind.

His researches established that 'Dr. Merchant' came to London in 1886, from a 'provincial practice'. 'Provincial' may refer to Liverpool, since Mr. Reilly mentions earlier that the doctor had a 'Liverpool connection'. (Two of the Ripper letters were sent from Liverpool.) Merchant wrote a number of pamphlets, and had letters published in professional journals. Mr. Reilly finds a breathless, headlong style in these letters, indicating a 'garrulous and fatuous' personality. He would have been thirty-seven at the time of the murders, and descriptions of the 'well-dressed man' mentioned by witnesses suggest a man in his mid-thirties. Spicer said that his Brixton doctor had 'rosy cheeks', which would be consistent with tuberculosis ... 'Is it not conceivable,' asks Mr. Reilly, 'that, knowing himself to be gravely ill, the "Brixton doctor" ran amok, and dealt with the social outcasts of Victorian London as his father's regiment had treated the military outlaws in the Mutiny . . .?'

The theory is fascinating and plausible, but the objections to it are strong. To begin with, the Spicer story must be regarded as doubtful, since it was first told forty-three years after the murders. There is no actual record of it at the time. But even assuming it to be true, there are many objections. The Ripper had committed two murders just before Spicer arrested 'Dr. Merchant', the last only about half an hour earlier. After the second, he had washed blood off his hands in a nearby sink; it seems likely that he would have blood on other places besides his cuffs. *If* the man seen talking to the prostitute 'Rosy' was Jack the Ripper, he would hardly have felt happy to be arrested by a young policeman, knowing that he had a bloodstained knife in his bag; it seems more likely he would have attacked Spicer, or at least tried to run away. Instead he followed him without protest, and was so self-possessed that he was allowed to go immediately. (This certainly lays Spicer's story open to doubt; would eight inspectors have allowed a man with blood on his cuffs to leave the station without even asking to look into his bag?) Mr. Reilly mentions the description of the unknown doctor as having 'rosy cheeks', and suggests that this could have been the result of his tubercular complaint. Spicer's actual description says that the man 'wore a high hat, a black suit with silk facings, and a gold watch and chain. He was about five feet eight inches, weighed around twelve stone, had a fair moustache, high forehead, rosy cheeks.' Read in context, the 'rosy cheeks' does not suggest a down-and-out doctor dying of tuberculosis, but a 'toff' in the best of health – in fact, the Duke of Clarence rather than Dr. Merchant.

But the strongest argument against the Merchant theory was contained in the following issue of *City*, in a piece by I. M. Bartlett. Mr. Bartlett simply points out that in P.C. Spicer's original account (in the *Daily Express*, 16th March, 1931), Spicer adds that he left the force five months after the episode, and 'I saw the man several times after this at Liverpool Street Station, accosting women. I would remark to him: "Hello Jack! Still after them?" He would immediately bolt.' If Spicer saw the man more than five months after the night of the double murder, then it could not have been 'Dr. Merchant', who died less than three months later.

Most of the above account appeared in *The Leicester Chronicle* for 29th January, 1971. I wrote it because I had heard that Dr. Stowell's son had destroyed his papers; the report that mentioned this (*Times*, 14th November, 1970) added that now no one could ever be certain that Stowell's suspect *was* the Duke of Clarence. And that should have been the end of the story.

In fact, it was only the preface to new developments.

I have already mentioned Michael Harrison, the expert on the Victorian era, who commented on Clarence's homosexual tendencies in *London by Gaslight*. In 1971, Michael Harrison began to write a biography of the Duke of Clarence.[3] Inevitably, he had to make some reference to the theory that 'Eddie' was the Ripper. He felt, as I did, that the theory was basically absurd. There remained the interesting question of why Stowell had come to hold it. Mr. Harrison studied Stowell's *Criminologist* article, and my own *Leicester Chronicle* piece, and came to some interesting conclusions.

First, we know that Stowell based his theory on something he had seen in Sir William Gull's papers, shown to him by Gull's daughter. And whatever Gull said involved Jack the Ripper, the Duke of Clarence, and some scandal. Stowell thereupon formulated the interesting hypothesis that Clarence was the Ripper. Stowell obviously took notes, for his account of 'S's' career in his *Criminologist* article is detailed and precise.

But, having made a study of Eddie's life, Michael Harrison instantly saw that Eddie's career and that of 'S' are quite different.

This had not struck me; I didn't know enough about Clarence's life to see the divergencies. I simply assumed that Stowell was drawing upon his own knowledge of Clarence's life. He wasn't; he was drawing upon the notes he made from Gull's papers.

Why, Michael Harrison wondered, did Stowell decide to call his suspect 'S'? By chance? Or did Gull refer to the suspect as 'S'?

The next question was obvious. If the biography of 'S' didn't fit the Duke of Clarence, then who did it fit?

Having studied Clarence's life, the answer was immediately clear to Mr. Harrison. Clarence's closest friend – and at one time his lover – James Kenneth Stephen, the son of the judge Sir James Fitzjames Stephen. There was a great deal of mental illness in the Stephen family – which Mr. Harrison details in his book – including the suicide of Stephen's cousin, Virginia Woolf, and the breakdown of his father, the judge, which caused his premature retirement. 'Jim Stephen' was handsome, brilliant and talented; he seemed set for a successful career at the bar. But a blow on the head in 1886 – in a riding accident – changed his personality. He became increasingly bitter and violent, and died in a mental home at Northampton, exactly twenty-two days after Eddie's death (which took place in the palace at Sandringham, not in a mental home). Stephen had starved himself to death; he began his 'hunger strike' when he saw the news of Clarence's death in the newspaper – or so Mr. Harrison convincingly argues.

Until he was nineteen, the Duke of Clarence was more or less inseparable from his younger brother George. Then the decision was taken to commission George as a sub-lieutenant in the navy, and to send Eddie to Trinity College, Cambridge. It was felt that Eddie needed a substitute for George, someone who could be friend, adviser and tutor. J. K. Stephen – only slightly Eddie's senior – was chosen. He 'crammed' Eddie for three months before he started at Cambridge, in the Autumn of 1883. And at Cambridge, says Mr. Harrison, Eddie became a member of a 'crypto-queer' group which included Stephen and a sinister character named Oscar Browning, who had been sacked from his housemastership at Eton for 'undue familiarity' with one of the boys, but nevertheless admitted to a Fellowship at Trinity.

Michael Harrison argues – although final proof is, of necessity, lacking – that Stephen became Eddie' lover. Eddie was bisexual – 'panerotic', Mr. Harrison calls his intense preoccupation with sex. So, to a lesser extent, was Stephen. (Michael Holroyd, in his biography of Lytton Strachey, claims that Stephen made 'violent advances' to Virginia Woolf's half-sister, Stella Duckworth, not long before his mental collapse.) The Stephen family was ambitious; Jim Stephen was no exception. He saw himself as the power behind the throne at some future date. But this was not to be. Eddie was not really suited to the effete, rather 'aesthetic', greenery-yallery literary set into which Stephen introduced him. When J. K. Stephen was called to the bar in 1884, and Eddie became a lieutenant in the Royal Artillery, they drifted apart. Stephen, says Michael Harrison, took it badly, and was intensely jealous and resentful.

The blow on the head which occurred in 1886, caused an abscess of the brain, and Stephen became a patient of Sir William Gull. ('Jack the Ripper was obviously Gull's patient', says Stowell.)

But what definite evidence is there that Stephen was Jack the Ripper? It is mostly circumstantial. To begin with, Stephen was a poet – he published two volumes of verse. Mr. Harrison examines some of the verses attributed to the Ripper, and parallels them with verses written by Stephen and reveals striking similarities. Then there is the famous Ripper verse which states 'I'm not a butcher, I'm not a Yid/Nor yet a foreign skipper'. Queen Victoria had written a letter to the Home Secretary suggesting that the police check on all foreign skippers – but this was not known to the press. *If* the Ripper was referring to it, he must have learned it direct from some member of the royal family. Stephen apparently developed a fierce hatred of women, says Mr. Harrison. One poem, called 'In the Backs', describes how he 'met a woman whom I did not like'. She is described with a kind of savage mockery, 'Loose-hipped, big-boobed, disjointed, angular' (she sounds like Elizabeth Stride), and after a dozen or so lines like this, he adds: 'I did not like her, and I should not mind/If she was done away with, killed or ploughed'. The poem seems to have no point except to record his sudden loathing for this cloddish, working-class woman. A much earlier poem (1882) describes his feelings about a man who accidentally stood on his foot in a train, and the hatred is distinctly paranoid:

> 'Oh, may'st thou suffer tortures without end:
> May fiends with glowing pincers rend thy brain,
> And beetles batten on thy blackened face!'

I must admit that these poems are, for me, the most convincing part of Michael Harrison's theory. They convey a picture of the Ripper, a man twisted with hate, burning with it.

Another poem – an 'innocent' one – is intended to be sung to the tune of 'Kaphoozelum' – 'Kaphoozalem' being a long, bawdy poem about the murder of ten little harlots of Jerusalem. Mr. Harrison believes that Stephen committed ten murders between 1888 and 1891 (the last one being that of 'Carroty Nell'). Stephen's mind collapsed completely in 1890, and he was confined in an institution. Mr. Harrison argues convincingly that the dates of the various murders were dates when Stephen was in London, and that during the periods when there were no murders, he was known to be elsewhere.

One of the odder points, which Mr. Harrison has mentioned to me in correspondence (although he does not mention it in his books) is that Stephen was also indirectly connected with the school at Blackheath at which Montague John Druitt was a master. Could Druitt and Stephen have been friends? Is this why the police suspected Druitt of being the Ripper?

It is difficult, at this stage, to pass judgement on Mr. Harrison's theory. I believe he has proved, beyond reasonable doubt, that Stephen *was* the 'S' whom Sir William Gull believed to be the Ripper, and circumstantial evidence is strong. But whether Stephen really *was* the Ripper seems to me more doubtful. If he hated women, why did he make 'violent advances' to Stella Duckworth? If he had broken with Eddie by 1888, how did he get to know of Queen Victoria's letter about 'foreign skippers'? Is it likely that Sir William Gull, Sir James Stephen, and various other members of the Stephen clan, all *knew* that J. K. was Jack the Ripper, yet could not prevent more murders?

But at least there is reason to hope that the Stephen theory might definitely be proved or disproved one day – which would distinguish it from most of the others. Stephen was a writer; so were many members of his family. One of his descendants may possess documents that confirm or deny the identification. I can only say that Mr. Harrison has advanced the most convincing theory to date.

1. Mr. David Streatfield, the librarian at New Scotland Yard, was kind enough to trace the reference for me. It was in *Tit-bits* for 23rd September, 1939, and was by Commissioner David C. Lamb of the Salvation Army, not General Booth, as I had wrongly recalled. The suspect was a 'highly skilled sign writer', not a male secretary. But I had remembered correctly the 'visions of blood', and his remark 'Carroty Nell will be the next one to go'.
2. I am also indebted to David Streatfield for sending me the relevant copies of *City*.
3. *Clarence*, by Michael Harrison, W. H. Allen, 1972.

Bibliography

ANONYMOUS: *My Secret Life*. 2 vols. Grove Press, N.Y., 1966.

ARDREY, ROBERT: *The Social Contract*. Collins, 1970.

CAMPS, FRANCIS E.: *The Investigation of Murder*. Michael Joseph, 1966. *Medical and Scientific Investigation in the Christie Case*. Medical Publication Ltd., 1953.

DONOVAN, ROBERT J.: *The Assassins*. Elek Books, 1956.

FRANKL, VIKTOR: *Man's Search for Meaning*. Washington Square Press, N.Y., 1965.

GELLER, STEVE: *Musical Impressions of Murder* (the Manson Case), not yet published.

HYAMS, EDWARD: *Killing No Murder*. Nelson, 1969.

IRVING, H. B.: *Studies of French Criminals*. Heinemann, 1901.

JACKSON, R. L.: *Criminal Investigation*. 5th ed. Sweet and Maxwell, 1962.

JESSE, F. TENNYSON: *Murder and its Motives*. Dolphin Books, N.Y., 1965.

JONAS, DAVID and KLEIN, DORIS: *Man Child*. Cape, 1971.

KENNEDY, LUDOVIC: *10 Rillington Place*. Gollancz, 1961.

LELY, GILBERT: *The Marquis de Sade*. Elek, 1961.

LEWIS, BERNARD: *The Assassins*. Weidenfeld & Nicolson, 1967.

LORENZ, KONRAD: *On Aggression*. Harcourt Brace & Co. N.Y., 1963.

MACDOUGALD, DAN: *Handbook for Emotional Maturity Development Profile*, etc. (published by: Emotional Maturity Instruction, P.O. Box 33065, Decatur, Georgia 30033, USA).

MACKENZIE, NORMAN: *Secret Societies*. Aldus, 1967.

MANNHEIM, HERMANN: *Comparative Criminology*. 2 vols. Routledge & Kegan Paul, 1965.

MARCHBANKS, DAVID: *The Moors Murders*. Frewin, 1966.

MASLOW, ABRAHAM: *The Farther Reaches of Human Nature*. Viking, N.Y., 1971. *Toward a Psychology of Being*. Van Nostrand, 1968.

MORLAND, NIGEL. *ed*: *The Criminologist*. Wolfe, 1971.

POTTER, JOHN DEANE: *The Monster of the Moors*. Elek, 1966.

ROSE, JOHN DU: *Murder was My Business*. W. H. Allen, 1971.

SADE, MARQUIS DE: Selected Works. 2 vols. Grove Press, N.Y., 1966.

SLEEMAN, J.: *Thug, or a Million Murders*. Sampson Low, London, 1933.

SANDERS, ED: *The Family*. [Charles Manson]. Hart-Davis, 1972.
SARTRE, JEAN-PAUL: *Sketch for a Theory of the Emotions*. Methuen, 1962.
SCHILLER, LAWRENCE: *The Killing of Sharon Tate*. New American Library, 1970.
WILLIAMS, JOHN: *Heyday for Assassins*. Heinemann, 1958.

Fascinating Non-fiction Reading in Panther Books

THE MARIJUANA PAPERS	Edited by David Solomon	75p	☐
THINK: *the story of IBM*	William Rogers	60p	☐
LA VIDA	Oscar Lewis	60p	☐
SOUL ON ICE	Eldridge Cleaver	35p	☐
POST-PRISON WRITINGS AND SPEECHES	Eldridge Cleaver	40p	☐
THE UNDERGROWTH OF LITERATURE	Gillian Freeman	50p	☐
BLACK LIKE ME	John Howard Griffin	40p	☐
MEN IN GROUPS	Lionel Tiger	60p	☐
SKIN DEEP IN SOHO	Richard Wortley	45p	☐
THE SHAPE OF MINDS TO COME	John Taylor	50p	☐
THE DOOMSDAY BOOK	G. Rattray Taylor	45p	☐
THE BIOLOGICAL TIME BOMB	G. Rattray Taylor	50p	☐
INTRODUCTION TO PSYCHOLOGY	D. E. James	75p	☐
THE IMMORTALIST	Alan Harrington	50p	☐
THE CHOSEN PEOPLE	John M. Allegro	60p	☐
THE SEA AROUND US	Rachel Carson	30p	☐
THE EDGE OF THE SEA	Rachel Carson	40p	☐
THE ENVIRONMENT GAME	Nigel Calder	42p	☐
THE DAY THEIR WORLD ENDED	Gordon Thomas & Max Morgan-Witts	30p	☐
THE RED BOOK AND THE GREAT WALL: *an impression of Mao's China*	Alberto Moravia	40p	☐